"I KNOW THAT I AM CHALLENGING THE CULTURAL TRADITION OF TWO AND A HALF THOUSAND YEARS."

--said Ayn Rand when she wrote ATLAS SHRUGGED.

Ayn Rand has become a legend in her own lifetime. Her best-selling novels have launched a nationwide intellectual movement that is rapidly growing.

In WHO IS AYN RAND?, Nathaniel Branden offers a brilliant analysis of Ayn Rand's books, from the standpoint of ethics, politics, psychology and literature. In Barbara Branden's penetrating and revealing biographical study, you will meet a person as heroic, intransigent and unique in our time as are her fictional characters.

IF YOU HAVE READ ATLAS SHRUGGED, YOU KNOW WHO IS JOHN GALT. NOW DISCOVER WHO IS AYN RAND.

ABOUT THE AUTHORS

NATHANIEL BRANDEN was born in Brampton, Ontario, and studied psychology at the University of California at Los Angeles and at New York University. In 1958, he closed his practice of psychotherapy to devote his time to writing on psychology and to the establishment of the Nathaniel Branden Institute, Inc. The Institute gives lecture courses, in New York and other major cities, on Ayn Rand's philosophy, Objectivism, and its application to the social sciences. Nathaniel Branden is also co-editor with Ayn Rand of *The Objectivist Newsletter,* a monthly journal of ideas. At present, he is completing a book on his theory of neurosis.

BARBARA BRANDEN (Mrs. Nathaniel Branden) was born in Winnipeg, Manitoba, and studied philosophy at the University of Manitoba, the University of California at Los Angeles and New York University. At present, she is vice-president of the Nathaniel Branden Institute and managing editor of *The Objectivist Newsletter.* Barbara Branden's chief interests are philosophy and literature; she is planning the career of a novelist.

WHO IS AYN RAND?

An Analysis of the Novels of Ayn Rand
by Nathaniel Branden

With a Biographical Essay
by Barbara Branden

PAPERBACK LIBRARY
New York

PAPERBACK LIBRARY EDITION

First Printing: *May, 1964*
Second Printing: *April, 1965*
Third Printing: *February, 1967*
Fourth Printing: *April, 1968*
Fifth Printing: *April, 1969*

Library of Congress Catalog Card Number:
62-10336.

**This Paperback Library Edition is published by
arrangement with Random House, Inc.**

Paperback Library is a division of Coronet Communications, Inc. Its
trademark, consisting of the words "Paperback Library" accompanied by
an open book, is registered in the United States Patent Office. *Coronet
Communications, Inc., 315 Park Avenue South, New York, N.Y. 10010.*

Preface

In the winter of 1961, at the University of Wisconsin, more than twelve hundred students, faculty members and visitors sat listening to a lecture that was part of the university's symposium on "Ethics in Our Time." It was the most technical of the papers presented, but the symposium had found it necessary to hold the lecture in its largest auditorium. In the lobby of the building, a hundred students who had waited in line to be admitted but could not be accommodated in the overcrowded auditorium, stood listening to the address through loud-speakers.

The address was entitled "The Objectivist Ethics." The lecturer was Ayn Rand.

This attendance at a lecture by Ayn Rand was typical. On campuses across the country, her appearances invariably attract record audiences. No other modern writer has displayed a comparable capacity to generate intellectual excitement.

The members of her audiences are far from philosophically homogeneous. Some have read her books and are in total or substantial agreement with her philosophy. Others—who may or may not have read her books—are fanatically antagonistic. Still others have little or no knowledge of her philosophy, but come because they hear her ideas debated violently and know that the name of Ayn Rand stands for something challenging and extraordinary. Like the hero of her novel *Atlas Shrugged*, Ayn Rand has become a legend in her own lifetime.

The Nathaniel Branden Institute, which offers lecture courses on Ayn Rand's philosophy, receives thousands of letters annually from all over the world, requesting information on her philosophy. With the exception of Ayn Rand's books, no other source material has been available. This present book is offered as an initial step toward filling that gap.

The first essay, "The Moral Revolution in *Atlas Shrugged*," discusses the essentials of Ayn Rand's ethics and its crucial relevance to our present intellectual, moral and political crisis. The essay is not intended as a detailed, systematic exposition of her ethics. Nor does it include a presentation of the base of her moral philosophy: Objectivist epistemology. This essay is a commentary on the historical and cultural significance of her ethics and the view of man which her ethics holds as a moral ideal.

"Objectivism and Psychology" briefly indicates some of the major implications of Objectivism for the science of psychology, and the potential contribution which it has to offer that science.

"The Literary Method of Ayn Rand" analyzes the underlying esthetic principles of Ayn Rand's novels, and discusses her concept of man's relationship to existence, which holds the key to her literary method.

The title essay, "Who is Ayn Rand?", written by Barbara Branden, is a biographical study which deals primarily with Ayn Rand's intellectual and artistic development.

What does Ayn Rand advocate? What does she challenge? Why are her books frequently and hysterically denounced—and why do they sell in the millions? What is it, as thinker and artist, that Ayn Rand offers men? What is the cause of the admiration and enthusiasm that her novels have inspired? These are the questions this book was written to answer.

An Analysis of the
Novels of Ayn Rand

by Nathaniel Branden

I

The Moral Revolution
in *Atlas Shrugged*

At a few minutes to eight, on an evening twelve years from tonight, the people of the United States are sitting at their radio and television sets, waiting to hear a broadcast by the head of their government—Mr. Thompson. They are waiting in silent despair to learn the answer they seek: the explanation of what has happened to the world.

For years they have been witnessing a process of ever-accelerating disintegration. They have seen the rest of the earth sink into the chaos, the brutality, the terror and starvation of collectivism. In the United States, they have watched the steps of the same process, the growing power of the government, the contracting sphere of freedom, the expanding tentacles of controls and regulations reaching out to encoil every life. But the disintegration of America is following a mysterious time schedule of its own, that has no historical precedent, moving at a faster rate than anyone can explain: the gates of factories are closing, conveyor belts are turning still, roads are growing empty, buildings are crumbling, weeds are crawling over the abandoned ruins of great industries; and certain men silently and inexplicably are vanishing—inventors, industrialists, artists, engineers, philosophers, scientists—men who have one attribute in common: ability. The lights of America are going out, darkness is swallowing the last of the civilized world, as if the motor of the world had stopped.

The people who are awaiting the broadcast have never known or wondered what *is* the motor of the world. They have taken industrial civilization for granted, as an irreducible fact of nature. And at the sight of every new disaster, at the news of every train wreck, every plane crash, every oil-tank explosion, every business collapsed into bankruptcy, at

7

the failure of every hope, they have heard the voices of their political and intellectual leaders declaring that *selfishness* is the cause of their plight, that *self-sacrifice* is the road to prosperity, that brotherly love and wider government power are the solution to all the problems of the world.

It is an age of cynicism—and of terror; of skepticism—and of hysteria; of exhausted resignation—and of frantic efforts to evade the knowledge of that to which men have become resigned. Now, in the midst of the last impoverished remnants of what had been America's greatness, in a mood of gray hopelessness and embittered passivity, they await the speech which—their government has promised them for weeks— will show them the path to recovery.

The speech is scheduled for eight o'clock. But at a few minutes to eight, every broadcasting station across the country suddenly goes dead; all sound has been cut off—jammed and silenced by an unknown transmitter that has taken control of the air waves. And then the hand of the clock reaches the dot of eight.

" 'Ladies and gentlemen,' said a voice that came from the radio receiver—a man's clear, calm, implacable voice, the kind of voice that had not been heard on the airwaves for years—'Mr. Thompson will not speak to you tonight. His time is up. I have taken it over. You were to hear a report on the world crisis. That is what you are going to hear. . . .

" 'For twelve years, you have been asking: Who is John Galt? This is John Galt speaking. I am the man who loves his life. I am the man who does not sacrifice his love or his values. I am the man who has deprived you of victims and thus has destroyed your world, and if you wish to know why you are perishing—you who dread knowledge—I am the man who will now tell you.' "

These are the words that begin the climax of the most original and challenging novel of our age—Ayn Rand's *Atlas Shrugged*. The radio speech that brings the events of this book to their climax is not addressed merely to the people in the story: it is addressed to *you*.

The world in which you live has not reached the physical disintegration of that projected in *Atlas Shrugged*—but it has reached the *cultural* disintegration. It is the prevalent ideas of a culture that determine its direction and its fate—and the ideas that dominate the culture in *Atlas Shrugged*, dominate your culture today.

In the world of the present, we are told by our leading philosophers and intellectuals that factual certainty is impossible, that the contents of man's mind need bear no necessary relationship to the facts of reality, that the concepts of "facts of reality" is an old-fashioned superstition, that reality is "mere appearance," that man can *know* nothing—that to feel uncertain, as one's chronic state, is the insignia of enlightened intellectuality.

We are told that personal happiness, self-interest and the profit motive are ignoble, that man must live for others, that the competent must exist for the sake of the incompetent, that those who suffer or are in need have first claim on the lives and energy of all the men around them, that theirs is the right superseding all other rights—that man's mind and effort are the property of the community, of the nation, of the globe. We are told that none of this is demonstrable in reason, but that morality is outside the province and judgment of reason.

We are told, by theologians and philosophers alike—by Niebuhr and by Ayer, by Tillich and by Russell, by Brunner and by Carnap, by Buber and by Reichenbach—that reason cannot provide man with a code of values: reason deals only with means, not with ends. Ethics, we are told, is a matter of faith and feelings—and the collective faith of mankind, the consensus of its noblest feelings, has revealed the standard by which good and evil are to be judged: the good is that which is motivated by concern for the interest of *others;* the evil is that which is motivated by concern for the interests of *self.* And our political leaders are putting these principles into action by moving toward a society in which self-interest *is* forbidden, in which profit *is* impossible, in which no man is permitted to exist for his own sake and all are sacrificed to all—that is, toward a society of collectivism, toward the totalitarian state.

In all the plans to redistribute the wealth of the world, in the endless debates which one hears today about whose need is greater than whose and who should have first right to someone else's property, in the innumerable schemes for the enslavement of man in the name of the public good, there are certain questions that no one cares to ask or think about: Where does wealth come from? Who produces it? What human faculty makes production possible? These are the questions that are raised and answered in *Atlas Shrugged.*

The question and issue at the root of these questions—and the theme of *Atlas Shrugged*—is: What makes *human survival* possible?

Atlas Shrugged is a novel about man's relationship to existence. It is a novel about the nature of man, the nature of the world, and the actions, values and goals necessary and proper to man if he is to sustain and further his life. It is the dramatization of a new system of ethics: a morality of reason.

Atlas Shrugged identifies and demonstrates that which has never been fully grasped by men: the philosophical meaning of the Industrial Revolution. After centuries of stagnation and unspeakable poverty, men witnessed—in the past two hundred years, since the birth of the "Machine Age"—a sudden stream of material abundance unprecedented in human history. But they stared at that abundance—and at everything which it made possible—and never identified its source. It was said that wealth is the product of brute muscular labor. It was said that wealth is acquired by the exploitation of workers and the expropriation of the "surplus value" of their efforts. It was said that wealth is created by the beneficence of governments. It was said that inquiries into the source of wealth are ignoble or vulgar, and that such concerns are unworthy of the attention of civilized men. It was said that "the goods are here" and that it does not matter how they got here.

But factories and generators are not raw materials or "natural resources." They are not a "given" of human existence. Wealth—material goods—is a necessity of man's survival, and it has to be produced. Those who view wealth in the manner described above, do not care to ask: What faculty makes the production of wealth possible?—because the answer is: *Man's mind—human intelligence.* They do not care to ask: Who produces it?—because the answer is: *The men of ability.* They do not care to ask: What condition of existence is necessary for production?—because the answer is: *Freedom;* the freedom to think, to act on one's own judgment, to explore, to create, to attempt the unprecedented—and to earn one's reward. The question they would dread most is: What would happen to the world if the men of the mind refused to function? *That* is the story of *Atlas Shrugged.*

"There is only one kind of men," states John Galt, "who have never been on strike in human history. Every other kind and class have stopped, when they so wished, and have presented demands to the world, claiming to be indispensable—except the men who have carried the world on their shoulders, have kept it alive, have endured torture as sole payment, but have never walked out on the human race. Well, their turn has come. Let the world discover who they are, what they do and what happens when they refuse to function. This is the strike of the men of the mind . . . This is the mind on strike." *

John Galt, the hero of *Atlas Shrugged,* is a physicist and

---

* All subsequent quotations in this essay, unless otherwise indicated, are from *Atlas Shrugged.*

10

inventor of genius. He is the leader of the strike. He convinces the other creators, the originators in every line of rational endeavor, to leave their businesses, their laboratories, their concert halls, their classrooms, and silently to withdraw—to refuse to work or offer any intellectual benefits to a world that regards them as serfs. One by one, the men of ability vanish —and what follows is the breakdown and disintegration of society, a society deprived of the mind.

When the world has collapsed into chaos, helplessness and ruins, Galt makes the radio speech in which he tells mankind what he has done—and why:

"Men do not live by the mind, you say? I have withdrawn those who do. The mind is impotent, you say? I have withdrawn those whose mind isn't. There are values higher than the mind, you say? I have withdrawn those for whom there aren't. . . . Do not cry that it is our duty to serve you. We do not recognize such duty. Do not cry that you need us. We do not consider need a claim. Do not cry that you own us. You don't. Do not beg us to return. We are on strike, we, the men of the mind. . . . We are on strike against self-immola-tion. We are on strike against the creed of unearned rewards and unrewarded duties. We are on strike against the dogma that the pursuit of one's happiness is evil. We are on strike against the doctrine that life is guilt."

The moral code that Galt is challenging—that *Atlas Shrugged* and Ayn Rand are challenging—is the creed which, in one form or another, has dominated mankind's history: the doctrine that man has no right to exist for his own sake.

All the ethical systems that achieved any degree of world influence, were, at root, variations on the theme of self-sacri-fice. Unselfishness was equated with virtue; selfishness was made a synonym of evil. In such systems, *man* has always been the victim, twisted against himself and commanded to be "unselfish" in sacrificial service to some allegedly higher value called God or Pharaoh or Emperor or King or Society or the State or the Race or the Proletariat.

It was a nineteenth-century advocate of collectivism and totalitarianism, Auguste Comte, who coined the term that names the essence of this concept of morality: *"Altruism."* Today, the average man often takes "altruism" to mean simply benevolence or kindness or respect for the rights of others. But that is not the meaning Comte intended and that is not the term's actual philosophical meaning. Altruism—as an ethical principle—holds that man must make the welfare of others his primary moral concern and must place their interests above his own; it holds that man has no right to

11

exist for his own sake, that service to others is the moral justification of his existence, that self-sacrifice is his foremost duty and highest virtue.

It is a curious paradox of human history that this doctrine —which tells man that he is to regard himself as a sacrificial animal—has been accepted as a doctrine representing benevolence and love for mankind. One need only consider the consequences to which this doctrine has led, to estimate the nature of its "benevolence." From the first individual, thousands of years ago, who was sacrificed on an altar for the good of the tribe—to the heretics and dissenters burned at the stake for the good of the populace or the glory of God— to the millions exterminated in gas chambers or slave-labor camps for the good of the Race or of the Proletariat—it is this morality that has served as justification for every dictatorship and every atrocity, past or present. Yet men fought only over particular applications of this morality, they fought over who should be sacrificed to whom and for whose benefit, they expressed horror and indignation when they did not approve of someone's particular choice of victims and beneficiaries— but they did not question the basic principle: that man is an object of sacrifice.

The majority of men do not, of course, attempt to practice the doctrine of altruism consistently in their everyday lives. By its nature, that would not be possible. It is not a code to live by—only to die by. But because men have accepted it as *right*, because they view "altruism" and "morality" as synonyms, they are left in a moral vacuum: they have no moral principles to guide their choices and actions in practical reality. In their human relationships, they do not know what demands they can permit themselves and what demands they must grant to others; they do not know what is theirs by right, what is theirs by favor, what is theirs by someone's sacrifice. They fluctuate between sacrificing themselves to others and sacrificing others to themselves—under the guidance of conflicting social pressures and conflicting subjective whims— in no case feeling in rational control of their lives. They are forced into the position of *a*moralists, not by desire but by default. The door to morality has been closed—by a doctrine that offers them self-immolation as a moral ideal.

What made such a doctrine possible? It was mysticism that gave birth to altruism and it is mysticism that sustains it. The doctrine that man has no right to exist for his own sake, that his foremost duty and virtue is to serve others, cannot be defended in reason. Few of its advocates have even attempted such a defense. They have known that reason and their moral-

12

ity are incompatible, that there is no conceivable justification for turning men into sacrificial animals and no valid cause for men willingly to accept such a role. They have known that they have no answer to the dying screams of *"Why?"* echoing from the flames of burning stakes or the dark cellars of torture chambers, erected as monuments to their love of humanity. But the declarations that faith is superior to reason, the demands that man throttle his intellect in awe before projections of the supernatural, the attacks on the efficacy of man's mind and senses, the claims to an "Aryan logic" or a "Proletarian logic" that represents a special, higher form of knowledge above the criticism or judgment of those who are denied this revelation—all have worked to obviate the necessity of a rational defense of their ethical doctrine. Mysticism has made it possible for wealth to be expropriated, whims to be indulged, minds to be choked and lives to be destroyed—for men to be left struggling helplessly in the chaos of a moral jungle—and for the beneficiaries of the creed of self-sacrifice to declare: "To those who understand, no explanation is necessary; to those who do not, none is possible."

When philosophers announced that ethics is outside the province of reason and science—that the realm of *values* is the realm of *faith* and *feeling*—they delivered morality to the monopoly of mysticism, and affixed their signature under the mystics' claims. They declared to mankind: here, reason may not enter. And a glance at history is sufficient to establish the fact that reason *hasn't*. Whatever parts of the legacy of mysticism men have challenged and overthrown, the morality of altruism remains untouched; it is regarded as a self-evident absolute, as an axiom not to be questioned or doubted.

In Western civilization, the reign of mysticism reached its height in the stagnation and brutality of the Dark and Middle Ages—with its worship of the supernatural, its hostility toward the mind, its prohibition of scientific inquiry, its restrictions on production and trade, its rigid society of status. The reign of mysticism was maintained by the rule of physical force, and it was against the rule of force that men were struggling—for the right to live on earth. As the official voice and dominant power of the culture, mysticism died with the Renaissance, though the echoes of its death rattle lasted for centuries. With the rebirth of reason and science, men began the slow, faltering, upward climb toward a society in which the self-assertive, creative power of man's mind could find expression.

For man to be in control of his own existence and to achieve—psychologically and in external reality—a human

13

state of life and civilization, three conditions are necessary: the acceptance of the supremacy of reason; freedom; and a rational code of moral principles to guide his actions.

With the Enlightenment, the Industrial Revolution, and the rise of capitalism in the nineteenth century, the first two of these conditions were achieved, to a considerable extent. The result was the transformation of the world.

With the collapse of the absolute state and the development of the free-market society, men saw the sudden release of productive energy that had previously had no outlet. They saw life made possible for countless millions who could have had no chance at survival in pre-capitalist economies. They saw mortality rates fall and population growth rates explode upward. They saw machines—the machines that many of them had cursed, opposed and tried to destroy—cut their workday in half while multiplying incalculably the value and reward of their effort. They saw themselves lifted to a standard of living no feudal baron could have conceived. With the rapid development of science, technology and industry, men saw, for the first time in history, man's liberated mind taking control of his material existence.

To the extent that various countries adopted capitalism, the rule of brute force vanished from men's lives. Capitalism abolished slavery and serfdom in all of the civilized nations. *Trade*, not violence, became the ruling principle of human relationships. Intellectual freedom and economic freedom rose and flourished together. Men had discovered the concept of individual *rights*.

Individualism was the creative power revolutionizing the world.

A system in which wealth and position were inherited or acquired by physical conquest or political favor, was replaced by one in which values had to be earned by productive work. In closing the doors to force, capitalism threw them open to achievement: it offered men a *market* instead of a gun. Rewards were tied to production, not to extortion; to ability, not to brutality; to man's capacity for furthering life, not for inflicting death.

It was the United States of America, with its system of limited, constitutional government, that implemented the principle of capitalism—of free trade on a free market—to the greatest extent. In America, during the nineteenth century, men's productive activities were *predominantly* left free of governmental regulations, controls and restrictions; men considered themselves emancipated from the thoroughly discredited economic policies of medievalism, mercantilism and pre-

14

capitalist statism. In the brief period of a century and a half, the United States created a level of freedom, of progress, of achievement, of wealth, of physical comfort—a standard of living—unmatched and unequaled by the total sum of mankind's development up to that time.

Much has been written concerning the harsh conditions of life during the early years of capitalism. Yet when one considers the level of material existence from which capitalism raised men, and the comparatively meager amount of wealth in the world when the Industrial Revolution began, what is startling is not the *slowness* with which capitalism liberated men from poverty, but the *speed* with which it did so. Once man was free to act, individual ingenuity and inventiveness proceeded to raise the standard of living to heights which, a century earlier, would have been judged fantastic. It would be difficult to name an event of history more impressive than this—or less appreciated.

Capitalism was achieving miracles before men's eyes. Yet, from its beginning, the majority of nineteenth-century intellectuals were vehemently antagonistic to it. Their writings were filled with denunciations of the free-market economy. Broadly speaking, the antagonism came from two camps: the medievalists and the socialists.

The medievalists found the disintegration of feudal aristocracy, the sudden appearance of fortune-makers from backgrounds of poverty and obscurity, the emphasis on merit and productive ability, the concern with science and material progress—and, above all, the pursuit of *profit*—spiritually repugnant. Many of them—such as Richard Oastler, Wordsworth, Coleridge, Carlyle, Robert Southey, William Cobbett, Thomas Hood and Thomas Love Peacock—unleashed scathing attacks on the factory system. They were avowed enemies of the Age of Reason. They declared individualism vulgar. They longed for a return to a status society. "Commerce or business of any kind"—wrote John Ruskin—"may be the invention of the Devil." Few of his contemporaries revered the Middle Ages more intensely than Ruskin, who longed to live in the thirteenth century and who, in the spirit of that longing, implored the designers of railroad trains to shape the trains as dragons—evidently to make Ruskin feel more at home in an industrial age.

The medievalists dreamed of abolishing the Industrial Revolution. The socialists wished to take it over. Both camps dismissed, or gave only grudging acknowledgment to, the achievements of capitalism; they preferred to eulogize the living conditions of previous ages. Friedrich Engels—along with

Carlyle—regarded the domestic industries system of the pre-industrial era as the Golden Age of the working classes. The criticisms leveled against capitalism by both camps were remarkably similar: the "dehumanizing" effect of the factory system upon the worker, the "alienation" of man from nature, the "cold impersonality" of the market, the "cruelty" of the law of supply and demand—*and the evil of the pursuit of profit.*

The "rights of the individual," which was the principle at the base of capitalism, seemed to these critics to be merely a license to immorality: a system whose generator was the *profit motive* was self-evidently iniquitous. Cardinal Newman and Karl Marx were of one mind in this issue.

The socialists were rhapsodic in their projections of what the future would make possible, once the profit motive was abolished. Discussing their enraptured flight from reality, in his treatise *Socialism,* an analysis of collectivist economic doctrines, Ludwig von Mises writes: "In Fourier's state of the future all harmful beasts will have disappeared, and in their places will be animals which will assist man in his labors—or even do his work for him. An anti-beaver will see to the fishing; an anti-whale will move sailing ships in a calm; an anti-hippopotamus will tow the river boats. Instead of the lion there will be an anti-lion, a steed of wonderful swiftness, upon whose back the rider will sit as comfortably as in a well-sprung carriage. 'It will be a pleasure to live in a world with such servants.' Godwin even thought that men might be immortal after property had been abolished. Kautsky tells us that under the socialist society 'a new type of man will arise . . . a superman . . . an exalted man.' Trotsky provides even more detailed information: 'Man will become incomparably stronger, wiser, finer. His body more harmonious, his movements more rhythmical, his voice more musical . . . The human average will rise to the level of an Aristotle, a Goethe, a Marx. Above these other heights new peaks will arise.' "

The medievalists claimed for their position the sanction of traditional authority and mystical revelation. The Marxian socialists—the *neo*-mystics—claimed the sanction of dialectical materialism and polylogism. No less than Tertullian, they were sensitive to the obstacles that reason placed in the path of their aims. Dialectical materialism asserts that man's mind and its content are determined by the material factors of production of a given period; that philosophical thought is the mere "ideological superstructure" of economic forces; that those forces direct the flow of historical events, and man is

16

impotent to intervene; and that historical providence has ordained the inevitable coming of socialism and has informed its prophets—the Marxists—accordingly. Polylogism asserts that there is no single, objective and universal logic; that one's concept of the logical is determined by one's class membership; and that since all criticisms of socialist economic policies are merely manifestations of corrupt "bourgeois logic," it is unnecessary to answer those criticisms or refute them.

In the writings of both medievalists and socialists, one can observe the unmistakable longing for a society in which man's existence will be automatically guaranteed to him—that is, in which man will not have to bear responsibility for his own survival. Both camps project their ideal society as one characterized by that which they call "harmony," by freedom from rapid change or challenge or the exacting demands of competition; a society in which each must do his prescribed part to contribute to the well-being of the whole, but in which no one will face the necessity of making choices and decisions that will crucially affect his life and future; in which the question of what one has or has not earned, and does or does not deserve, will not come up; in which rewards will not be tied to achievement and in which someone's benevolence will guarantee that one need never bear the consequences of one's errors. The failure of capitalism to conform to what may be termed this *pastoral* view of existence, is essential to the medievalists' and socialists' indictment of a free society. It is not a Garden of Eden that capitalism offers men.

Commenting on a discussion between Werner Sombart, a Marxist turned Nazi, and Othmar Spann, a confirmed medievalist—Professor Mises writes (in a letter to Ayn Rand concerning her *For the New Intellectual*): "More than thirty years ago, I heard two of the most eminent eulogists of Attilaism bemoan the decay of civilization. 'Everything that happened since the Renaissance,' said Sombart, 'is decay and disintegration of the true and eternal Values.' 'You are mistaken,' replied Othmar Spann, 'the decadence started already in the thirteenth century when the lofty ideals of chivalry began to give way to selfish commercialism.' In Sombart's eyes the antithesis was: 'Heroes or Hucksters' as expounded in his book *Händler und Helden.*"

Whatever the differences that otherwise divided them, the critics of capitalism tacitly agreed on one thing: the basic evil of capitalism—with its profit-seeking, its individualism, its implicit affirmation of man's right to exist for his own sake —is that it represents a system of *institutionalized selfishness*.

What answers were given to these criticisms by the *de-*

fenders of capitalism? Consider the statements of two of its most famous advocates, John Stuart Mill and Herbert Spencer.

Mill's essay *On Liberty* is generally regarded as one of the classic defenses of the rights of the individual. But individual *rights* is precisely the concept that Mill does *not* support. His ethical standpoint is that of Utilitarianism. In *On Liberty*, he argues that society should leave men free. But as justification for his position, he projects an essentially collectivist premise: the premise that the group should permit the individual to be free because that will allow him *best to serve its interests*—thus implying that man does not in fact have the *right* to freedom, but is, morally, the property of the collective. Not astonishingly, Mill ended his life as a socialist.

Spencer defended capitalism by means of spurious analogies to animals in a jungle and "the survival of the fittest"— which implied a complete misrepresentation of the nature of capitalism, one that was thoroughly in accord with the views of its enemies. An animal's method of survival is not man's; men do not survive by fighting over a static quantity of meat (or wealth); their rational interests are not at war; they do not prosper at one another's expense and sacrifice; men survive by *producing* the values, the goods, their life requires. What was Spencer's ultimate moral justification for a free-market economy? Not the rights of the individual—but the purification of the *race;* the "weeding out of the unfit," in alleged accordance with the principles of evolution; that is, the good of the collective, of the *human species*.

It is historically, philosophically and psychologically significant that not one of the defenders of *laissez faire* chose to attack the position of his opponents at the root, on the level of basic premises; not one of them challenged the altruist-collectivist frame of reference in which all discussions concerning the value of capitalism were held.

Today, capitalism has been all but extinguished. Throughout the world, the rule of brute force is returning. In many major countries, the institution of slave labor has been reestablished, as a planned part of their economic program. Mankind is falling back to the statism of pre-capitalist centuries, as if the concept of a free society had never existed.

Yet *economically*, the case for capitalism has never been refuted. The advocates of *laissez faire* provided an unanswerable demonstration that a free-market economy is incomparably the most efficient and productive, that government controls and regulations do not raise but *lower* the standard of living, that government interventionism is responsible for the evils popularly ascribed to "unregulated" capitalism, such as depressions, protracted unemployment, militarism and aggressive nationalism. If, today, their arguments are swept aside; if modern teachers of economics prefer to speak as if the refutations of socialism and interventionism, offered by such writers as Ricardo, Say, Bastiat, Cobden, Böhm-Bawerk and Mises, did not exist; if students are now taught the dictatorial schemes of neo-barbarism, which economists in their great-grandfathers' time had recognized as such, and which are currently hailed as "liberal" and "progressive"; if the nature of capitalism is now forgotten or ignored—it is not because of the superior economic logic of its opponents. Capitalism was not defeated on economic grounds, but on *moral* grounds.

The tragedy of Western civilization is that while men rejected the *theology* of mysticism, they did not reject its *ethics*. They still clung to the creed of sacrifice. What changed was merely the name of the beneficiary. Not God but *Society* was to be the collector and recipient of man's sacrifices. But capitalism did not rest and could not survive on an altruist base. Capitalism implied and required a system of ethics that did not yet exist: a morality of *rational self-interest*. It was the absence of such a morality that made capitalism philosophically helpless against its enemies. If altruists assert that the profit motive is evil, that the competent and able must work and live for the good of Society, that intelligence is a "natural resource," that self-interest is anti-social—so do the rulers of the modern totalitarian state.

"The world seen through Fascism"—writes Benito Mussolini—"is not this material world which appears on the surface, in which man is an individual separated from all others and standing by himself . . . The man of Fascism is an individual who is nation and fatherland, which is a moral law, binding together individuals and the generations into a tradition and a mission, suppressing the instinct for a life enclosed within the brief round of pleasure in order to restore within duty a higher life free from the limits of time and space: a life in which the individual, through the denial of himself, through the sacrifice of his own private interests, through death itself, realizes that completely spiritual existence in which his value as a man lies."

"To be a socialist"—states Joseph Goebbels—"is to submit the I to the thou; socialism is sacrificing the individual to the whole."

"In the hunt for their own happiness"—declares Adolf Hitler—"people fall all the more out of heaven into hell."

19

Would Augustine or Calvin or John Kenneth Galbraith or Khrushchev disagree?

As to communism, its connection to the altruist morality is too obvious and too well known to require lengthy discussion. The sacrifice of the individual to the collective, the renunciation of all personal interests and motives, the individual's service to society as the sole justification of his existence, society's right to sacrifice him at any moment, in any manner it pleases, for the sake of any social goal—this is the essence of communism. "From each according to his abilities, to each according to his needs," is the altruist-collectivist slogan picked up from antiquity and introduced into modern culture by Karl Marx. "In a country where the sole employer is the State," writes Leon Trotsky, with uncharacteristic candor, "opposition means death by slow starvation. The old principle, who does not work shall not eat, has been replaced by a new one: who does not obey shall not eat." When, during his visit to the United States in 1959, Khrushchev declared, in effect, that communism merely puts into practice the precepts of the Bible, he revealed a better grasp of ethical principles than those who listened to him, aghast.

If one studies the manner in which the United States moved from its original policy of almost complete *laissez faire* to its present position of accelerating statism, if one analyzes the reasons offered for the judicial decisions that sanctioned the imposition of wider and wider government controls, one will see, graphically and specifically, why altruism and freedom are incompatible and by what steps the logic of altruism leads to the doctrine of government omnipotence. The implicit justification offered for those controls was the premise that the individual must be subordinated to the "public welfare"; which amounted, in application, to the premise that the competent must be sacrificed to the incompetent, that weakness and need—not objective justice—must be given first consideration in any dispute.

There is, perhaps, no more eloquent illustration of the intellectual and moral bankruptcy of our present culture, than a news story which appeared in *Time* on July 29, 1957:

"Recalling his tortuous postwar discussions with Zhukov—a 'confirmed Communist' but an 'honest man'—Dwight Eisenhower went on: 'One evening we had a three-hour conversation. We tried each to explain to the other just what our systems meant . . . to the individual, and I was very hard put to it when he insisted that their system appealed to the idealistic and we completely to the materialistic, and I had a very tough time trying to defend our position because he said:

20

"You tell a person he can do as he pleases, he can act as he pleases, he can do anything. Everything that is selfish in man you appeal to him, and we tell him that he must sacrifice for the state. . . ." '

"Asked by the New York *Times's* James Reston if he meant to imply that democracy was more difficult to defend than Communism, the President patiently explained: 'Look, Mr. Reston, I think you could run into people you have a hard time convincing that the sun is hot and the earth is round. . . . Against that kind of belief you run against arguments that almost leave you breathless. You don't know how to meet them.' "

Clearly, this is not an answer, but an evasion. Eisenhower *did not know how to meet* Zhukov's arguments.

Such is the moral chaos to which the ethics of altruism has led: the President of the greatest, noblest, freest country on earth has no moral defense to offer—against the bloodiest dictatorship in history, whose representative proudly boasts of *his* country's moral superiority; and, by the standards of altruism, *Zhukov is right.*

Capitalism—and civilization—are perishing, because men failed to achieve the *third* condition necessary for a human state of existence: a rational code of morality appropriate to man's nature and to this earth.

It is this that Ayn Rand has provided in *Atlas Shrugged.*

In the face of centuries of the worship of self-sacrifice as a moral ideal, as the highest good man can reach, Ayn Rand has risen to ask: *Good? By what standard?* She demonstrates with irrefutable logic that the morality of altruism is incompatible with the requirements of man's existence and survival. What she offers instead is that which had been declared impossible: a scientific ethics—a code of moral values based, not on revelation or subjective whim or social tradition, but on man's nature as a *living being.*

The philosophical and historical importance of the ethical system presented and dramatized in *Atlas Shrugged* does not consist only of the specific *conclusions* advocated, but of their manner of derivation—the epistemological and metaphysical foundation, the starting point, the place at which the system begins, and the method of its development.

Ayn Rand does not begin by taking the phenomenon of "values" as a given; that is, she does not begin merely by observing that men pursue various values and by assuming that the first question of ethics is: What values ought man to pursue? She begins on a far deeper level, with the question: What are values and why does man need them? Her approach is not

21

statistical, sociological or historical, but metaphysical; her concern is: What are the facts of reality—the facts of existence and of man's nature—that necessitate and give rise to values?

A *value,* she states, is that which one acts to gain and/or to keep. A value is the object of an action. " 'Value' presupposes an answer to the question: of value to whom and for what? 'Value' presupposes a standard, a purpose and the necessity of action in the face of an alternative. Where there are no alternatives, no values are possible." An entity who—by its nature—had no purposes to achieve, no goals to reach, could have no values and no need of values. There would be no "for what." An entity incapable of initiating action, or for whom the consequences would always be the same, *regardless* of its actions—an entity *not confronted with alternatives*—could have no purposes, no goals, and hence no values. Only the existence of alternatives can make purpose—and therefore values—*possible and necessary.*

"There is only one fundamental alternative in the universe: existence or non-existence—and it pertains to a single class of entities: to living organisms. The existence of inanimate matter is unconditional, the existence of life is not: it depends on a specific course of action. Matter is indestructible, it changes its forms, but it cannot cease to exist. It is only a living organism that faces a constant alternative: the issue of life or death. Life is a process of self-sustaining and self-generated action. If an organism fails in that action, it dies; its chemical elements remain, but its life goes out of existence. It is only the concept of 'Life' that makes the concept of 'Value' possible. It is only to a living entity that things can be good or evil."

It is only a living entity that can have needs, goals, *values* —and it is only a living entity that can generate the actions necessary to achieve them.

A plant does not possess consciousness; it can neither experience pleasure and pain nor have the concepts of life and death; nevertheless, plants can die; a plant's *life* depends on a specific course of action. "A plant must feed itself in order to live; the sunlight, the water, the chemicals it needs are the values its nature has set it to pursue; its life is the standard of value directing its actions. But a plant has no choice of action; there are alternatives in the conditions it encounters, but there is no alternative in its function: it acts automatically to further its life, it cannot act for its own destruction."

Animals possess a primitive form of consciousness; they cannot know the issue of life and death, but they can know

22

pleasure and pain; an animal's life depends on actions automatically guided by its sensory mechanism. "An animal is equipped for sustaining its life; its senses provide it with an automatic code of action, an automatic knowledge of what is good for it or evil. It has no power to extend its knowledge or to evade it. In conditions where its knowledge proves inadequate, it dies. But so long as it lives, it acts on its knowledge, with automatic safety and no power of choice, it is unable to ignore its own good, unable to decide to choose the evil and act as its own destroyer."

Given the appropriate conditions, the appropriate physical environment, all living organisms—with one exception—are set by their nature to originate automatically the actions required to sustain their survival. The exception is *man*.

Man, like a plant or an animal, must act in order to live; man, like a plant or an animal, must gain the values his life requires. But man does not act and function by automatic chemical reactions or by automatic sensory reactions; there is no physical environment on earth in which man could survive by the guidance of nothing but his involuntary sensations. And man is born without innate ideas; having no innate knowledge of what is true or false, he can have no innate knowledge of what is good for him or evil. *Man has no automatic means of survival.*

For man, survival is a question—a problem to be *solved*. The perceptual level of his consciousness—the level of passive sensory awareness, which he shares with animals—is inadequate to solve it. To remain alive, man must *think*—which means: he must exercise the faculty which he alone, of all living species, possesses: the faculty of abstraction, of *conceptualizing*. The *conceptual* level of consciousness is the human level, the level required for man's survival. It is upon his ability to think that man's life depends.

"But to think is an act of choice. The key to . . . human nature is the fact that *man is a being of volitional consciousness.* Reason does not work automatically; thinking is not a mechanical process; the connections of logic are not made by instinct. The function of your stomach, lungs or heart is automatic; the function of your mind is not. In any hour and issue of your life, you are free to think or to evade that effort. But you are not free to escape from your nature, from the fact that *reason* is your means of survival—so that for *you*, who are a human being, the question 'to be or not to be' is the question 'to think or not to think.'"

A being of volitional consciousness, a being without innate ideas, must discover, by a process of thought, the goals, the

23

actions, the values on which his life depends. He must discover what will further his life and what will destroy it. If he acts against the facts of reality, he will perish. If he is to sustain his existence, he must discover the *principles of action* required to guide him in dealing with nature and with other men. His need of these principles is his need of a code of values.

Other species are not free to *choose* their values. Man is. "A code of values accepted by choice is a code of morality."

The reason of man's need for morality determines the purpose of morality as well as the standard by which moral values are to be selected. Man needs a moral code in order to live; that is the purpose of morality—for every man as an individual. But in order to know what are the values and virtues that will permit him to achieve that purpose, man requires a standard. Different species achieve their survival in different ways. The course of action proper to the survival of a fish or an animal, would not be proper to the survival of man. Man must choose *his* values by the standard of that which is required for the life of a *human being*—which means: he must hold *man's life* (man's survival *qua* man) as his standard of value. Since reason is man's basic tool of survival, this means: the life appropriate to a rational being—or: that which is required for the survival of man *qua* rational being.

"All that which is proper to the life of a rational being is the good; all that which destroys it is the evil."

To live, man must think, he must act, he must *produce* the values his life requires. This, metaphysically, is the *human* mode of existence.

"Man's life, as required by his nature, is not the life of a mindless brute, of a looting thug or a mooching mystic, but the life of a thinking being—not life by means of force or fraud, but life by means of achievement—not survival at any price, since there's only one price that pays for man's survival: reason."

Thinking is man's basic virtue, the source of all his other virtues. "Reason is the faculty that perceives, identifies and integrates the material provided by his senses." Thinking is the activity of perceiving and identifying that which exists—of integrating perceptions into concepts, and concepts into still wider concepts, of constantly expanding the range of one's knowledge to encompass more and more of reality. The tool of thought is logic—"logic is the art of *non-contradictory identification*." Evasion, the refusal to think, the willful rejection of reason, the willful suspension of consciousness, the willful defiance of reality, is man's basic vice—the source of all his evils.

When men attempt to survive, not by thought and productive work, but by parasitism and force, by theft and brutality, it is still the faculty of reason that they are secretly counting on: the reason that some moral man had to exercise in order to create the goods which the parasites propose to loot or expropriate.

Man, like every other living species, has a specific manner of survival which is determined by his nature. Man is free to act against the requirements of his nature, to reject his means of survival: his mind—but he is not free to escape the consequence: misery, anxiety, destruction. When men attempt to exist by a means other than reason, it becomes a matter of little more than chance who lasts a decade and who lasts a year, who is wiped out by whom and who is able to consume some part of his gains before the club descends on *him*. Man's life depends on thinking, not on acting blindly; on achievement, not on destruction; nothing can change that fact. Mindlessness, passivity, parasitism, brutality are not and cannot be principles of survival; they are merely the policy of those who do not wish to face the issue of survival.

"Man's life" means: life lived in accordance with the *principles* that make man's survival *qua* man possible.

Just as man is alive, physically, to the extent that the organs within his body function in the constant service of his life, so man is alive, as a total entity, to the extent that, in addition to his heart, lungs and other vital organs, his *mind* functions in the constant service of his life. The mind, too, is a vital organ—the one vital organ whose function is *volitional*. A man encased in an iron lung, whose own lungs are paralyzed, is not dead; but he is not living the life proper to man. Neither is a man whose *mind* is volitionally paralyzed.

If a man is to live, he must recognize that facts are facts, that A is A, that *existence exists*—that reality is an absolute, not to be evaded or escaped—and that the task of his mind is to perceive it, that *this* is his primary responsibility. "A rational process is a *moral* process." He must recognize that his life requires the pursuit and achievement of rational values, values consonant with his nature and with reality—that life is a process of self-sustaining and self-generated action. He must recognize that *self*-value is the value without which no others are possible, but it is a value that has to be earned—and the virtue that earns it is thinking. "To live, man must hold three things as the supreme and ruling values of his life: Reason—Purpose—Self-esteem. Reason, as his only tool of knowledge— Purpose, as his choice of the happiness which that tool must proceed to achieve— Self-esteem, as his inviolate certainty that his mind is competent to think and his person is worthy of happiness, which means: is worthy of living."

The traditional mystics have declared that if God did not exist, morality would be unnecessary—everything would be "permissible." The neo-mystics have declared that if *Society* did not exist, morality would be unnecessary—any course of action would be as valid as any other. *Would it?* asks Ayn Rand. It is not for the purpose of satisfying the wishes of a supernatural being that man needs a code of moral values— she demonstrates—nor for the purpose of satisfying the wishes of his neighbors. The source and justification of values is neither God nor Society. Morality is neither mystical nor social. It is a practical, *selfish* necessity. Alone on a desert island, man would face constant alternatives requiring moral choice: to think—or not to think; to perceive reality, identify facts and act accordingly—or to sulk and pray; to work and produce—or to demand a miracle that would spare him the effort; to act on the judgment of his mind—or to surrender to terror; and his life would hang in the balance.

The cardinal principle at the base of Ayn Rand's ethical system is the statement that "It is only the concept of 'Life' that makes the concept of 'Value' possible. It is only to a living entity that things can be good or evil." This is the identification that cuts through the Gordian knot of past ethical theorizing, that dissolves the mystical fog which enveloped the field of morality, and refutes the contention that a rational morality is impossible and that values cannot logically be derived from facts.

It is the nature of living entities—the *fact* that they must sustain their life by self-generated action—that makes the existence of *values* possible and necessary. For each living species, the course of action required is specific; what an entity *is* determines what it *ought* to do.

By identifying the context in which values arise existentially, Ayn Rand refutes the claim—especially prevalent today —that the ultimate standard of any moral judgment is "arbitrary," that *normative* propositions cannot be derived from *factual* propositions. By identifying the genetic roots of "value" epistemologically, she demonstrates that *not* to hold man's life as one's standard of moral judgment is to be guilty of a *logical contradiction*. It is only to a living entity that things can be good or evil; life is the basic value that makes all other values possible; the value of life is not to be justified

26

by a value beyond itself; to demand such justification—to ask: Why *should* man choose to live?—is to have dropped the meaning, context and source of one's concepts. *"Should"* is a concept that can have no intelligible meaning, if divorced from the concept *and value* of life.

If life—existence—is *not* accepted as one's standard, then only one alternative standard remains: *non*-existence. But non-existence—death—is not a standard of value: it is the negation of values. The man who does not wish to hold life as his goal and standard is free not to hold it; but he cannot claim the sanction of reason; he cannot claim that his choice is as valid as any other. It is not "arbitrary," it is not "optional," whether or not man accepts his nature as a living being—just as it is not "arbitrary" or "optional" whether or not he accepts reality.

The concept of an ethics based on man's metaphysical nature is not, as such, new. Many philosophers of antiquity, as well as many of the post-Renaissance system builders, claimed to have derived their systems of ethics from such a base. In their attempts logically to connect the specific values they advocated with their descriptions of man's metaphysical nature, one may discern two major trends.*

Some philosophers ascribed to man, as a metaphysical attribute, a particular *desire* or *conatus;* they declared it to be universal and innate; then they stated that an objective ethics, one genuinely based on man's nature, would be one that enabled man to achieve this desire or striving. Aristotle spoke of the universal desire for *eudaimonia* (happiness or well-being); Epicurus—of the universal desire for pleasure; the Stoics—of the universal desire for serenity; Spinoza—of the universal *conatus* toward self-preservation. But none of these philosophers ever succeeded in demonstrating that any such desire or striving *is* universal and innate in man; nor could such a claim be proved. (The fallacy of treating desires as innate or as irreducible primaries is discussed in Chapter II.) Observe, further, that these philosophers were not so much *deducing* from man's nature the values man should choose, as claiming to find values *pre-existing* in man's nature.

Other philosophers attempted a different solution. (Some attempted to combine both.) They declared that individual man is not an autonomous entity metaphysically, but is merely a fragment or aspect or manifestation or appearance of some higher, unified, transcendent entity or dimension which constitutes "true reality"—and that virtue consists of acting in

---

* I am indebted to my associate Leonard Peikoff for the identification of these two trends.

27

accordance with the purposes of, or principles governing, this transcendent reality. Plato spoke of acting in accordance with the Form of Man and the Form of the Good; the Stoics—of acting in accordance with the purposes of the Cosmic Organism; Spinoza—of acting in accordance with the Logic of Eternity; Hegel—of acting in accordance with the dialectical procession of the Absolute. This, of course, is not an objective ethics, but merely a retreat into mysticism. And here again one may observe, in the theories of these philosophers, the assumed pre-existence of values in man's nature and in the nature of the universe, rather than a genuine deducing of values from the facts of man's nature.

In no sense does Ayn Rand regard any particular value as a metaphysical given, as pre-existing in man or in the universe. She begins by observing the facts that create the *need* for values. The basic facts of man's nature from which her ethics proceeds, are: that man's life, like that of any other organism, must be sustained by self-generated action; that the course of action required is *specific,* as it is specific for every species; that man is a being of volitional consciousness; that man has no automatic code of behavior, but must discover the actions and values his life requires; that reason is man's basic means of survival. She answers the question "What are values and why does man need them?" by analyzing man's distinctive nature in the context of the universal class of living organisms. That is the great originality of her approach. She does not advocate a single moral principle that cannot be traced back, by an unbroken logical chain, to the demonstrable requirements of man's survival *qua* man.

What are the major virtues man's survival requires? Rationality—independence—honesty—integrity—justice—productiveness—pride. Rationality is the unreserved commitment to the perception of reality, to the acceptance of reason as an absolute, as one's only guide to knowledge, values and action. Independence is reliance upon one's own mind and judgment, the acceptance of intellectual responsibility for one's own existence. Honesty is the refusal to seek values by faking reality, by evading the distinction between the real and the unreal. Integrity is loyalty *in action* to the judgment of one's consciousness. Justice is the practice of identifying men for what they *are* and treating them accordingly. Productiveness is the act of supporting one's existence by translating one's thought into reality, of setting one's goals and working for their achievement, of bringing knowledge or goods into existence. Pride is *moral ambitiousness,* the recognition "that as man must produce the physical values he needs to sustain

28

his life, so he must acquire the values of character that make his life worth sustaining—that as man is a being of self-made wealth, so he is a being of self-made soul . . ."

In elaborating the meaning and application of these virtues, Ayn Rand makes clear that they are all expressions or derivatives of the primary virtue: rationality. The manner in which these virtues relate to the issue of man's survival is discussed in principle in Galt's speech and illustrated in detail in the events of *Atlas Shrugged*.

The virtue of *productiveness* is the basic expression of rationality in man's relationship to nature—and it is obvious why a morality of survival would attach especial importance to this virtue. All the characters whom Ayn Rand presents as representatives of her morality—philosopher-scientist John Galt, industrialists such as Hank Rearden, Francisco d'Anconia and Dagny Taggart, a composer such as Richard Halley, or men of lesser ability and a smaller scale of ambition such as Eddie Willers—have one conspicuous attribute in common: a passionate love of their work, a dedication to achieving the utmost possible to them, a profound sense that thought and effort constitute, not a burden or a duty, but the source of their enjoyment of existence.

In asserting the efficacy of his intellect through the act of supporting his life, man gains a control over his own existence that no other species can achieve. Productive work is the supremely *human* act; animals must adjust themselves to their physical background; man adjusts his physical background to himself. Man has the capacity of giving psychological and existential unity to his life by integrating his actions to goals projected across a life span.

Morally, it is not the *degree* of a man's productive ability that matters, but his choice to exercise such ability as he does possess. It is not the *kind* of work a man selects that determines his moral stature, but whether or not he seeks a work that requires and expresses the fullest, most conscientious use of his mind. The mere physical motions of an unthinking zombie repeating a routine he does not care to understand or improve upon, do not represent the virtue of productiveness.

If life on earth is the standard, then it is not the man who *sacrifices* values who is moral, but the man who *achieves* them; not the man who renounces, but the man who creates; not the man who forsakes life, but the man who makes life possible.

Man—every man—is an end in himself, not a means to the ends of others. *He is not a sacrificial animal.* As a living being, he must exist for his own sake, neither sacrificing himself to others nor sacrificing others to himself. The achievement of his own happiness is man's highest moral purpose.

To live for his own happiness imposes a solemn responsibility on man: he must learn what his happiness objectively requires. It is a responsibility that the majority of men have not chosen to assume. No belief is more prevalent—or more disastrous—than that men can achieve their happiness by the pursuit of any random desires they experience. The existence of such a profession as psychotherapy is an eloquent refutation of that belief.

Happiness is the state of consciousness that proceeds from the achievement of one's values. "Happiness is the successful state of life, pain is an agent of death. . . . But neither life nor happiness can be achieved by the pursuit of irrational whims. Just as man is free to attempt to survive in any random manner, but will perish unless he lives as his nature requires, so he is free to seek his happiness in any mindless fraud, but the torture of frustration is all he will find, unless he seeks the happiness proper to man. The purpose of morality is to teach you, not to suffer and die, but to enjoy yourself and live."

In a lecture on her moral philosophy at the 1961 Wisconsin Symposium on Ethics, at the University of Wisconsin, Ayn Rand stated:

"The maintenance of life and the pursuit of happiness are not two separate issues. To hold one's own life as one's ultimate value, and one's own happiness as one's highest purpose are two aspects of the same achievement. Existentially, the activity of pursuing rational goals is the activity of maintaining one's life; psychologically, its result, reward and concomitant is an emotional state of happiness. It is by experiencing happiness that one lives one's life, in any hour, year or the whole of it. And when one experiences the kind of pure happiness that is an end in itself—the kind that makes one think: *This* is worth living for'—what one is greeting and affirming in emotional terms is the metaphysical fact that *life* is an end in itself.

"But the relationship of cause to effect cannot be reversed. It is only by accepting 'man's life' as one's primary and by pursuing the rational values it requires that one can achieve happiness—*not* by taking 'happiness' as some undefined, irreducible primary and then attempting to live by its guidance. If you achieve that which is the good by a rational standard of value, it will necessarily make you happy; but that which makes you happy, by some undefined emotional standard, is not necessarily the good. To take 'whatever makes one

30

happy' as a guide to action means: to be guided by nothing but one's emotional whims. Emotions are not tools of cognition; to be guided by whims—by desires whose source, nature and meaning one does not know—is to turn oneself into a blind robot, operated by unknowable demons (by one's stale evasions), a robot knocking its stagnant brains out against the walls of a reality which it refuses to see.

"*This* is the fallacy inherent in *hedonism*—in any variant of ethical hedonism, personal or social, individual or collective. 'Happiness' can properly be the *purpose* of ethics, but *not* the *standard*. The task of ethics is to define man's proper code of values and thus to give him the means of achieving happiness. To declare, as the ethical hedonists do, that 'the proper value is whatever gives you pleasure' is to declare that 'the proper value is whatever you happen to value'—which is an act of intellectual and philosophical abdication, an act which merely proclaims the futility of ethics and invites all men to play it deuces wild." *

In declaring that the achievement of his happiness is man's highest moral purpose, Ayn Rand advocates an ethics of *selfishness* or *egoism*. To be selfish means to be motivated by concern for one's self-interest; egoism, as an ethical doctrine, holds that self-interest is man's proper moral goal.

But only reason can judge what is or is not objectively to man's self-interest; the question cannot be decided by feeling or whim. To act by the guidance of feelings and whims is to pursue a course of self-destruction; and self-destruction is not to man's self-interest. Self-interest cannot be divorced from reason, or from man's nature, or from the nature of reality; it cannot be divorced from *objective facts*.

Now, in what manner have philosophers traditionally presented the issue of selfishness versus unselfishness, or egoism versus altruism? Selfishness has been represented to mean: acting on one's own desires, regardless of the facts of reality and regardless of the rights of others. *Un*selfishness has been defined as: sacrificing one's own desires and serving the desires of others, instead. Ethicists have commonly declared or implied that man's basic moral alternative is: to sacrifice others to himself (which they call egoism)—or to sacrifice himself to others (altruism). The overwhelming majority of ethicists, of course, have insisted that man practice the latter alternative; the few exceptions have been the philosophers,

---

* Ayn Rand, "The Objectivist Ethics," New York: Nathaniel Branden Institute, 1961.

such as Nietzsche* and Max Stirner, who recommended the former. But observe the two crucial issues on which both sides agree: (1) that feelings and whims are the proper guides of man's actions and the basic concern of ethics, and that the only question is: Whose whims are to be satisfied and whose are to be sacrificed? (2) that sacrifices are *necessary*, that by the nature of human existence, someone must inevitably be sacrificed to someone.

The second of their assumptions is the inevitable product of the first. If men choose their goals by *whim*, without regard for reason and reality, then, in the moral wilderness that will result, their "interests" will necessarily clash; and men will have no choice but to view one another with fear, suspicion and hatred, as potential victims or executioners.

It is because Ayn Rand rejects the *first* of these two assumptions that she does not fall into the trap of accepting the *second*. Here again one may observe her distinctive approach, which was noted earlier: in no issue does she take a *desire* as a primary ethical consideration; her focus is *fact*-centered, *reality*-centered, not *wish*-centered. Just as she begins her treatment of ethics with the question: What *facts of reality* give rise to and necessitate values?—so, in her treatment of the specific issue of selfishness, she asks: What *in fact* constitutes man's self-interest?—*not*: Is it moral for a man to act on his *desires*?

As a consequence, she does not accept the tenet that human existence is an amoral jungle, that life requires the practice of human sacrifices, and that man's basic moral choice is to be a sadist or a masochist. She recognizes both sadism and masochism as a disease, as two variations of the same evil. The root of that evil is *whim-worshipping*.

To think, is to man's self-interest; to suspend his consciousness, is not. To choose his goals in the full context of his knowledge, his values and his life, is to man's self-interest; to act on the impulse of the moment, without regard for his long-range context, is not. To exist as a productive being, is to man's self-interest; to attempt to exist as a parasite, is not. To seek the life proper to his nature, is to man's self-interest; to seek to live as an animal, is not.

The man who sacrifices others is no more concerned with his self-interest *in fact* than the man who sacrifices himself; no man who pursues a policy of irrationality, evasion, parasitism and destructiveness can be said to be objectively concerned

---

* At least in some of his works; his position is rather equivocal.

with his self-interest. Sadism and masochism are merely two different forms of *failing* to be concerned with one's self-interest.

If, as altruism claims, to be motivated by self-interest is evil, then *life and that which it objectively requires* is evil. If self-sacrifice is the essence of virtue, then it is *death* that altruism offers men as a moral ideal.

In one of the most brilliant passages of Galt's speech, Ayn Rand subjects the ethics of altruism—the code of "sacrifice" —to a detailed analysis of its exact meaning and implications for man's life on earth. She demonstrates that it is an inverted morality: a morality that holds the evil as the good, and the good as the evil. It holds as vices the things on which man's life depends, and as virtues, the things that lead to man's destruction: it denounces reason and demands faith; it scorns achievement and extols renunciation; it attacks self-esteem and commends guilt; it penalizes ability and rewards incompetence; it damns happiness and worships suffering.

No man of reason and self-esteem, she states, expects others to exist for his welfare, or to regard his pain as their burden or his needs as a claim on their life; nor is he willing to assume the role of sacrificial animal in relation to them. The oath taken by John Galt and all the men whom he leads on strike, is: "I swear—by my life and my love of it—that I will never live for the sake of another man, nor ask another man to live for mine."

If men are to live together as civilized beings, then *justice,* not sacrifice, must be the ruling principle among them. Just as productiveness is the primary expression of man's rationality in his relationship to nature, so justice is the primary expression of man's rationality in his relationship to other men.

To be just, is to deal with men as they objectively deserve, which means: never to grant or demand the unearned, neither in matter nor in spirit—to recognize each man's right to exist for his own sake and never to ask that he exist for yours—to reward the actions and traits of character in men which are pro-life, and to condemn those which are anti-life—to offer men admiration for their virtues and contempt for their vices —and never to turn virtue into a *liability,* and vice into an *asset,* by supporting or sanctioning any doctrine which proposes to sacrifice the men of virtue, intelligence and ability, for the benefit of the evil, the stupid, the incompetent.

"The symbol of all relationships among [rational] men, the moral symbol of respect for human beings, is *the trader.* . . . A trader is a man who earns what he gets and does not give or take the undeserved. A trader does not ask to be paid for

33

his failures, nor does he ask to be loved for his flaws. A trader does not squander his body as fodder or his soul as alms. Just as he does not give his work except in trade for material values, so he does not give the values of his spirit—his love, his friendship, his esteem—except in payment and in trade for human virtues, in payment for his own selfish pleasure, which he receives from men he can respect. The mystic parasites who have, throughout the ages, reviled the traders and held them in contempt, while honoring the beggars and the looters, have known the secret motive of their sneers: a trader is the entity they dread—a man of justice."

The principle of justice, which is central in the ethical philosophy of Ayn Rand, is the principle most conspicuously avoided in the ethics of altruism. The question of justice is one which the advocates of altruism clearly prefer not to hear raised. Their reticence is not difficult to understand, when one remembers what altruism advocates. Just as altruism teaches that wealth does not have to be earned, so it teaches that love does not have to be earned. Just as it teaches that the able must be sacrificed to the incompetent, so it teaches that values must be sacrificed to flaws, that virtue consists of loving without standards, of offering one's love as alms to whoever may claim to need it. "A morality that professes the belief that the values of the spirit are more precious than matter, a morality that teaches you to scorn a whore who gives her body indiscriminately to all men—this same morality demands that you surrender your soul to promiscuous love for all comers." Just as altruism seeks to divorce wealth from achievement, so it seeks to divorce love from values—so that men will be paid for the goods they have not produced, and loved for the qualities of character they do not possess.

One of the foremost contemporary spokesmen for this "non-commercial" view of human relationships is psychologist Erich Fromm, who, with impressive consistency, is a socialist, a devotee of Zen Buddhism and an advocate of the theory that love should be liberated from such unspiritual concepts as the "deserved" and the "undeserved." "In essence, all human beings are identical," he declares in *The Art of Loving.* "We are all part of One; we are One. This being so, it should not make any difference whom we love." Fromm criticizes capitalism for what he (correctly) terms its *"fairness ethics."* It is capitalism, he holds, that makes the practice of love so difficult. He writes: "It may even be said that the development of fairness ethics is the particular ethical contribution of capitalist society. The reasons for this fact lie in the very nature of capitalist society. In pre-capitalist

34

societies, the exchange of goods was determined either by direct force, by tradition, or by personal bonds of love or friendship. In capitalism, the all-determining factor is the exchange on the market. Whether we deal with the commodity market, the labor market, or the market of services, each person exchanges whatever he has to sell for that which he wants to acquire under the conditions of the market, without the use of force or fraud. . . . If our whole social and economic organization is based on each one seeking his own advantage, if it is governed by the principle of egotism tempered only by the ethical principle of fairness, how can one do business, how can one act within the framework of existing society and at the same time practice love? . . . The *principle* underlying capitalistic society and the *principle* of love are incompatible." It is socialism, he argues, that will make love possible, by annihilating the concepts of the "earned" and the "unearned" by means of which capitalism has poisoned the development of ideal love.

Here one may observe, in unusually explicit statement, the diametrical opposite of Ayn Rand's view of proper human relationships as expressed by the "trader principle." Ayn Rand does not believe that fairness (justice) "tempers" or "limits" self-interest, as Fromm evidently does; she regards fairness or justice as indispensable to, *and inseparable from*, self-interest. Nor does she think that, in regard to moral worth, "all human beings are identical." She draws moral distinctions between a hero and a scoundrel, or a murderer and his victim. Nor does she think that "it should not make any difference whom we love." In her ethics, it should and does make a difference.

To love, she states, is to *value;* love, properly, is the consequence and expression of admiration—"the emotional price paid by one man for the joy he receives from the virtues of another." Love is not alms, but a moral tribute.

If love did *not* imply admiration, if it did not imply an acknowledgment of moral qualities that the recipient of love possessed—what meaning or significance would love have, and why would Fromm or anyone consider it desirable? Only one answer is possible, and it is not an attractive one: when love is divorced from values, then "love" becomes, not a tribute, but a moral blank check: a promise that one will be forgiven anything, that one will not be abandoned, that one will be taken care of.

There are characters in *Atlas Shrugged* who would agree with Fromm's view of love, enthusiastically and unreservedly. One of these characters is James Taggart. "Don't bother me,

don't bother me, don't bother me," are the first words uttered
by Taggart, when he is introduced in the story; they contain
the essence of his soul and of his chronic sense of life; they are
addressed to the universe in general and to anyone's demand
that he think, in particular. Taggart is the president of a great
railroad, which he had inherited; his wife, Cherryl, a young,
intensely idealistic girl, had married him, believing him to be
a brilliant industrialist; gradually she discovers that he is only
a pretentious parasite who has taken credit for the achievements of others. When she confronts Taggart with her knowledge of the truth about him, he answers:

" 'You don't love me' . . .

" 'I did love you once,' she said dully, 'but it wasn't what
you wanted. I loved you for your courage, your ambition,
your ability. But it wasn't real, any of it.'

"His lower lip swelled a little in a faint, contemptuous
thrust. 'What a shabby idea of love!' he said.

" 'Jim, what is it that you want to be loved for?'

" 'What a cheap shopkeeper's attitude!'

"She did not speak; she looked at him, her eyes stretched
by a silent question.

" 'To be loved *for!*' he said, his voice grating with mockery
and righteousness. 'So you think that love is a matter of mathematics, of exchange, of weighing and measuring, like a pound
of butter on a grocery counter? I don't want to be loved *for*
anything. I want to be loved for myself—not for anything I
do or have or say or think. For myself—not for my body or
mind or words or works or actions.'

" 'But then . . . what *is* yourself?'

" 'If you loved me, you wouldn't ask it. . . . You wouldn't
ask. You'd know. You'd *feel* it. Why do you always try to tag
and label everything? Can't you rise above those petty materialistic definitions? Don't you ever feel—just *feel?*' "

"Love," declares Erich Fromm, "is an act of faith." So
does James Taggart.

There is another contemporary figure whom it is appropriate to quote in this connection—philosopher Bertrand Russell. He, too, conveys impatience with such distinctions as the
earned and the unearned; it is suffering and need, he declares
—not justice—that must be given first consideration. In his
essay "A Free Man's Worship," he writes: "The life of Man
is a long march through the night, surrounded by invisible
foes, tortured by weariness and pain, towards a goal that few
can hope to reach, and where none may tarry long. One by
one, as they march, our comrades vanish from our sight,
seized by the silent orders of omnipotent Death. Very brief is

the time in which we can help them, in which their happiness or misery is decided. Be it ours to shed sunshine on their path, to lighten their sorrows by the balm of sympathy, to give them the pure joy of a never-tiring affection, to strengthen failing courage, to instill faith in hours of despair. Let us not weigh in grudging scales their merits and demerits, but let us think only of their need—of the sorrows, the difficulties, perhaps the blindnesses, that make the misery of their lives; let us remember that they are fellow-sufferers in the same darkness, actors in the same tragedy with ourselves."

One would think that a man of such compassion, with as great a concern for the misery of his fellow-sufferers, would be anxious to inquire about the *cause* of their sorrows, difficulties and blindnesses, and to discover whether the merits and demerits, which he brushes aside so airily, have some relationship to it—whether the uncondemned demerits are causing the darkness and the tragedy which the unrecognized merits could have had the power to eliminate. But Mr. Russell—and those who share his viewpoint—are clearly impatient of such questions.

Who can measure virtues in the midst of a catastrophe?— is an attitude that one frequently encounters among those who offer, as justification for altruism, the view of man's life as metaphysically tragic. The tragic view of human existence is, along with the morality of sacrifice, among the foremost parts of the legacy left to civilization by mysticism. In bewailing the misery of the human condition, Augustine was vehement; to imagine that one is happy, he declared, is to confess that one is devoid of all human feeling. Not to think that man's life is tragic, is commonly regarded as proof of one's superficiality; certainly it is the proof that one is not fashionable. That Existentialism has enthusiastically embraced the metaphysics of catastrophe and wailing, is well known. But even such anti-Existentialist, "modern" philosophers as Sidney Hook and Ernest Nagel have felt obliged, in papers respectively entitled "Pragmatism and the Tragic Sense of Life" and "Naturalism Reconsidered," to defend Pragmatism (or "Naturalism") against the charge that it is insufficiently tragic in its view of life, and to protest that Pragmatists (or "Naturalists") are fully as cognizant of the tragic aspects of existence as anyone else.

If theologians, philosophers and moralists were less eager to damn existence, man's nature and his life on earth, if they were less willing to conclude that suffering is man's inevitable fate—they would perhaps notice that the predominant cause of such suffering as they do observe is not any sort of meta-

37

physical necessity, but the *philosophies* men have been offered as a guide by which to live. If men are taught that faith is superior to reason, that man's intellect is impotent to solve the fundamental problems of his existence, that virtue consists of sacrifice; if men believe that it is immoral to pass moral judgments, that one must not draw moral distinctions between the practitioners of irrationality and their victims, since "all men are equally unworthy in the sight of God"; if men, accepting the doctrine that they are helpless, believe that life on earth is misery—it *will be*. So long as mysticism and altruism are offered to the world as antidotes to the disasters of which they are the cause, man's life can be *nothing but* tragic. But the fault does not lie in human nature, nor in the nature of existence.

If one is genuinely concerned with the alleviation of human suffering, one must begin by recognizing that to live *"non-tragically,"* man requires a rational view of existence and a rational code of moral values. And included in such a code must be the recognition that one does not alleviate suffering by refusing to distinguish between innocence and guilt; man must judge and be willing to be judged.

An unearned forgiveness of evil, holds Ayn Rand, is a shrug of indifference toward the pain of the innocent. The magnanimity, generosity and sympathy exhibited by Ayn Rand's heroes toward those who are the innocent victims of injustice or who are putting up an honest battle against adversity—and her heroes' merciless condemnation of those who are the conscious, willful perpetrators of injustice—proceed from a single premise: loyalty to life and to those who are struggling to preserve it. *Because* her heroes have sympathy for man the victim, they have none for man the killer.

Just as Ayn Rand rejects mysticism and the morality of altruism, so she rejects their product: the tragic view of life. Ayn Rand does not see man as a being metaphysically torn by impossible contradictions, she does not see his nature as depraved, she does not see him as doomed, she does not see life as frustration and futility. In *Atlas Shrugged*, she has created a glowing tribute to the potentialities of man's existence, to the greatness, happiness, fulfillment and mutual benevolence possible to men who choose to live by the principles, not of faith and sacrifice, but of reason, justice and the inviolate supremacy of man's right to exist for his own sake.

What she offers men, is a philosophy for living on earth.

It is significant that she chose industry as the background against which to dramatize her ethics, and an industrialist

38

—Hank Rearden—as one of her central heroes. Of any one class or profession, industrialists have been the most exploited victims of the mystic-altruist code—and, simultaneously, they have been, by the nature of their activity, one of the most eloquent refutations of that code.

It is shocking but true that the majority of men have never grasped the fact that the food they eat, the clothing they wear, the building they live in, the refrigerators, the automobiles, the can openers, the radio and television sets they enjoy—are the products of human *intelligence*. They regard material production as some sort of "animal instinct" unrelated to man's mind. They have reserved the concepts of "genius" and "spiritual greatness" for the philosopher, the theoretical scientist and the artist; they have never grasped that the concepts apply to Hank Rearden.

It is mysticism that has made this failure of understanding possible. Specifically, it is a result of the mystics' *soul-body* dichotomy—with its damnation of this earth as an "inferior realm," its contempt for production, trade and profit-seeking as "ignoble" and "vulgar," and its longing for a "higher dimension" where men will be unencumbered by such unworthy, material concerns. How many persons, who would consider themselves thoroughly emancipated from any trace of mysticism or supernaturalism, still cling to and perpetuate this remnant of the Dark Ages?

The soul-body dichotomy has worked hand in hand with the ethics of altruism to support the creed of the unearned: since, it is claimed, industrialists are mindless barbarians engaged in activities which "superior spirits" despise—why *shouldn't* they be chained, commanded, expropriated?

In *Atlas Shrugged,* Ayn Rand shows the qualities of *spirit* —of mind and of character—that material production requires. She dramatizes and makes graphically real the independence, the courage, the integrity, the ambition, the intellectual power of the men who create and sustain an industrial civilization—the men who are *not* helpless, who are *not* impotent, who do not regard work and effort as an imposition or a burden, who do not passively submit to disaster while moaning that life is tragedy—the men who transform the materials of nature for the purpose of man's enjoyment and comfort—the men *who do not long for a Garden of Eden*— the men who are in love with this earth.

And, in Galt's radio speech, Ayn Rand asks: "You, who claim that you long to rise above the crude concerns of the body, above the drudgery of serving mere physical needs— *who* is enslaved by physical needs: the Hindu who labors from sunrise to sunset at the shafts of a hand-plow for a bowl of rice, or the American who is driving a tractor? *Who* is the conqueror of physical reality: the man who sleeps on a bed of nails or the man who sleeps on an inner-spring mattress? *Which* is the monument to the triumph of the human spirit over matter: the germ-eaten hovels on the shorelines of the Ganges or the Atlantic skyline of New York?"

Atlas Shrugged is profoundly anti-mystical, not only in its unreserved advocacy of reason, but in its overall projection of man's relationship to existence: in its *man-centeredness*, its celebration of human efficacy, its presentation of this earth as a realm benevolently open to man's achievement and enjoyment.

The actual hero of *Atlas Shrugged* is: man's mind. The novel dramatizes what reason is, how it functions and what happens to the world when the men of the mind—the men who create motors, railroads, metals, philosophies and symphonies—refuse to be martyred by the rule of irrationalism. It is in defense of such men—the men of ability and of "unrequited rectitude"—that *Atlas Shrugged* is written.

Such grudging admiration as has been given man's mind, has been reserved exclusively for the abstract theoretician; intelligence has been admired only when it was aimed at the stars, never when it was aimed at this earth—on the premise that thinking can be of moral significance only to the extent that it appears to dissolve into mysticism in its lack of concern for the problems of man's practical existence. Hence the scorn of technology or applied science as against "pure" science. *Every* productive use of the mind, either theoretical or practical, requires and expresses ability; and *all* knowledge, however abstract, ultimately does have practical application to man's existence. But the concept of *ability*, in its prevalent and popular usage, more specifically denotes the achievements of human intelligence and ingenuity in the direct service of man's practical needs. And it is to *this* that men have been morally indifferent.

In basing ethics on the requirements of man's survival, in demonstrating the role of man's mind in human existence, in exalting human ability and in defining a morality of rational self-interest, Ayn Rand has provided the intellectual foundation of an industrial civilization, a civilization geared to the creative assertion of man's intellect. In *Atlas Shrugged*, the Industrial Revolution, capitalism—and man's life on earth—have found that which they lacked and desperately needed: a *philosophical* spokesman and defender.

The moral principles men accept, their view of what is

right or wrong for man, determines the kind of society they will create and the kind of laws that will govern that society. A political system is the expression and product of a code of ethics. Just as collectivism is the expression of the ethics of altruism, so individualism—capitalism—is the expression of the ethics of rational self-interest.

The essence of the social system Ayn Rand advocates, the system derived from and necessitated by her ethics, is contained in a single principle: *No man—or group of men—may seek to gain values from others by the use of physical force.*

When men enter into social relationships, when they choose to deal with one another, they face a fundamental alternative: to deal with men by means of reason—or by means of force. Reason and force are opposites; either a man seeks to gain values from others by their voluntary consent, by persuasion, by appealing to their mind—or he seeks to gain values *without* the voluntary consent of the owner, that is, by coercion or fraud. This is the issue at the base of all social relationships and all political systems.

The choice to deal with men by reason, by persuasion, rests on the recognition that every man is the owner of his own life and person, that he is an end in himself and exists for his own sake, that his mind is no one else's to command. The choice to deal with men by force rests on the rejection of reason as man's means of survival, the rejection of man's right to exist, the acceptance of the tenet that men may be treated as sacrificial animals whose lives are at the disposal of others.

It is at the *mind* that every gun is aimed. Every use of force is the attempt to compel a man to act against his own judgment; if he were *willing* to take the action, force would not be required.

In a moral society, holds Ayn Rand, force may be used only as *retaliation* and only against the man who *initiates* its use. The principle involved is that which distinguishes murder from self-defense. The man who resorts to the initiation of force seeks to gain a value by so doing; the man who retaliates in self-protection does not seek to gain a value, but to *keep* a value that is rightfully his. "A holdup man seeks to gain wealth by killing me; I do not grow richer by killing a holdup man."

The policy of seeking values from men by means of force, when practiced by an individual, is called crime; when practiced by a government, it is called Statism—or Totalitarianism or Collectivism or Communism or Socialism or Nazism or Fascism or the Welfare State.

Force is the instrument by which the ethics of altruism—

41

the creed of the unearned—is translated into political reality.

It is to those who believe they have the right to force the minds of others that Galt is speaking when, in his address to a world whose motor he has stopped, he states: "If you want to know what you lost when I quit and when my strikers deserted your world—stand on an empty stretch of soil in a wilderness unexplored by men and ask yourself what manner of survival you would achieve and how long you would last if you refused to think, with no one around to teach you the motions, or, if you chose to think, how much your mind would be able to discover—ask yourself how many independent conclusions you have reached in the course of your life and how much of your time was spent on performing the actions you learned from others—ask yourself whether you would be able to discover how to till the soil and grow your food, whether you would be able to invent a wheel, a lever, an induction coil, a generator, an electronic tube—then decide whether men of ability are exploiters who live by the fruit of *your* labor and rob you of the wealth that *you* produce, and whether you dare to believe that you possess the power to enslave them. . . . When you clamor for public ownership of the means of production, you are clamoring for public ownership of the mind. I have taught my strikers that the answer you deserve is only: 'Try and get it.'"

The moral-political concept that forbids the initiation of force, and stands as the guardian and protector of man's life, freedom and property, is the concept of *rights*.

If life on earth is the standard, states Ayn Rand, man has a *right* to live and pursue values, as his survival requires; he has a *right* to think and to act on his judgment—the right of liberty; he has a *right* to work for the achievement of his values and to keep the results—the right of property; he has a *right* to live for his own sake, to choose and work for his own personal goals—the right to the pursuit of happiness.

Without property rights, no other rights are possible. If one is not free to use that which one has produced, one does not possess the right of liberty. If one is not free to make the products of one's work serve one's chosen goals, one does not possess the right to the pursuit of happiness. And—since man is not a ghost who exists in some non-material manner—if one is not free to keep and to consume the products of one's work, one does not possess the right of life. In a society where men are not free privately to own the material means of production, their position is that of slaves whose lives are at the absolute mercy of their rulers. It is relevant here to remember the statement of Trotsky: "Who does not obey shall not eat."

Just as Ayn Rand demonstrates that morality is neither mystical nor social nor subjective, but is a practical, objective necessity of man's existence—so she demonstrates that *rights* are neither arbitrary nor "stipulational" nor provisional, but are logically derivable from man's nature and needs as a living being. ". . . the source of man's rights is not divine law or congressional law, but the law of identity. A is A—and Man is Man. *Rights* are conditions of existence required by man's nature for his proper survival."

Traditionally, the source of rights *has* been described as "divine law or congressional law." That is, rights have been represented as a gift of God or a gift of Society. To validate rights by claiming to derive them from a supernatural being, is to base them on *mysticism*—and thus to declare that there is no *rational* justification for rights, no *rational* proof why men should not murder and enslave one another. To validate rights by claiming that they are a gift of Society is to *deny* the concept of rights and to declare that man exists, not by right, but by *permission*. A permission can be revoked. If man's life and property are a gift from society, then man is the *property* of society. To exist by permission, is to be a slave.

In Ayn Rand's approach to the issue of rights, as in so many other issues, one can observe how radical is her break with the traditional defenders of individualism and capitalism. In fundamental premises she is as distant from the traditional defenders of capitalism as she is from its enemies.

In a political-economic context, freedom, she states, means one thing and one thing only: *freedom from physical compulsion.* There is nothing that can deprive man of his freedom except other men—and no means by which they can do it except through the use of force. It is only by the initiation of force (or fraud, which is an indirect form of force) that man's rights can be violated.

A society's choice is not whether or not it will *grant* man rights, but whether or not it will *recognize* that he possesses them. "*Rights* are a moral concept—and morality is a matter of choice. Men are free not to choose man's survival as the standard of their morals and their laws, but not free to escape from the fact that the alternative is a cannibal society, which exists for a while by devouring its best and collapses like a cancerous body, when the healthy have been eaten by the diseased, when the rational have been consumed by the irrational."

The only proper and justifiable purpose of a government,

holds Ayn Rand, is to protect man's rights; to protect man from physical violence. It is the fact that man's rights *can* be violated by other men that necessitates the institution of government. "A proper government is only a policeman, acting as an agent of man's self-defense, and, as such, may resort to force *only* against those who *start* the use of force." The function of a government is to protect men from criminals, to protect men from foreign invaders, and to provide a system of courts for the protection of property and contracts against breach or fraud.

In a society where men's rights are protected by objective law, where the government has no other function or power, men are free to choose the work they desire to do, to trade their effort for the effort of other men, to offer ideas, products and services on a market from which force and fraud are barred, and to rise as high as their ability will take them. Because they deal with one another as producers, not as masters or slaves, they are able to achieve the full advantages of social existence: the advantages made possible by the human capacity to transmit knowledge, and by specialization and exchange under a division of labor. Among men who do not seek the unearned, who do not long for contradictions or wish facts out of existence, who do not regard sacrifice and destruction as a valid means to gain their ends—there is no conflict of interests. Such men deal with one another by voluntary consent to mutual benefit. They do not reach for a gun —or a legislator—to procure for them that which they cannot obtain through voluntary exchange.

It is a widely held belief, inherited from Marx, that government is necessarily an agent of economic interests, and that political systems are to be defined in terms of whose economic interests a government serves. Thus, capitalism is commonly regarded as a system in which the government predominantly acts to serve the interests of businessmen; socialism, as a system in which the government serves the interests of the working class. It is this concept of government that Ayn Rand rejects.

The fundamental issue, she demonstrates, is not what *kind* of economic controls a government enforces nor on whose behalf; the issue is a controlled economy versus an *un*controlled economy—that is, slavery versus freedom. *Laissez faire* capitalism is *not*—as its enemies have inexcusably attempted to maintain—government control of economics for the benefit of businessmen; it is the complete *separation* of State and Economics. This is implicit in the nature of capitalism, but historically it was not identified in such terms nor

44

adhered to consistently. In *Atlas Shrugged*, this concept is made explicit and basic. What Ayn Rand establishes is that the separation of State and Economics is a *defining principle* of capitalism.

One of the consequences of men's confusion on this issue and of their failure sharply to distinguish between the principle of free trade and the principle of statism, is that capitalism is blamed for evils which in fact were caused by the *abrogation* of capitalism—for instance, governmental intervention to foster coercive monopolies or cartels.* But A is A—and free trade is *free* trade. Essential to Ayn Rand's political philosophy is that a proper government must *have no economic favors to dispense*—it must be constitutionally forbidden to abridge the freedom of production and trade on *anyone's* behalf.

The battle in *Atlas Shrugged*—and in the world today—is not between businessmen and workers. It is between men who *earn* values and men who seek the unearned; between men who wish to deal by trade and men who wish to deal by force; between the kind of businessman or worker who seeks to profit by honest productive ability, and the kind who seeks to profit by political power: by means of franchises, subsidies, tariffs, compulsory unionism, minimum wage laws, and other such government regulations.

Who profits in a world where men are free to seek profits? Who benefits in a society where the initiation of force—either by individuals or by the government—is forbidden? In Galt's speech Ayn Rand presents with irrefutable logic that which she has thoroughly dramatized and illustrated in the events preceding the speech: the essential nature and operation of a free-market society. The passage is worth quoting at length:

"Look past the range of the moment, you who cry that you fear to compete with men of superior intelligence, that their mind is a threat to your livelihood, that the strong leave no chance to the weak in a market of voluntary trade. What determines the material value of your work? Nothing but the productive effort of your mind—if you lived on a desert island. The less efficient the thinking of your brain, the less your physical labor would bring you . . . But when you live in a rational society, where men are free to trade, you receive an incalculable bonus: the material value of your work is de-

---

* For a discussion of how economic evils resulting from government interventionism have been used as an indictment of *laissez faire* and made the excuse for *increasing* interventionism, see Ayn Rand, *Notes on the History of American Free Enterprise*, New York: Nathaniel Branden Institute, 1959. In these *Notes,* the early history of the American railroads is used as illustration.

termined not only by your effort, but by the effort of the best productive minds who exist in the world around you.

"When you work in a modern factory, you are paid, not only for your labor, but for all the productive genius which has made that factory possible: for the work of the industrialist who built it, for the work of the investor who saved the money to risk on the untried and the new, for the work of the engineer who designed the machines of which you are pushing the levers, for the work of the inventor who created the product which you spend your time on making, for the work of the scientist who discovered the laws that went into the making of that product, for the work of the philosopher who taught men how to think . . .

"The machine, the frozen form of a living intelligence, is the power that expands the potential of your life by raising the productivity of your time. If you worked as a blacksmith in the mystics' Middle Ages, the whole of your earning capacity would consist of an iron bar produced by your hands in days and days of effort. How many tons of rail do you produce per day if you work for Hank Rearden? Would you dare to claim that the size of your pay check was created solely by your physical labor and that those rails were the product of your muscles? The standard of living of that blacksmith is all that your muscles are worth; the rest is a gift from Hank Rearden.

"Every man is free to rise as far as he's able or willing, but it's only the degree to which he thinks that determines the degree to which he'll rise. Physical labor as such can extend no further than the range of the moment. The man who does no more than physical labor, consumes the material value-equivalent of his own contribution to the process of production, and leaves no further value, neither for himself nor others. But the man who produces an idea in any field of rational endeavor—the man who discovers new knowledge—is the permanent benefactor of humanity. Material products can't be shared, they belong to some ultimate consumer; it is only the value of an idea that can be shared with unlimited numbers of men, making all sharers richer at no one's sacrifice or loss, raising the productive capacity of whatever labor they perform. It is the value of his own time that the strong of the intellect transfers to the weak, letting them work on the jobs he discovered, while devoting his time to further discoveries. This is mutual trade to mutual advantage; the interests of the mind are one, no matter what the degree of intelligence, among men who desire to work and don't seek or expect the unearned.

"In proportion to the mental energy he spent, the man who creates a new invention receives but a small percentage of his value in terms of material payment, no matter what fortune he makes, no matter what millions he earns. But the man who works as a janitor in the factory producing that invention, receives an enormous payment in proportion to the mental effort that his job requires of *him*. And the same is true of all men between, on all levels of ambition and ability. The man at the top of the intellectual pyramid contributes the most to all those below him, but gets nothing except his material payment, receiving no intellectual bonus from others to add to the value of his time. The man at the bottom who, left to himself, would starve in his hopeless ineptitude, contributes nothing to those above him, but receives the bonus of all of their brains. Such is the nature of the 'competition' between the strong and the weak of the intellect. Such is the pattern of 'exploitation' for which you have damned the strong.

"Such was the service we had given you and were glad and willing to give. What did we ask in return? Nothing but freedom. We required that you leave us free to function—free to think and to work as we choose—free to take our own risks and to bear our own losses—free to earn our own profits and to make our own fortunes—free to gamble on *your* rationality, to submit our products to your judgment for the purpose of a voluntary trade, to rely on the objective value of our work and on your mind's ability to see it—free to count on your intelligence and honesty, and to deal with nothing but your mind. Such was the price we asked, which you chose to reject as too high. You decided to call it unfair that we, who had dragged you out of your hovels and provided you with modern apartments, with radios, movies and cars, should own our palaces and yachts—you decided that *you* had a right to your wages, but *we* had no right to our profits, that you did not want us to deal with your mind, but to deal, instead, with your gun. Our answer to *that*, was: 'May you be damned!' Our answer came true. You are."

In the world of the present, men regard the right of a government to initiate force against its citizens as an absolute not to be debated or challenged. They stipulate only that force must be used "for a good cause." Precisely because capitalism forbids men the use of force to gain their ends, intellectuals dismiss *laissez faire* as "antisocial" and "unprogressive." All the enemies of the free-market economy—communists, socialists, fascists, welfare statists—openly aspire to a single goal: to reach a position where they will be empowered to impose their ideas on others at the point of a gun. Whether

47

they propose to take over the economy outright, in the manner of communists and socialists, or to maintain the pretense of private property while dictating prices, wages, production and distribution, in the manner of fascists and welfare statists —it is a gun, it is the rule of physical force that they consider "kind," they who consider the free market "cruel."

Whatever the differences in their specific programs, they are unanimous in their belief that they have a *right* to dispose of the lives, property and future of others, that private ownership of the means of production is a selfish evil, that the more a man has achieved, the greater is his debt to those who have not achieved it, that men can be compelled to go on producing under any terms or conditions their rulers decree, that freedom is a luxury which may have been permissible in a primitive economy, but for the running of giant industries, electronics factories and complex sciences, nothing less than slave labor will do.

Since the moral justification offered for the rule of force is mankind's *need* of the things which the men of ability produce, it follows that the greater a man's productive ability, the greater are the penalties he must endure, in the form of controls, regulations, expropriations. An obvious application of this principle is the progressive income tax: those who produce the most, are penalized accordingly; those who produce nothing, receive a subsidy, in the form of relief payments. Or consider the enthusiastic advocacy of socialized medicine. What is the justification offered for placing the practice of medicine under government control? The *importance* of the services that physicians perform—the urgency of their patients' *need*. Physicians are to be penalized precisely because they have so great a contribution to make to men's welfare; thus is virtue turned into a liability.

Today, men have all but lost the knowledge of what capitalism is, how it functions and what it achieved. The truth about its nature and history has been drowned in a wave of misrepresentation, distortion, falsification and almost universal ignorance. Only within the past few decades has there been the beginning of a serious movement among historians to expose and correct the gross factual errors in the literature purporting to describe nineteenth-century capitalism. Almost everyone today takes it as axiomatic that capitalism results in the vicious exploitation of the poor; that it leads to monopoly; that it necessitates periodic depressions; that it starts wars; that it resisted and opposed the workers' rising standard of living; that that standard of living was the achievement, not of capitalism, but of labor unions and humanitarian labor

48

legislation. Not one of these claims is true; but they are among the commonest bromides of our culture. People do not feel obliged to question such bromides, since they "know" in moral principle that capitalism *must* result in evils: capitalism is based on the profit motive and appeals to men's self-interest; that alone is sufficient to damn it. The soul-body dichotomy and the ethics of altruism permit intellectuals—when discussing politics and economics—to indulge an unconcern for knowledge, facts, evidence or proof, that would be universally recognized as shockingly irresponsible were it directed at any other science.

If freedom, capitalism and civilization are to survive, it is the legacy of mysticism—in epistemology, in metaphysics, in ethics, in politics—that men must reject.

The world will not be saved by that alleged defense of freedom (by "conservatives") which consists of arguing that man should not be sacrificed to the State, he should sacrifice himself to God instead. It was the mystics' morality of sacrifice that *delivered* the world to collectivism. The basic question is not: To whom should man be sacrificed? The basic question is: Is man an object of sacrifice?

It is *here*, Ayn Rand has shown, that the moral line must be drawn: between all the anti-mind, anti-man, anti-life contingents that preach self-sacrifice for the sake of heaven or of posterity, for the sake of God or of Society—and the men of self-esteem who will proudly assert a morality of reason, individualism, self-interest and man's happiness on earth.

The name that Ayn Rand has chosen for her system is Objectivism. The concept is applicable to her theory of existence, of knowledge and of values. In metaphysics, it is the principle that reality is objective and absolute, that it exists independent of anyone's consciousness, perceptions, beliefs, wishes, hopes or fears—that that which is, is what it is—that "existence is identity"—that A is A. In epistemology, it is the principle that man's mind is competent to achieve objectively valid knowledge of that which exists. In ethics, it is the principle that the values proper to man are objectively demonstrable.

Ayn Rand's opposition to contemporary epistemological theory is no less profound than her opposition to contemporary ethical and political theory. The same rejection of reason which in politics is expressed in the resurgence of the rule of brute force throughout the world, is expressed in philosophy in the cult of uncertainty and epistemological agnosticism; the first is made possible only by the second. At a time when the need for answers to crucial questions is a matter of life and death, modern philosophy has nothing to offer men but a choice of mysticisms: the neo-mysticism of Pragmatism and Positivism, which teaches that it is meaningless to speak of "facts of reality" and/or futile to imagine that man can know any facts—and the old-fashioned mysticism of Existentialism, which teaches (in its more optimistic moods) that man *can* know reality, but not by means of reason, only through his "blood and bowels." The analysis of this resurgence of irrationalism, which has been growing since the time of Kant (and usually parading as the voice of science), constitutes one of the most important epistemological issues presented in *Atlas Shrugged*. In Galt's speech, Ayn Rand develops the essential similarities between the traditional mystics, whom she calls the "mystics of spirit," and the neo-mystics, whom she calls the "mystics of muscle." "For centuries, the mystics of spirit have proclaimed that faith is superior to reason, but have not dared deny the existence of reason. Their heirs and products, the mystics of muscle, have completed their job and achieved their dream: they proclaim that everything is faith, and call it a revolt against believing. As revolt against unproved assertions, they proclaim that nothing can be proved; as revolt against supernatural knowledge, they proclaim that no knowledge is possible; as revolt against the enemies of science, they proclaim that science is superstition; as revolt against the enslavement of the mind, they proclaim that there is no mind."

The ability to think outside the frame of reference of one's predecessors and contemporaries, to question their implicit assumptions, to challenge their standard definitions and to look at the facts of reality with an unobstructed glance—is a defining characteristic of an innovator; one finds this ability made manifest on every page of *Atlas Shrugged*. Encyclopedic in its philosophic and psychological range, the novel deals with the widest and most basic problems of human existence—and to those problems Ayn Rand brings an inexhaustible richness and originality of perception and analysis. There is no issue that she does not treat in a fresh and startlingly illuminating way. One of the slogans of the heroes of the novel is "Check your premises"—and it is this that Ayn Rand demands of her readers: to check, to re-examine, to re-think the most fundamental premises at the root of their convictions and of their culture.

It is overwhelmingly apparent that such an act of reappraisal is necessary—when one considers the present state of the world and the disaster to which its prevalent ideas have brought it.

No single book has ever challenged so many traditional beliefs in so many areas of human life, and it was inevitable that *Atlas Shrugged* should become a storm center of intellectual controversy. It is hard to say which is the more eloquent proof of its signal relevance to the crucial issues of our age: the widespread enthusiasm and admiration it has inspired—or the hysteria of the attacks unleashed against it.

The nature of those attacks is an instructive index of the current intellectual condition of our culture.

Ayn Rand's antagonists have unfailingly elected to pay her what is, perhaps, the greatest tribute one can offer to a thinker whom one opposes: they have all felt obliged to misrepresent her ideas in order to attack them.

No one has dared publicly to name the essential ideas of *Atlas Shrugged* and to attempt to refute them. No one has been willing to declare: "Ayn Rand holds that man must choose his values and actions exclusively by reason, that man has the right to exist for his own sake, that no one has the right to seek values from others by physical force—and I consider such ideas wrong, evil and socially dangerous."

Ayn Rand's opponents have found it preferable to debate with straw men, to equate her philosophy with that of Spencer or Nietzsche or Spinoza or Hobbes and thus expose themselves to the charge of philosophic illiteracy—rather than identify and publicly argue against that for which Ayn Rand actually stands.

Were they discussing the ideas of an author whose work was not known to the general public, their motive would appear obvious. But it is a rather grotesque spectacle to witness men seemingly going through the motions of concealing from the public the ideas of an author whose readers number in the millions.

When one considers the careful precision with which Ayn Rand defines her terms and presents her ideas, and the painstaking manner in which each concept in concretized and illustrated—one will search in vain for a non-psychiatric explanation of the way in which her philosophy has been reported by antagonists. Allegedly describing her concept of rational self-interest, they report that Ayn Rand extols disregard for the rights of others, brutality, rapacity, doing whatever one feels like doing and general animal self-indulgence. This, evidently, is the only meaning they are able to give to the concept of self-interest. One can only conclude that this is how they conceive their own self-interest, which they altruistically and self-sacrificially renounce. Such a viewpoint

51

tells one a great deal about the man who holds it—but nothing about the philosophy of Ayn Rand.

In Ayn Rand's earlier novel, *The Fountainhead*, altruist-collectivist Ellsworth Toohey makes an observation that is singularly appropriate here: ". . . just listen to any prophet and if you hear him speak of sacrifice—run. Run faster than from a plague. It stands to reason that where there's sacrifice, there's someone collecting sacrificial offerings. Where there's service, there's someone being served. The man who speaks to you of sacrifice, speaks of slaves and masters. And intends to be the master. But if ever you hear a man telling you that you must be happy, that it's your natural right, that your first duty is to yourself—that will be the man who's not after your soul. That will be the man who has nothing to gain from you. But let him come and you'll scream your empty heads off, howling that he's a selfish monster. So the racket is safe for many, many centuries."

Ayn Rand's antagonists have cried that the heroes of *Atlas Shrugged* are ruthless, unfeeling, devoid of compassion. The first of the antagonists who cried it was James Taggart. Those who share his viewpoint feel that the generosity of Ayn Rand's heroes is heartlessly selective: it is not offered indiscriminately to good and evil alike, it is offered only to those who deserve it. Evidently they have sensed that, by Ayn Rand's ethics, a moral flaw they did not care to correct would not be forgiven them; and they find this monstrous. Doubtless, they have their reasons, as James Taggart has his.

Theirs is the mentality which asserts that the proof of the cruelty of Ayn Rand's ethics is the willingness of her heroes to withdraw from the world and see it collapse in chaos, famine and ruins. If the men of ability in *Atlas Shrugged* are immoral because they refuse to go on producing under the rule of force, then this charge is equally applicable to any individuals who flee from a dictatorship. Consider the example of East Germany. The economy of this collectivist dictatorship collapsed as a result of the flight of its most independent and talented citizens. If their refusal to be martyrs and to sacrifice themselves for the sake of whatever benefits they might have brought to the people left behind, is regarded as cruel—then *there* is the proof that Ayn Rand is right in describing altruism as a creed of *moral cannibalism*.

In their commitment to non-perception, the enemies of *Atlas Shrugged* have denounced its ethical philosophy as "materialistic." Remembering that Ayn Rand's ethics holds *thinking* as man's highest virtue, one might be tempted to assume that the charge of "materialism" is made *in spite of* this fact; the truth is that it is made *because of* it. To think, is to identify the facts of reality. Man's life, states Ayn Rand, depends on his mind; the purpose of thought is knowledge; the purpose of knowledge is action and achievement; the purpose of action and achievement is man's life and happiness on earth. The person who regards this as "materialistic" is merely confessing that he does not wish to know that the question of moral values *is* the question of life or death; he does not want the issue of survival (or of reality) to arise; he wants the problem of survival to have been solved, somehow, by someone, so that he will not have to be restricted by such "vulgar" concerns and his soul will be free to contemplate the "higher" issues that "really" matter. What have thought and achievement got to do with *ethics?* he cries petulantly. Why should I be judged by what I think or do? What about my *feelings?* I want to be loved for myself!

While it is not true that Ayn Rand is concerned only with "matter," it *is* true that she is concerned only with *reality,* that is, with *existence.* She willingly leaves non-existence to her antagonists.

Just as Ayn Rand presents a new code of morality, so, emerging from the pages of *Atlas Shrugged,* is a new concept of man, a new concept of the human potential—of the human ideal. And if one wishes to understand the cause of the great enthusiasm that *Atlas Shrugged* has inspired—as well as the cause of the virulent hatred—one will find the key in the nature of the ideal man that Ayn Rand projects.

He is the man who is passionately in love with existence, and passionately in love with his own consciousness—the man of intransigent rationality and inviolate self-esteem. When Dagny Taggart sees John Galt for the first time, this is the description given of him: ". . . a face that bore no mark of pain or fear or guilt. The shape of his mouth was pride, and more: it was as if he took pride in being proud. The angular planes of his cheeks made her think of arrogance, of tension, of scorn—yet the face had none of these qualities, it had their final sum: a look of serene determination and of certainty, and the look of a ruthless innocence which would not seek forgiveness or grant it. It was a face that had nothing to hide or to escape, a face with no fear of being seen or of seeing, so that the first thing she grasped about him was the intense perceptiveness of his eyes—he looked as if his faculty of sight were his best-loved tool and its exercise were a limitless, joyous adventure, as if his eyes imparted a superlative value to himself and to the world—to himself for

53

his ability to see, to the world for being a place so eagerly worth seeing."

An unreserved commitment to reason and the acceptance of reality as an absolute, are the hallmark of the Ayn Rand hero. He is the man who faces existence in full mental focus —who accepts the responsibility of being *conscious.*

He is the man who holds nothing above the rational judgment of his mind—neither wishes nor whims nor the unproved assertions of others. He is not the man without desires; he is the man who has no desires held in defiance of reason. He is not the man without emotions; he is the man who does not substitute his emotions for his mind. He is not the man without passion; he is the man without arbitrary whims. He is not the man without the capacity to feel; he is the man with the highest capacity for feeling—because his feelings are the product of rational, non-contradictory values.

The most crucially important *psychological* concept in Galt's speech, is the definition of man as a being of *volitional consciousness*, the definition of free will as consisting of one choice and one choice only, which confronts man in every moment and issue of his life: to think or not to think—to focus his mind or to suspend it—to perceive or to blank out —to achieve the human state of awareness, to *conceptualize,* or to remain on the involuntary, automatic, concrete-bound level of an animal's awerness. The heroes of Ayn Rand's novels are the men who consistently choose to think; the villains are the men who choose not to. This is the choice at the base of morality and of all of a man's subsequent actions; it is the choice that determines his character; it is the gauge of his virtue. The villains are the men who *resent* the effort of consciousness, who resent the "restrictions" of logic, who treat their feelings as tools of cognition and their wishes as superior to facts, longing for a universe in which their whim would be omnipotent, and striving to blank out the distinction between the real and the unreal, the achieved and the faked, the earned and the unearned. If the Ayn Rand hero is the man who is pro-consciousness, then his antipode is the man who regards consciousness as an irritating imposition. If the Ayn Rand hero is the man who never places his desires above reality, then his antipode is the man who, in any clash, regards his desires as untouchable absolutes and reality as expendable.

Ayn Rand is not the first writer to project a hero who is a genius; nor is she the first writer to project a hero who fights courageously to achieve his chosen goals. But she *is* the first to project a hero who is a hero *all of the time*—that is, a hero who does not go out to fight a great battle and then come home to marry a hausfrau and to live his *private* life by a less demanding code of values.

Mankind has moved forward by the grace of the men who chose to be rational about one thing only: their work—but who, as their biographies reveal, were often quite conventional or irrational in all the other aspects of their lives. The heroes in *Atlas Shrugged* are distinguished by the fact that they have chosen to exercise their rational faculty in *every* aspect of their lives—not only their work, but also their character, their romantic choices, their personal relationships, that which they seek for enjoyment and emotional consumption. In their work, they are men of limitless ambition, for whom achievement is the meaning of life. In their human relationships, what they expect from and offer to those they love is not forgiveness or compassion, but admiration—an admiration that has to be earned. They judge others by rational standards—and they expect others to judge them by rational standards.

Just as, in their relationship to nature, it is not a pastoral existence they long for, but an existence that will make the fullest demands on their consciousness, on the efficacy of their minds—so, in their relationships with other human beings, it is not an escape from values they long for, but the highest and most demanding values possible.

The Ayn Rand hero is the man to whom every moment of his life is important—because it is *his* life. He is the man to whom every aspect of his character is important—because it is *his* character.

He is the man who has been denounced as heartless, inhuman, antisocial, cruel, unbelievable, unreal. He is called heartless, because he lives by the judgment of his mind. He is called inhuman, because the irrational does not tempt him, because he has no inner conflicts to evade and no secret vices to conceal. He is called antisocial, because he holds that man has the right to exist. He is called cruel, because he does not believe in human sacrifices. He is called unbelievable, because in his most passionate or spontaneous moments he does not lose the knowledge of what he is doing. He is called unreal, because he possesses a degree of self-esteem that those who attack him could not begin to conceive—a self-esteem that is not at the trembling mercy of anyone's chance appraisal, of anyone's approval or condemnation—a self-esteem whose source and motor is his intransigent determination to think and to act on his rational judgment.

He is the man whom the moral code of the centuries has been designed to destroy—and, simultaneously, the man whom it has declared to be impossible. Has it been said that a John Galt could not possibly exist? This means that a man of reason could not possibly exist—that a man whose mind and emotions are not at war could not possibly exist—that a man who wishes to be neither slave nor master could not possibly exist—that parasitism is possible, but independence is not—that disease is possible, but health is not—that a scoundrel is possible, but a hero is not—that evil is possible, but virtue is not—that self-loathing is possible, but self-esteem is not—that the sub-human is possible, but the human is not. The Ayn Rand hero is not, as those who attack him have asserted, the man who is "beyond good and evil." He is that which, to them, is much more terrifying: a man who takes the issue of good and evil seriously—and assumes the responsibility of identifying what *is* the good and the evil.

Such is the moral ideal that Ayn Rand has brought to the world. Such is the standard that she has chosen to raise in the growing darkness of a bankrupt culture.

No one can predict the speed with which new ideas will be grasped and accepted by men, most particularly ideas that oppose a tradition thousands of years old. But in *Atlas Shrugged* the mystic-altruist-collectivist ethics has received an analysis from which that ethics will not recover.

In an age when their ideals have turned most of the earth into a slaughterhouse, the worn-out, fifty-year-old, collectivist intellectuals, posturing as daring, idealistic, adolescent rebels, have become grotesque. They are the representatives of an exhausted, cynical, bloodstained *status quo*. Today, Objectivism is the new radicalism.

Some of those who read *Atlas Shrugged* will recognize that they are being offered that which had never existed before: a rational morality proper to man's nature and to his life on earth. Some of those who read *Atlas Shrugged* will cry—as James Taggart cries, after hearing Galt's speech—"We don't have to believe it! Nobody's ever said it before! We don't have to believe it!" No, they don't have to believe it. They are free to think or not to think. They are free to hold life —or death—as their standard of value.

But the moral revolution in *Atlas Shrugged* is not to be stopped. The mystics' monopoly on morality has been broken. Man the rational being has found his spokesman and defender, and has been released from his moral underground. That is the imperishable achievement of Ayn Rand.

II
Objectivism and Psychology

The belief that moral values are the province of faith and
that no rational, scientific code of ethics is possible, has had
disastrous effects in virtually every sphere of human activity. But there is one profession for which the consequences
of this belief have been particularly acute: the science of
psychology.

As a theoretical discipline, pyschology is concerned with
studying and defining the nature of consciousness: the volitional and automatic functions of consciousness, the source
and nature of emotions, the principles of character-formation,
the principles of motivation. As a therapeutic discipline, it is
concerned with the diagnosis and treatment of the malfunc-
tions of consciousness, of mental and emotional disturbances,
of character and motivational disorders.

The central problem of the science of psychology is the
issue of *motivation*. The base of the science is the need to
answer two fundamental questions: Why does a man act as he
does? What would be required for a man to act differently?
These questions are directed, not only at man's physical actions, but at the actions of his consciousness—at the whole of
his mental life.

The key to motivation lies in the realm of *values*.

Within the context of his inherent needs and capacities as
a specific kind of living organism, it is man's premises—
specifically his *value*-premises—that determine his actions
and emotions. Whether his value-premises are rational or
contradictory and self-defeating, whether they are held consciously or subconsciously, whether they are explicit or implicit, whether they were chosen independently and by deliberation or were uncritically absorbed from other men by a
process of cultural osmosis—it is a man's notion of what is
for him or against him, what is conducive or inimical to his
welfare, that determines the goals he will pursue and the
emotions he will experience.

Just as man's knowledge of reality is not innate, but must
be *acquired* by a process of thought—so the moral values by

which man guides his life, the principles on which he acts and the ends he seeks to reach, are not "instinctive," but must be *chosen*.

If man chooses values that are consonant with the facts of reality and the needs of his own nature, these values will work in the service of his life. If he chooses values that are in contradiction to reality and to his nature, they will work for his own destruction. No man whose values were *consistently* irrational could continue to exist. The majority of men hold values that are part-rational, part-irrational—part-consonant with and part-inimical to man's nature and needs—and they spend their lives in anxiously precarious fluctuation between life and destruction, neither dying immediately nor achieving their full human potential; they pay the price of their unresolved contradictions in frustration, in misery and in neurosis.

Contradictions in one's values result in contradictions in one's emotions: *philosophical* conflicts are the base of *psychological* conflicts. A *neurotic* conflict is a philosophical conflict that has not been faced or resolved. The existence of neurosis, of mental and emotional disturbances, is one of the most eloquent proofs that man *needs* an integrated, objective code of moral values—that a haphazard collection of subjective or collective whims will not do—that a rational ethical system is as indispensable to man's psychological survival as it is to his existential survival.

The paradox—and the tragedy—of psychology today is that *values* is the one issue specifically banned from its domain.

The majority of psychologists—both as theoreticians and as psychotherapists—have accepted the premise that the realm of science and the realm of ethics are mutually inimical, that morality is a matter of faith, not of reason, that moral values are inviolately subjective, and that the therapist must cure his patients without appraising or challenging their fundamental moral beliefs.

Guilt, anxiety and self-doubt—the neurotic's chronic complaints—entail *moral* judgments. The psychotherapist must deal with such judgments constantly. The conflicts that torture patients are *moral* conflicts: *Is* sex evil, or is it a proper human pleasure?—*Is* the profit motive evil, or do men have the right to pursue their own interests?—*Must* one love and forgive everybody, or is it ever justifiable to feel violent indignation?—*Must* man blindly submit to the teachings of his religious authorities, or dare he subject their pronouncements to the judgment of his own intellect?—*Is* it one's duty to remain with a husband or wife one despises, or is divorce a valid solution?—*Should* a woman regard motherhood as her noblest function and duty, or may she pursue an independent career?—*Is* man "his brother's keeper," or does he have the right to live for his own happiness?

It is true that patients frequently repress such conflicts and that the repression constitutes the major obstacle to the conflicts' resolution. But it is not true that merely bringing such conflicts into conscious awareness guarantees that the patients will resolve them. The answers to moral problems are not self-evident; they require a process of complex philosophical thought and analysis.

Nor does the solution lie in instructing the patient to "follow his deepest feelings." That frequently is the policy that brought him to disaster in the first place. Nor does the solution lie in "loving" the patient and, in effect, giving him a moral blank check (which is one of the approaches most commonly advocated today). Love is not a substitute for reason, and the suspending of all moral estimates will not provide the patient with the code of values that his mental health requires. The patient feels confused, he feels uncertain of his judgment, he feels he does not know what is right or wrong; if the therapist, to whom the patient has come for guidance, is professionally *committed* to not knowing, the impasse is total.

To the extent that the therapist acts on the principle that he must be silent in moral issues, he tacitly confirms and sanctions the monopoly on morality held by mysticism—more specifically, by religion. Yet no conscientious therapist can escape the knowledge that religious teachings frequently are instrumental in *causing* the patient's neurosis.

In fact, there is *no way* for a psychotherapist to keep his own moral convictions out of his professional work. By countless subtle indications he reveals and makes the patient aware of his moral estimates—through his pauses, his questions, the things he chooses to say or not to say, etc. But because —for both parties—this process of communication is subconscious, the patient is being guided emotionally rather than intellectually; he does not form an independent, self-conscious appraisal of the therapist's value-premises; he can only accept them, if he accepts them at all, on *faith,* by *feeling,* without reasons or proof, since the issues are never named explicitly. This makes of the therapist, in effect, a religious authority— a *subliminal* religious authority, as it were.

A therapist who approaches moral problems in this manner will, most commonly, encourage conformity to and acceptance of the prevailing moral beliefs of the culture, without regard for the question of whether or not those beliefs are compatible with psychological health. But even if the values the therapist communicates are rational, the method of "persuasion" is not—and thus fails to bring the patient any closer to authentic, *independent* rationality.

In the professional literature of recent years, a number of psychologists have begun to acknowledge that their science cannot dispense with moral questions and judgments. Viktor E. Frankl's *The Doctor and the Soul* and O. H. Mowrer's *The Crisis in Psychiatry and Religion* are examples of this trend. But the solution most typically offered—as in the case of these two authors—is some form of reunion with the values of traditional religion (modified, it is sometimes claimed, by "common sense"). Erich Fromm is currently seeking some sort of rapprochement between psychology and Zen Buddhism. If most psychologists—properly—recoil from any suggestion of mysticism being introduced into their work, and if they do not assume the responsibility of seeking a *rational* code of ethics, then they are left in a moral vacuum where they are powerless to deal effectively with their patients' most fundamental problems. If psychotherapists are not always cognizant of the tragedy of this vacuum, their patients *are*. The degree of success attained by current therapeutic systems is not impressive.

For these reasons, the ethical theory of Objectivism is of profound significance for the science of psychology. In defining the principles of a scientific morality and in demonstrating why man's life must be its standard of value, Ayn Rand has stripped away the veil of mysticism and subjectivity that has enshrouded the most urgent questions of man's existence; she has brought them into the context of reason, reality and man's actual and demonstrable needs. The psychologist who studies her work will discover an invaluable analysis of the issues that confront him in his daily practice: the relation of reason and emotions—the role of productive work in human life—the relationship of man to the society in which he lives—the nature and meaning of sexual love— the existential and psychological consequences for those who attempt to practice and live by today's moral doctrines—the motivation of those who seek power over others and take pleasure in acts of destruction—the motivation of those who dread the responsibility of independence—the motivation of those who revolt against reason—the factors that create or destroy self-esteem. The psychologist will find a matchless delineation of the morality of survival and mental health—

and a projection and concretization of the self-esteem possible to men who choose to live by the judgment of their mind. He will find that "there *is* a morality of reason, a morality proper to man"—and that he, the psychologist, cannot function effectively without it.

There is one science that does hold man's life as its standard of value: the science of medicine. A physician judges the action of every organ within man's body by a single standard: for or against the life of the organism? If he did not—if he maintained that health and disease should be judged by some "other" or "higher" standard—men would regard him as a murderer.

Neither a physician nor a psychologist can—or should attempt to—force his views on a patient who is unwilling to accept them. Nothing can compel a mind to work, to think, to accept reason; that is a matter of a man's own choice. But this does not mean that health or disease—good or evil—are subjective and "personal." If a physician sees a patient who suffers from pneumonia wandering with inadequate clothing in the rain, he does not say: "It seems to me that that is bad for the patient—but who am I to pass value-judgments?" But as psychotherapy is currently practiced, psychologists utter the equivalent of such statements every day, as when they declare that one must not "tamper" with a patient's religious beliefs. Or again: if an individual came to a physician and requested to be cured of a disease that had already infected two-thirds of the population, the physician would not reply: "Adjust to your environment. Do you want to be a non-conformist?" But what might a modern psychologist reply to *his* patient?

The Objectivist ethics is especially significant for the psychotherapist because it is the first *psychological* morality. It is the first morality to define the issue of good and evil in terms of the *actions of one's consciousness*—that is, in terms of the manner in which one *uses* one's consciousness. It ties virtue and vice to the action directly subject to man's volition: the choice to think or not to think. The evils that a man may commit existentially, in action, are made possible only by the primary evil committed inside his consciousness: evasion, the refusal to think, the rejection of reason—just as the good that a man may achieve is made possible by his choice to think, to identify, to integrate, to accept reason as an absolute.

The Objectivist morality does not require infallibility or omniscience of man: it merely requires that he choose to be conscious—that is, to perceive reality. The issue is a *moral* one, because man is a being who has to be conscious *by choice*.

This approach to morality is reflected in the Objectivist treatment of desires. Altruistic moralities tell man to sacrifice his desires. Hedonistic moralities tell man to indulge them. Other schools of morality tell man to seek a compromise, to mediate among his desires and the other claims upon him. But all of these schools share a fundamental premise, whether one consults Plato, Epicurus, Augustine, Calvin, Hobbes, Hume, Kant, Bentham, Nietzsche or Dewey: they all, implicitly or explicitly, regard desires and emotions as irreducible primaries, as the given—then proceed to tell man what attitude to take toward them. The Objectivist morality recognizes that man's desires and emotions proceed from and are caused by his premises, that his premises are the result of his thinking—and that the issue of morality is not to be fought over desires and emotions (which are only a consequence), but over the thinking a man has done or has failed to do. Objectivism teaches man that his mind and his emotions do not have to be antagonists, that his conscious convictions and his desires do not have to clash; it teaches man how they are to be *integrated*, how to bring them into noncontradictory harmony; it teaches man how *he* can determine the *content* of his desires and emotions. (It defines the principles involved; to develop their full implementation is the task of the science of psychology.)

Ayn Rand does not take up or discuss the nature of mental health explicitly. But by defining the principles of an objective morality, by identifying the fact that man is a being of volitional consciousness, and by stressing the crucial and fundamental importance of this fact, she has provided the philosophical foundation for a definition of mental health and for the standard by which it is to be judged.

It is a bromide of modern psychology that mental health cannot be defined. That which we call "healthy" or "normal," psychologists commonly declare, is determined by the culture or society in which one happens to live; what is healthy in one society is not healthy in another; it is all "relative"—there can be no universal and objective standard of mental health, they declare, just as there can be no universal and objective standard of moral values. This view is expressed, for instance, by Karen Horney when, in *The Neurotic Personality of Our Time*, she writes: "With us a person would be neurotic or psychotic who talked by the hour with his deceased grandfather, whereas such communication with ancestors is a recognized pattern in some Indian tribes. A person who felt mortally offended if the name of a deceased relative were mentioned we should consider neurotic indeed, but he would be absolutely normal in the Jicarilla Apache culture." Dr. Horney speaks for the majority of her profession when she concludes that almost every statement about normalcy or mental health must be qualified by the expression "in this society" or "in this culture."

Psychological relativism is a corollary of moral relativism —and contains the same fallacies.

Just as the nature of mental health is not determined by *individual* preference, so it is not determined by social, cultural or historical preference; it is determined by the nature of man. That some hallucinating savage lives on an island where hallucinations are fashionable, does not alter the fact that hallucinations are the proof and the product of an aberrated mind. A leper cannot make himself healthy by joining a leper colony where his disease is shared by everyone; neither can a schizophrenic. Health is not adherence to a statistical norm. A healthy *body* is one whose organs function efficiently in maintaining the life of the organism; a diseased body is one whose organs do not. The standard by which health and disease are to be measured is *life,* for it is only the alternative of life or death that makes the concept of health or disease meaningful or possible. Just as medical science evaluates man's body by the standard of whether or not his body is functioning as man's life requires, so psychological science must uphold the standard of life in appraising the health or disease of man's consciousness. The health of man's consciousness must be judged, like the health of any other organ, by how well it performs its proper function; and the function of consciousness is perception, cognition, and the initiation and direction of action. An unobstructed consciousness, an integrated consciousness, a thinking consciousness, is a *healthy* consciousness. A blocked consciousness, an evading consciousness, a self-blinding consciousness, a consciousness disintegrated by fear or immobilized by depression, a consciousness dissociated from reality, is an *unhealthy* consciousness.

If man's consciousness were not volitional, if man did not have the power to reject sight in favor of blindness, and reality in favor of unreality—evasion and repression would not be possible. If evasion and repression were not possible, neurosis would not be possible. A consciousness that functioned automatically would not face the problem of mental illness—not *psychogenic* mental illness.

Neurotic and psychotic manifestations are the *symptoms*

of a mind's malfunctioning. In order to learn whether a particular action or belief *is* an expression of such malfunctioning, it may be necessary to evaluate and interpret that action or belief in a social, cultural or historical context. This is an issue of *diagnosis*—not of the *nature* of mental health. It is *not* an indication of neurosis, for instance, for a man to believe, in the sixth century, that the world is flat; but to believe it in the twentieth century, *is*. The diagnostician has to take into consideration the *knowledge* available to the patient (or person being studied). Ignorance or honest errors of knowledge are not intrinsic signs of disease; only errors due to evasion, to the rejection of available evidence, are. The concept of mental health pertains to the manner in which a consciousness *functions;* this determines the degree of its health.

What, in essence, does mental health depend on and require? It requires of man that he place no value above perception, which means: no value above consciousness, which means: no value above reality.

Every neurosis entails a break with reality. A neurotic is a man who, when his desires clash with reality, considers reality expendable. This is the attitude that the psychotherapist must seek to correct. But he cannot do so except by challenging (a) the patient's manner of using his consciousness, the abuses to which he subjects it, the evasions, the emotion-worshipping, the policy of mental inertia, and (b) the *values* that create the patient's emotions and set his purposes and goals.

No one is in a better position than the psychologist to appreciate the tragic fallaciousness of the claim that men can survive in any random manner they please. The psychologist is confronted daily with the kind of "survival" achieved by those who do not choose to live by the guidance of reason —with the sight of mental and emotional cripples caught in the wreckage of moral subjectivity and of the belief that life does not require consciousness.

If the patient is to be cured of his neurosis, he must learn to distinguish between a *thought* and a *feeling,* between a *fact* and a *wish,* and to recognize that nothing but destruction can result from sacrificing one's sight of reality to any other consideration. He must learn to seek his sense of self-esteem in the productive use of his mind, in the achievement of rational values, on whatever his level of ability. He must learn that the approval of others cannot be a substitute for self-esteem, and that only anxiety is possible to those who attempt such a substitution. He must learn to allow himself no contradictions in his values or actions. He must learn not to seek the fraud of unearned love, and not to grant it. He must learn not to be afraid to question and challenge the most fundamental beliefs of his culture. He must learn to reject the claims of those who demand his agreement *on faith*. He must learn to fight for his own happiness and to deserve it. He must learn that the irrational *will not work*—and that so long as any part of him desires it, that desire is the cause of his suffering.*

One of the most interesting and productive of Ayn Rand's specifically psychological theories is presented in *Atlas Shrugged*—in her treatment of the psychology of sex. Has it been claimed by advocates of an arch-physicalistic interpretation of sex that a man's philosophical convictions are the reflection and product of his sexual psychology? Ayn Rand demonstrates that a man's sexual psychology, his sexual desires, values and practices are the product and the expression of his most profound philosophical convictions. She goes considerably beyond the theorists who have recognized that sexual neuroses proceed from personality neuroses rather than vice versa. She shows how a man reveals his deepest premises and values in that which he finds sexually attractive or desirable; she shows that a man's sexual psychology is the most revealing index of his character; that it is the reward or the nemesis of the ideas he has consciously or subconsciously accepted; that there is no activity more eloquently spiritual than this allegedly "physical" pursuit.

Ayn Rand is a master of motivational psychology. In this respect, she stands in the literary tradition of Dostoyevsky (with the important difference that her psychological acuity is not restricted to the presentation of depravity and disease, but includes the presentation of the genius, the hero, the *healthy*). The extraordinary sensitivity and originality of her approach to characterization and motivation are undoubtedly

---

* I was very interested to learn, from four different students attending my lectures on Objectivism in New York City, that they had come at the specific advice of the psychiatrists who were treating them and who had suggested that a study of Objectivism would help them with their personal problems. Some years ago, a Los Angeles psychiatrist told of the following case: he had been treating an extremely unresponsive neurotic who suffered from an almost total passivity; then someone gave the patient a copy of *The Fountainhead;* the patient was struck with the novel's emphasis on the importance of man's creative faculty, he renewed his interest in a career he had wanted years earlier, and was thus started toward recovery. In New York City, Dr. Allan Blumenthal is doing very impressive work in applying Objectivist principles to the treatment of anxiety disorders and character neuroses.

one of the major reasons why her work is studied not only in philosophy, political science and literature courses in universities, but in psychology courses as well.

If, for instance, one wishes to understand the psychology of the type of man who is popularly described today as a "conformist," let him study the characterization of Peter Keating in *The Fountainhead*. Let him study the scene in which Keating, on his first day at work, begins to ingratiate himself with Guy Francon, the architect, Keating's employer, whom Keating despises, envies and seeks to emulate; or the scene of Keating's first encounter with Ellsworth Toohey, the architectural critic, whom Keating dreads, hates and whose sanction and guidance he desperately craves; or the scene of Keating's last meeting with Catherine Halsey, the one girl whom he had loved, but had abandoned in order to enter a marriage that would grant him more prestige—the scene in which Keating finally perceives the abject selflessness of his entire life and the futility of his quest to survive by means of adjusting blindly to the values of others. "Katie, I wanted to marry you. It was the only thing I ever really wanted. And that's the sin that can't be forgiven—that I hadn't done what I wanted. It feels so dirty and pointless and monstrous, as one feels about insanity, because there's no sense to it, no dignity, nothing but pain—and wasted pain. . . . Katie, why do they always teach us that it's easy and evil to do what we want and that we need discipline to restrain ourselves? It's the hardest thing in the world—to do what we want. And it takes the greatest kind of courage. I mean, what we really want. As I wanted to marry you. Not as I want to sleep with some woman or get drunk or get my name in the papers. Those things—they're not even desires—they're things people do to escape from desires—because it's such a big responsibility, really, to want something."

Ayn Rand's concept of the "second-hander"—the man who lives through, by and for others—is a landmark of psychological analysis. By comparison with *The Fountainhead*'s approach to the psychology of the spiritual dependent, the psychology of the man who rejects the responsibility of living by the judgment of his own mind—an analysis in terms of men's fundamental attitude toward the problem of survival—the writings of professional psychologists and sociologists on the subject of "conformity" appear superficial and primitive.

If one wishes to understand the motivation of men who seek power, such as Hitler, Stalin or Khrushchev, let him study the characterization of Ellsworth Toohey, or, in *Atlas Shrugged*, of James Taggart and Wesley Mouch. What these characterizations make irresistibly real is the profound mediocrity of this type: the power-seeker's desperate sense of inferiority, his intellectual self-doubt, his furtive lust to deceive and manipulate the consciousness of others, his resentment toward anything confident, able, benevolent, self-assertive, living—and, above all, his virulent rebellion against reason and the "restrictions" of an objective reality. The power-seeker is shown to be a *psychological* mystic, regardless of whether or not he is *philosophically* committed to mysticism: that is, he is a man who regards *feelings* as his basic tool of cognition.

"A mystic is a man who surrendered his mind at its first encounter with the minds of others. Somewhere in the distant reaches of his childhood, when his own understanding of reality clashed with the assertions of others, with their arbitrary orders and contradictory demands, he gave in to so craven a fear of independence that he renounced his rational faculty. At the crossroads of the choice between 'I know' and 'They say,' he chose the authority of others, he chose to submit rather than to understand, to *believe* rather than to think. Faith in the supernatural begins as faith in the superiority of others. His surrender took the form of the feeling that he must hide his lack of understanding, that others possess some mysterious knowledge of which he alone is deprived, that reality is whatever they want it to be, through some means forever denied to him.

"From then on, afraid to think, he is left at the mercy of unidentified feelings. His feelings become his only guide, his only remnant of personal identity, he clings to them with ferocious possessiveness—and whatever thinking he does is devoted to the struggle of hiding from himself that the nature of his feelings is terror.

"When a mystic declares that he *feels* the existence of a power superior to reason, he feels it all right, but that power is not an omniscient super-spirit of the universe, it is the consciousness of any passer-by to whom he has surrendered his own. A mystic is driven by the urge to impress, to cheat, to flatter, to deceive, *to force* that omnipotent consciousness of others. 'They' are his only key to reality, he feels that he cannot exist save by harnessing their mysterious power and extorting their unaccountable consent. 'They' are his only means of perception and, like a blind man who depends on the sight of a dog, he feels he must leash them in order to live. To control the consciousness of others becomes his only passion; power-lust is a weed that grows only in the vacant lots of an abandoned mind.

"Every dictator is a mystic, and every mystic is a potential dictator. A mystic craves obedience from men, not their agreement. He wants them to surrender their consciousness to his assertions, his edicts, his wishes, his whims—as *his* consciousness is surrendered to theirs. He wants to deal with men by means of faith and force—he finds no satisfaction in their consent if he must earn it by means of facts and reason. Reason is the enemy he dreads and, simultaneously, considers precarious; reason, to him, is a means of deception; he *feels* that men possess some power more potent than reason—and only their causeless belief or their forced obedience can give him a sense of security, a proof that he has gained control of the mystic endowment he lacked. His lust is to command, not to convince: conviction requires an act of independence and rests on the absolute of an objective reality. What he seeks is power over reality and over men's means of perceiving it, their mind, the power to interpose his will between existence and consciousness, as if, by agreeing to fake the reality he orders them to fake, men would, in fact, create it.

"Just as the mystic is a parasite in matter, who expropriates the wealth created by others—just as he is a parasite in spirit, who plunders the ideas created by others—so he falls below the level of a lunatic who creates his own distortion of reality, to the level of a parasite of lunacy who seeks a distortion created by others."

If one wishes to understand the soul of a man of intransigent rationality, independence and self-esteem—if one wishes to understand his motivation, his goals, his manner of facing existence and his method of using his consciousness—let him study the characterization of Howard Roark in *The Fountainhead,* and Hank Rearden, Francisco d'Anconia and John Galt in *Atlas Shrugged*. Let him study, for instance, the opening chapter of *The Fountainhead,* in which Howard Roark—a young architect of genius—is introduced standing on the edge of a cliff and looking at the earth around him. "He looked at the granite. To be cut, he thought, and made into walls. He looked at a tree. To be split and made into rafters. He looked at a streak of rust on the stone and thought of iron ore under the ground. To be melted and to emerge as girders against the sky. . . . These rocks, he thought, are here for me; waiting for the drill, the dynamite and my voice; waiting to be split, ripped, pounded, reborn; waiting for the shape my hands will give them." Roark has just been expelled from architectural school—for refusing to design buildings in the tradition of the past, and for designing, instead, buildings such as had never before existed. When, later that day, he is summoned to the office of the Dean of the Institute and is informed that the Institute may re-admit him if, henceforward, he is willing to recognize that ". . . everything beautiful in architecture has been done already. . . . We can only choose from the great masters. Who are we to improve upon them?"—Roark tells the Dean, pointing to the window: "Look . . . Can you see the campus and the town? Do you see how many men are walking and living down there? Well, I don't give a damn what any or all of them think about architecture—or about anything else, for that matter. Why should I consider what their grandfathers thought of it? . . . I have, let's say, sixty years to live. Most of that time will be spent working. I've chosen the work I want to do. If I find no joy in it, then I'm only condemning myself to sixty years of torture. And I can find the joy only if I do my work in the best way possible to me. But the best is a matter of standards—and I set my own standards. I inherit nothing. I stand at the end of no tradition. I may, perhaps, stand at the beginning of one." Roark leaves the Dean's office, thinking that there is some important principle represented by the Dean and by men like him that he, Roark, must discover. He is struggling with the concept which, years later, he will identify as the phenomenon of the "second-hander." But in a moment the question ceases to concern him. "He saw the sunlight of late afternoon, held still in the moment before it was to fade, on the gray limestone of a stringcourse running along the brick wall of the Institute building. He forgot men, the Dean and the principle behind the Dean, which he wanted to discover. He thought only of how lovely the stone looked in the fragile light and of what he could have done with that stone."

Or consider the chapter that introduces Hank Rearden in *Atlas Shrugged*—on the night when Rearden Steel is pouring the first heat for the first order of Rearden Metal, the new alloy it has taken Rearden ten years of excruciating effort to develop. In honor of this night, and of the endurance which had been required to achieve it, Rearden thinks of the long struggle behind him and the steps of his rise. "He saw the day when he stood on a rocky ledge and felt a thread of sweat running from his temple down his neck. He was fourteen years old and it was his first day of work in the iron mines of Minnesota. He was trying to learn to breathe against the scalding pain in his chest. He stood, cursing himself, because he had made up his mind that he would not be tired.

After a while, he went back to his task; he decided that pain was not a valid reason for stopping." "He saw an evening when he sat slumped across his desk in that office. It was late and his staff had left; so he could lie there alone, unwitnessed. He was tired. It was as if he had run a race against his own body, and all the exhaustion of years, which he had refused to acknowledge, had caught him at once and flattened him against the desk top. He felt nothing, except the desire not to move. He did not have the strength to feel—not even to suffer. He had burned everything there was to burn within him; he had scattered so many sparks to start so many things—and he wondered whether someone could give him now the spark he needed, now when he felt unable ever to rise again. He asked himself who had started him and kept him going. Then he raised his head. Slowly, with the greatest effort of his life, he made his body rise until he was able to sit upright with only one hand pressed to the desk and a trembling arm to support him. He never asked that question again." Now, this night, walking home from his mills in the darkness, he turns and sees the neon sign against the sky: Rearden Steel. "He stood straight, as if before a bench of judgment. He thought that in the darkness of this night other signs were lighted over the country: Rearden Ore—Rearden Coal—Rearden Limestone. He thought of the days behind him. He wished it were possible to light a neon sign above them, saying: Rearden Life."

One of the most psychologically eloquent scenes in *Atlas Shrugged* occurs between John Galt and Dagny Taggart, in the underground tunnels of Taggart Transcontinental, at the start of their love affair. Galt had been watching Dagny silently for years, passionately in love with her but unable to approach her, unable to tell her of his battle and of the strike he was leading until she was ready to hear it. Now, they have just slept together for the first time—and he tells her serenely that he had known of her affair with Hank Rearden in the years when he could not approach her. "Do you want me to tell you what I did the night after I learned it? . . . I had never seen Hank Rearden, only pictures of him in the newspapers. I knew that he was in New York, that night, at some conference of big industrialists. I wanted to have just one look at him. I went to wait at the entrance of the hotel where that conference was held. There were bright lights under the marquee of the entrance, but it was dark beyond, on the pavement, so I could see without being seen, there were a few loafers and vagrants hanging around, there was a drizzle of rain and we clung to the walls of the building. One could tell the members of the conference when they began filing out . . . They were worn men, those industrialists, aging, flabby, frantic with the effort to disguise uncertainty. And then I saw him. He wore an expensive trenchcoat and a hat slanting across his eyes. He walked swiftly, with the kind of assurance that has to be earned, as he'd earned it. Some of his fellow industrialists pounced on him with questions, and those tycoons were acting like hangers-on around him. I caught a glimpse of him as he stood with his hand on the door of his car, his head lifted, I saw the brief flare of a smile under the slanting brim, a confident smile, impatient and a little amused. And then, for one instant, I did what I had never done before, what most men wreck their lives on doing—I saw that moment out of context, I saw the world as he made it look, as if it matched him, as if he were its symbol—I saw a world of achievement, of unenslaved energy, of unobstructed drive through purposeful years to the enjoyment of one's reward—I saw, as I stood in the rain in a crowd of vagrants, what my years would have brought me, if that world had existed, and I felt a desperate longing—he was the image of everything I should have been . . . and he had everything that should have been mine. . . . But it was only a moment. Then I saw the scene in full context again and in all of its actual meaning—I saw what price he was paying for his brilliant ability, what torture he was enduring in silent bewilderment, struggling to understand what *I* had understood—I saw that the world he suggested, did not exist and was yet to be made, I saw him again for what he was, the symbol of my battle, the unrewarded hero whom *I* was to avenge and to release—and then . . . then I accepted what I had learned about you and him. I saw that it changed nothing, that I should have expected it—that it was right. . . . Dagny, it's not that I don't suffer, it's that I know the unimportance of suffering, I know that pain is to be fought and thrown aside, not to be accepted as part of one's soul and as a permanent scar across one's view of existence." This last sentence of Galt names one of the most fundamental characteristics of the Ayn Rand hero.

Her ability to present, with overwhelming and persuasive reality, characters who *are* genuinely heroic, is undoubtedly one of the chief reasons for the enormous popularity of Ayn Rand's novels. Her characters have served as a source of moral and psychological inspiration for thousands of readers, particularly among the young. That she has been able convincingly to project such heroes is made possible not only by her literary skill, but by the nature of her philosophy—by

71

virtue of the fact that hers is a philosophy *for living on earth.*
It is not astonishing—when one considers the kind of moral
doctrines which men have accepted—that writers have been
far more successful in their projections of mediocrities, dope
addicts, homosexuals, murderers and psychotics, than in their
(rarely attempted) projections of ideal men.

It is impossible, in the space of a brief essay, to present
the full richness of Ayn Rand's thought in its implications for
the science of psychology; to develop those implications is the
task of more than one volume. It has been possible here to
indicate only a few basic issues in the most general terms.

But for the profession of psychology, *The Fountainhead,
Atlas Shrugged* and *For the New Intellectual* should properly
be regarded almost as textbooks. If the purpose of the psychologist is to help men to achieve their unbreached human
potential, then he will find in the works of Ayn Rand an
invaluable contribution to his goal.

III

The Literary Method of
Ayn Rand

"I decided to be a writer," states Ayn Rand, "at the age
of nine—it was a specific, conscious decision—I remember
the day and the hour. I did not start by trying to describe the
folks next door—but by inventing people who did things the
folks next door would never do. I could summon no interest
or enthusiasm for 'people as they are'—when I had in my
mind a blinding picture of people as they could be.

"I decided to become a writer—not in order to save the
world, nor to serve my fellow men—but for the simple, personal, selfish, egoistical happiness of creating the kind of
men and events I could like, respect and admire. I can bear
to look around me levelly. I cannot bear to look down. I
wanted to look up.

"This attitude has never changed. But I went for years
thinking that it was a strictly personal attitude toward fiction
writing, never to be discussed and of no interest to anyone
but me. Later I discovered I had accepted as the rule of my
lifework a principle stated by Aristotle. Aristotle said that
fiction is of greater philosophical importance than history,

because history represents things only as they are, while fiction represents them 'as they might be and ought to be.' If you wish a key to the literary method of [my novels], this is it."

The projection of "things as they might be and ought to be" names the essence of Ayn Rand's concept of literature. In the wave of Naturalism that has engulfed the literature of the twentieth century, her novels are an outstanding exception. They are at once a continuation of the Romantic tradition and a significant departure from the mainstream of that tradition: she is a *Romantic Realist*. "Romantic"—because her work is concerned with *values,* with the essential, the abstract, the universal in human life, and with the projection of man as a heroic being. "Realist"—because the values she selects pertain to this earth and to man's actual nature, and because the issues with which she deals are the crucial and fundamental ones of our age. Her novels do not represent a flight into mystical fantasy or the historical past or into concerns that have little if any bearing on man's actual existence. Her heroes are not knights, gladiators or adventurers in some impossible kingdom, but engineers, scientists, industrialists, men who belong on earth, men who function in modern society. As a philosopher, she has brought ethics into the context of reason, reality and man's life on earth; as a novelist, she has brought the dramatic, the exciting, the heroic, the stylized into the same context.

Just as in philosophy she rejects every version of the mystics' soul-body dichotomy: theory versus practice, thought versus action, morality versus happiness—so in literature she rejects the expression of this same dichotomy: the belief that a profound novel cannot be entertaining, and that an entertaining novel cannot be profound, that a serious, philosophical novel cannot have a dramatic plot, and that a dramatic plot-novel cannot possibly be serious or philosophical.

Atlas Shrugged—the greatest of her novels—is an action story on a grand scale, but it is a consciously philosophical action story, just as its heroes are consciously philosophical men of action. To those who subscribe to the soul-body dichotomy in literature, *Atlas Shrugged* is a mystifying anomaly that defies classification by conventional standards. It moves effortlessly and ingeniously from economics to epistemology to morality to metaphysics to psychology to the theory of sex, on the one hand—and, on the other, it has a chapter that ends with the heroine hurtling toward the earth in an airplane with a dead motor, it has a playboy crusader who blows up a multi-billion-dollar industry, a philosopher-turned-pirate who attacks government relief ships, and a climax that involves the rescue of the hero from a torture chamber. Notwithstanding the austere solemnity of its abstract theme, her novel—as a work of art—projects the laughing, extravagantly imaginative virtuosity of a mind who has never heard that "one is not supposed" to combine such elements as these in a single book. To those who believe that "one is not supposed to," Ayn Rand would answer: "Check your premises."

Ayn Rand has written four novels—*We the Living, Anthem, The Fountainhead, Atlas Shrugged*—and each of them has a major philosophical theme. Yet they are not "propaganda novels." The primary purpose for which these books were written was not the philosophical conversion of their readers. The primary purpose was to project and make real the characters who are the books' heroes. *This* is the motive that unites the artist and the moralist. The desire to project the ideal man, led to the writing of novels. The necessity of defining the premises that make an ideal man possible, led to the formulating of the philosophical content of those novels. "I had to [originate a philosophical framework of my own], because my basic view of man and of existence was in conflict with most of the existing philosophical theories," she writes in her Preface to *For the New Intellectual.* "In order to define, explain and present my concept of man, I had to become a philosopher in the specific meaning of the term." What then is the base of Ayn Rand the artist and Ayn Rand the philosopher? Ayn Rand, the worshipper and glorifier of man—in the most profound, metaphysical sense.

By its nature, every work of art projects, implicitly or explicitly, a metaphysics: that is, a fundamental view of man and of man's relation to existence. To be exact, it projects the *emotional corollary* of a metaphysics: a *"sense of life."* It can project a *tragic* sense of life or a *heroic* sense of life or a *benevolent* sense of life, etc., according to the artist's basic psychological state and conscious or subconscious view of reality. But *some* sense of life—*some* estimate of existence and of man's place in it—is inescapably implicit in an art work, by the nature of the creative process.

In a lecture on esthetics at the 1961 Creative Arts Festival of the University of Michigan, Ayn Rand defined her concept of art as follows: "Art is a re-creation of reality according to the artist's values. It is not a creation out of a void, but a *re-creation,* a selective rearrangement of the elements of reality, guided by the artist's view of existence. That view determines the subject he chooses to present and every detail of the manner in which he presents it; it determines both

74

the *"what"* and the *"how"* of his work. An artist declares his metaphysical estimates by means of that which he chooses to include or to omit, to emphasize or to ignore—by means of the subject he selects, of the particular aspect he stresses, of the specific attributes he features. One can make a statue of man as a Greek god or as a deformed Oriental monstrosity; both are metaphysical estimates of man. One can paint a still life of some fruit and flowers in a manner that will convey a benevolent, glowing, sunlit sense of life; one can paint the same fruit and flowers in a manner that will project decay, corruption and a sense of murky doom. An artist may or may not choose to include some explicit philosophical message in his work; that choice is optional. The real, basic, essential message, which every art work conveys, whether the artist intended it consciously or not, is *the concretization of a sense of life."*

As illustration of this principle, contrast the heroic sense of life projected in the novels of the great Romanticist, Victor Hugo, with the sordid and doomed sense of life conveyed in the novels of the arch-Naturalist, Emile Zola. Consider the literary means by which each writer's sense of life is projected. Where Hugo builds purposeful plot, Zola unravels calamitous contingency; where Hugo dramatizes the conflict of crucial values, Zola describes the horror of torpid depravity; where Hugo delineates characters in terms of their fundamental motivations, Zola lingers on the surface of accidental, journalistic minutiae; where Hugo presents life as exciting and man as a giant, Zola presents life as futility and man as a pygmy; where Hugo sees literature as artistic creation, Zola sees literature as history—*Police Gazette* history.

For good or evil, intentionally or otherwise, every work of art is a psychological confession. Through that which he chooses to present, an artist declares to the world: *"This is what I think is important—important for me to project and for others to perceive—this is the world as I see it—this is the essence of things—this is what matters."*

If a writer chooses to present—as the chief object of his focus—intelligence, ability, integrity, and the pursuit and achievement of great and demanding values, he reveals one kind of soul and view of life; if another writer chooses to present—as *his* chief object of focus—mediocrity, helplessness, depravity, suffering and defeat, he reveals a different kind of soul and view of life. In either case, what has been projected is a metaphysical estimate of man's existence—even if the author knows that estimate only in the form of

75

an emotion, of that which "feels right" to him in the creative process; emotions and feelings are not causeless. The most intensely anti-Romantic "slice of life" writer cannot escape the fact that art deals with *values,* and the artist's choice is only: what *kind* of values will be present? Art deals with the essence of things, and the choice is only: what does one take as the essence of things?—what kind of sense of life will one project? Is it the genius or the psychotic who is to be taken as the representative of man? Is it efficacy or helplessness that fundamentally characterizes man's relation to existence? Is it achievement and happiness—or failure and misery— that constitute the essence of life?

If every work of art is a psychological confession, so is every esthetic response. One responds esthetically to that which reflects and confirms one's own sense of life. (The pleasure one might happen to find in reading a novel because of the information it contains, is not an *esthetic* emotion.) That in which one finds enjoyment is the most eloquent indicator of one's fundamental values and philosophy. If one enjoys reading about men of integrity, ability and moral strength, and is bored by stories of men's helplessness and evil, one reveals one kind of soul; if one enjoys stories of men's helplessness and evil, and is bored by reading about men of integrity, ability and moral strength, one reveals another kind of soul. Artistic likes and dislikes are not "a matter of taste"—but a matter of metaphysics.

In the novels of Ayn Rand, the sense of life projected is conscious, deliberate, explicit and philosophically implemented. It is as unique and unprecedented in literature as the premises from which it proceeds. It is a sense of life untouched by tragedy, untouched by any implication of metaphysical catastrophe or doom. Its essence is an unclouded and exaltedly benevolent view of existence, the sense of a universe in which man *belongs,* a universe in which triumph, enjoyment and fulfillment are possible—although not guaranteed—to man, and are to be achieved by the efficacy of his own effort.

No matter how terrible their struggle, no matter how difficult the obstacles they encounter, the basic sense of life of Ayn Rand's heroes—as of the novels—is indestructibly affirmative and triumphant. Whether the characters achieve victory or, as in *We the Living,* suffer defeat, they do not regard pain and disaster as the normal, as the inevitable, but always as the abnormal, the exceptional, the *unnatural.*

Ayn Rand shares with the Romantic novelists of the nineteenth century the view of man as a being of free will, a being who is moved and whose course is determined, not by fate or the gods or the irresistible power of "tragic flaws," but by the *values* he has *chosen*. But she differs from those writers in the particular values she regards as proper to man; and, as a consequence, she differs in her view of the nature of man's life on earth.

Prior to the birth of the Romantic movement, the literature of Western civilization was dominated by the "fate" motif. Man was presented as the plaything—sometimes the defiantly rebellious, sometimes the sadly resigned, but almost always the defeated plaything—of an inexorable fate beyond his control, which determined the ultimate course of his life, regardless of his choices, wishes or actions. This is exemplified in the Greek tragedies, many of which were resolved by the arbitrary edict of a god, and, in a different form, in the plays of Shakespeare. In Shakespeare's dramas, man, for the most part, is not determined by the power of outside forces, but by uncontrollable passions or weaknesses within him, by the "tragic flaw," which he cannot resist and which defeats all his hopes, plans and intentions; Shakespeare presents heroic-sized figures, but he does not present man as a hero; he merely "holds up a mirror to life," it is said. In one form or another, the plays, epic poems, sagas and chronicles that preceded the rise of the novel carried the same message: man is the pawn of destiny, he is caught in a universe essentially inimical to his interests, and if he ever does succeed, it is not by his own efforts, but by fortuitous external circumstances.

Consistent with the metaphysics of fatalism or determinism, these literary works were dramatized *histories* or fictionalized *biographies*. They offered a recital of the events that had happened in the life of a man; the writer was, in effect, a biographer, a recorder of the given, the unalterable, the fated or determined. The emergence of a new literary form, the *novel,* in the late eighteenth century, represented a radical break with this tradition; the distinction of a novel is that it is a work of *pure fiction,* a story invented by its author and intended to be understood as such, rather than a fictionalized *chronicle* purporting to be a record of actual events.

Romanticism was a literary school whose authors discarded the role of transcriber and assumed the role of creator. For the first time in literary history, a sharp line was drawn between fiction and journalism, between artistic creation and historical reporting. The Romantic novelists did not make it their goal to record that which *had* happened, but to project that which *ought* to happen. They did not take the things

77

man had done as the given, as the unalterable material of existence, like facts of physical nature, but undertook to project the things that men should *choose* to do.

The concept of man as a being motivated by his chosen values lay at the base of the great artistic innovation and distinctive characteristic of the Romantic novel: *plot*. Whereas a story is a series of *contingently* connected events, plot is a series of *logically* connected events. In the Romantic plot-novel, the course of man's life is determined by his chosen purpose, which he pursues through a series of relevant problems that he has to solve, of non-accidental obstacles that he has to overcome, of conflicts that he has to win—conflicts among his own values and/or conflicts with the values and purposes of others—through a series of coherent, integrated events leading to the climax of a final resolution.

The concept of *values* as the crucial and determining element in human life is the central, dominant and logically implicit premise of the Romantic plot-novel. But from its beginning, the Romantic school harbored a contradiction, which ultimately defeated it: the contradiction between the requirements of man's life on earth and the mystic-altruist code of morality.

The writers who dramatized the principle of man's free will, of man's efficacy, of his power to achieve his values and determine the course of his life—found, consciously or subconsciously, that the values of traditional morality were not applicable to this earth, could not be practiced, could not serve as man's guide to success or happiness. This is the reason why so many Romantic novels, whose sense of life is essentially pro-man and pro-earth, have tragic endings, such as Hugo's *Notre Dame de Paris* or *The Man Who Laughs*. This is also the reason why so many Romantic novels are laid in the past, in some remote period of history—with a marked preference for medieval history—such as the novels of Walter Scott, or the "costume" novels of today, which are among the last remnants of the Romantic school. A novel dealing with the crucial problems of the author's time, such as Hugo's *Les Miserables*, is a rare exception. By escaping from the problems of the present, the Romanticists contradicted their own (implicit) basic philosophical belief in man's efficacy: they saw *man* as heroic, but *life* as tragic. They could not successfully project and concretize man's fulfillment on earth; neither the traditional values of mysticism nor the defiantly subjective values of their own could make such fulfillment possible. Taking flight into the historical past, or else taking refuge in novels of impossibly unrealistic sentimentality, the Romantic writers progressively became more vulnerable to the charge of "escapism" that was being raised against their work. The contradiction they were unable to resolve forced them to retreat further and further from the actual problems of human existence, and, ultimately, to abandon all serious issues and concerns; their work degenerated into the class of light fiction, which is its predominant status today.

Naturalism—the literary counter-revolution against Romanticism—was a regression to a pre-Romantic view of man, to a view lower than that against which the Romanticists had rebelled. It was Naturalism that reintroduced the "fate" motif into literature, and once more presented man as the helpless plaything of irresistible forces.

Consistent with the philosophical doctrines that were gaining ascendancy, the Naturalists gave "fate" a new form: it was not the omnipotent power of the gods, nor the omnipotent power of "tragic flaws," but the omnipotent power of *society*. It is society, the Naturalists declared—or family, or upbringing, or social caste, or economic status—that determines man's destiny.

Naturalists claim that the purpose of literature, including the novel, is to transcribe life "as it really is," meaning: as the people around them are living it; to present men "as they really are," meaning: as the men they observe are, *not* as they "ought to be." No "ought to be" is possible—assert the Naturalists—and no moral choice, and no values, because man cannot help being what he is; man is the product of his background; his life and character are determined by forces beyond his control. A writer must not take sides nor pronounce moral judgments nor hold any values (*qua* writer), but must, like a camera, reproduce impartially and indiscriminately whatever life happens to place before him.*

"The Naturalist school of writing," observes Ayn Rand in her Foreword to the new (1959) edition of *We the Living*, "consists of substituting statistics for one's standard of value, then cataloguing minute, photographic, journalistic details of a given country, region, city or back yard in a given decade, year, month or split-second, on the overall premise of: 'This

* "Naturalism," as used here, includes schools of writing sometimes classified as "Realism" or "Social Realism," because the fundamental literary principles are identical. Zola attempted to distinguish his "Naturalism" from the "Realism" of Flaubert; but observe that all the above comments are equally applicable to both writers; no literary historian has ever succeeded in drawing a *basic* distinction between their respective methods and approaches.

79

is what men have done'—as against the premise of: 'This is what men have *chosen* and/or *should* choose to do.' "

With the rise of this school in the second half of the nineteenth century, a writer, once more, became a man who "holds up a mirror to life," and, it was added, he must have the "courage" to let his mirror reflect the lowest, the ugliest, the most sordid aspects of nature—*human* nature. He must do so, because he must be "honest"—he must admit that the essence of existence is ugliness, futility, doom, defeat.

What followed, in the history of literature, is a procession of men with mirrors, which defies the laws of optics by the fact that the men and the mirrors shrink as they come closer to us, instead of growing larger in stature—so that what began as ballroom mirrors reflecting the destinies of nations is now dentists' mirrors in the hands of men peering into rat holes.

Today, the Romantic method of writing has been all but forgotten. Many commentators speak as if it were an axiom that all fiction is to be judged by the canons of Naturalism, as if no other school had ever existed. In their view—and by their sense of life—to project man as a being moved by his chosen values, and to show him at his heroic potential, is "unrealistic." Only the helpless, the passive, the sordid, the depraved are "real."

If Romanticism was defeated by the fact that its values were removed from this world, the alternative offered by Naturalism was to remove values from literature. The result today is an esthetic vacuum, left by the historical implication that men's only choice is between artistic projections of near-fantasy—or Sunday supplement exposés, gossip columns and psychological case-histories parading as novels.

It is against the background of the despair, the exhausted cynicism and the unremitting drabness that have settled over contemporary literature, that the novels of Ayn Rand have appeared.

Ayn Rand has brought values back to literature—and back *to this earth*. She has chosen to write about the most fundamental and urgent issues of our age, and to use them as the material of Romantic art. In her novels, the ruling values *are* applicable to reality, they *can* be practiced, they *can* serve as man's guide to success and happiness. As a result, her heroes predominantly *win* their battles, they *achieve* their goals, they succeed *practically* and in their own lives. *Anthem*, *The Fountainhead* and *Atlas Shrugged* do not end with heroic death, but with heroic victory.

Her work is an accomplished embodiment of Aristotle's

80

definition of the proper function of literature. "Things as they might be" is the principle of Realism: it means that fiction must stay within the bounds of reality, and not indulge in fantasies concerning the logically or metaphysically impossible. "Things as they ought to be" is the principle of Romanticism: it means things objectively possible and proper to man, things which he *can* and *ought to* choose.

She does not face man with the camera of a photographer as her tool, but with the chisel of a sculptor. Howard Roark, Hank Rearden, Francisco d'Anconia and John Galt are not statistical composites of men "as they are." They are projections of man as he might be and ought to be; they are projections of the human *potential*. On the premise of Naturalism, such heroes as these are incomprehensible: one does not meet them around every corner; one may never, in one's own lifetime, meet them at all. But in projecting such figures, Ayn Rand does not ask: *Do* such men exist? She asks: *Should* such men exist? *That* is the premise of art, as against the premise of history or biography. It is not a mirror reflecting the things behind them that her work holds up to men, but a beacon to be reached ahead.

An understanding of the principle by which her characters —heroes and villains—are created, is essential to an understanding of her literary method as a whole. Discussing this aspect of her work, she has written: "Readers have asked me whether my characters are 'copies of real people in public life' or 'not human beings at all, but symbols.' Neither is true. . . . What I did was to observe real life, analyze the reasons which make people such as they are, draw an abstraction and then create my own characters out of that abstraction. My characters are persons in whom certain human attributes are focused more sharply and consistently than in average human beings."

Whether she is presenting a Howard Roark or a Peter Keating, a John Galt or a Wesley Mouch, the principle of characterization is the same: to present a character by means of essentials, that is, to focus on the actions and attributes which reflect the character's basic values and premises—the values and premises that motivate him and direct his crucial choices. A successful characterization is one which makes a man distinguishable from all other men, and makes the causes of his actions intelligible. To characterize by essentials is to focus on the universal—to omit the accidental, the irrelevant, the trivial, the contingent—and to present the fundamental motivational principles which are potentially applicable to all men.

The characterization of Howard Roark, for instance, is a thoroughly individualized portrait; Roark is unique and unforgettable, in manner, in speech, in temperament, in personality. Yet, in his basic premises and goals, in the opposition he encounters and in the battle he fights, his life and struggle project an abstraction that is timeless: Roark is not "an American architect of the 1940's," he is the independent innovator of intransigent integrity in any profession and in any century.

Consider the scene in *The Fountainhead* in which Roark, at a time when he is destitute, is offered an enormously important commission, one which would virtually make his career. He is told that the commission is his—on one condition: that he agree to modify the unconventional design of his building. A member of the Board of Directors shows Roark a sketch of the kind of changes the Board desires:

"It was Roark's building on the sketch, very neatly drawn. It was his building, but it had a simplified Doric portico in front, a cornice on top, and his ornament was replaced by a stylized Greek ornament.

"Roark got up. He had to stand. He concentrated on the effort of standing. It made the rest easier. He leaned on one straight arm, his hand closed over the edge of the table, the tendons showing under the skin of his wrist."

Roark listens to their assurances that the changes do not "spoil anything." Then he answers.

"He spoke for a long time. He explained why this structure could not have a Classic motive on its facade. He explained why an honest building, like an honest man, had to be of one piece and one faith; what constituted the life source, the idea in any existing thing or creature, and why—if one smallest part committed treason to that idea—the thing or the creature was dead; and why the good, the high and the noble on earth was only that which kept its integrity."

They inform him that the Board's decision is unalterable —that Roark may be right, but "in practical life, one can't always be so flawlessly consistent."

" 'You understand the situation, Mr. Roark?'

" 'Yes,' said Roark. His eyes were lowered. He was looking down at the drawings [of his building].

" 'Well?'

"Roark did not answer.

" 'Yes or no, Mr. Roark?'

"Roark's head leaned back. He closed his eyes.

" 'No,' said Roark.

"After a while the chairman asked:

" 'Do you realize what you're doing?'

" 'Quite,' said Roark.

" 'Good God!' Weidler cried suddenly. 'Don't you know how big a commission this is? You're a young man, you won't get another chance like this. And . . . all right, damn it all, I'll say it! You need this! I know how badly you need it!'

"Roark gathered the drawings from the table, rolled them together and put them under his arm.

" 'It's sheer insanity!' Weidler moaned. 'I want you. We want your building. You need the commission. Do you have to be quite so fanatical and selfless about it?'

" 'What?' Roark asked incredulously.

" 'Fanatical and selfless.'

"Roark smiled. He looked down at his drawings. His elbow moved a little, pressing them to his body. He said:

" 'That was the most selfish thing you've ever seen a man do.' "

In this scene, the author, by the strict purposefulness of her writing, by that which she chooses to include and to omit, dramatizes and makes real the naked essence of Roark as a man: the sovereign consciousness; the unyielding independence of judgment; the passion for his work; the willingness to pay any price for that passion, for *his* work done *his* way. And because Roark is presented in this manner—because his is not a Naturalistic portrait, burdened with trivia—he is not less but *more* real to the reader: more real, because he is presented in the sharp focus of purposeful stylization.

To write and to characterize by means of essentials requires that one know what *is* essential and what is derivative, what is a cause and what is a consequence. It is by identifying causes that one arrives at basic principles. No such understanding is required by the Naturalist method of characterization.

A Naturalist observes that men act in a certain manner; he does not ask *why;* on the premise of determinism, he explicitly or implicitly assumes that somehow men's heredity and environment force them to act as they do. Since he sees himself as a historical observer, as a recorder of the given, what he offers as characterization and motivational explanation is a haphazard collection of surface details, a string of concretes without any abstract significance, such as a character's preference in automobiles, his use of the slang typical of a particular region in a particular year, his random thoughts while brushing his teeth, the restaurants he frequents, the newspapers he reads and the geographical location of his old high school. (Sometimes, if a contemporary writer feels that this is not quite adequate, he may toss in a few Freudian slogans, to add "depth" to his characterization.)

Any sort of causal analysis, beyond the most primitive and obvious level, is alien to the Naturalist approach. If, for instance, a Naturalist decides to write about "a Madison Avenue executive," he projects that a Madison Avenue executive does the things he does because—"well, *you* know, *because* he's a Madison Avenue executive!" Naturalist literature is filled with portraits on this level of profundity: "a typical Bronx housewife"—"a typical ruthless business tycoon"—"a typical French coal miner"—"a typical frustrated and bored French housewife, longing for a lover"—"a typical member of the Russian landed nobility"—etc. *This,* to a Naturalist, is characterization.

Aggressive social climbers—men such as Peter Keating— exist in large numbers. The type has been treated extensively in countless Naturalist novels. If Ayn Rand's presentation of this type has already achieved the status of a psychological classic, the reason is that Ayn Rand, observing the behavior of such men, asked *"Why?"*— and built Peter Keating's characterization on the answer. As illustration of the difference between the Naturalist method of cataloguing journalistic surface details and the Romantic method of characterization by essentials, contrast the innumerable Naturalist presentations of aggressive social climbers with the characterization of Peter Keating. If you have difficulty clearly calling to mind a *specific* Naturalist portrait to serve as contrast with Peter Keating, *that* is the point.

There have been superlatively observant Naturalist writers, such as Sinclair Lewis, who have provided impressively exact portraits of the manners, the speech habits, the practices of a certain type of American in a certain region of the country during a certain period. These portraits may have value as sociological reports, but then they should be identified as such. And if sociological instructiveness is the virtue to be claimed for Naturalism, then it should be recognized that Naturalism—and not Romanticism—deserves the charge of being "didactic."

To those who share the Naturalist view of literature and the view of life from which it comes, to whose who do not understand and/or who resent the principle of artistic stylization and the perspective of philosophical essentials, it is "superficial" and "unconvincing," for instance, to present John Galt as a man motivated by an inviolate self-esteem, an unlimited ambition, a passionate love of existence and a total commitment to reason—whereas it would be "profound," it would "add depth" to Galt's characterization, if he were shown combing his hair in the morning, drinking cough medicine when he has a cold and stopping to chat with the grocer when he buys a pound of coffee. After all, *doesn't* Galt comb his hair? *Doesn't* "even he" occasionally catch a cold? *Doesn't* he go to the grocer to buy coffee? Isn't this, too, part of life? Why does Ayn Rand choose to discriminate against such vital aspects of reality?

The answer, of course, is that such events are omitted because they are of no importance—neither to the plot nor to the theme nor to Galt's characterization *nor to Galt*. The standard by which events are selected, in a properly constructed novel, is objective importance and *relevance* to the purpose that is being dramatized.

Ayn Rand's attitude in this matter is perhaps best illustrated by the following incident. A young man once expressed concern as to whether he could live up to the heroes in her novels, and offered her this example: If John Galt (the young man said) were preparing to pour champagne for a girl, he would open the bottle swiftly, smoothly and efficiently, and the scene would be very glamorous; but in real life the cork might be stuck and he, the young man, would have difficulty in opening the bottle, and the mood of the occasion would be marred. Why cannot real life be more like art?—he wanted to know. Ayn Rand answered that the young man's error was in being upset if the cork stuck, that he was wrong to attach any importance to it; a John Galt might very well have trouble in opening the bottle if the cork stuck, she explained, but he would attach no significance to it, his attention and emotional focus would be on the girl and the evening, *that* is what would be important to him, not any momentary mishap. She formulated the principle thus: "In life, one *ignores* the unimportant; in art, one *omits* it."

Since art necessarily is selective, to include an incident in a novel is to make it important. To include the unimportant is to magnify it and give it equal status with the important, thus undercutting the important. Those who wish that Galt had been given a few accidental or irrelevant touches have but one basic motive, whether they choose to identify it or not: to see Galt undercut, to see his stature diminished, to see his certainty and self-esteem breached. They believe that what they are objecting to is his characterization. In fact, what they are objecting to is his character.

There is a scene in *The Fountainhead* in which Peter Keating resentfully asks Howard Roark: "'Can't you be human for once in your life? . . . Can't you ever relax? . . . Do you always have to be so damn serious? Can't you ever do things without reason, just like everybody else? . . . Everything's important with you, everything's great, significant in some way, every minute, even when you keep still. Can't you ever be comfortable—and unimportant?' " If one understands Keating's psychology in this scene, one understands the psychology of those who find Galt "unreal" or "inhuman."

The method by which Ayn Rand characterizes the villains in her novels is, following the same principle of selectivity, to focus on the actions and reactions that hold the key to their fundamental motivations. One of the most fascinating and complex of these characterizations is that of Dr. Robert Stadler in *Atlas Shrugged*. Dr. Stadler is shown as a great mind, genuinely devoted to science—but willing, in exchange for a laboratory, to work for the practitioners of brute force, the looters in control of the State. He is irresistibly and almost pathetically drawn to the intelligence of Dagny Taggart, in whose eyes he attempts to justify himself—but then snarls at her his contempt for all industrialists (of which she is one), because of their "vulgar" concern with "practical" pursuits. He worships and longs for the genius of his former student, John Galt—but, at the end of a long series of betrayals, he is driven by his own guilt to seek his idol's death. "What can you do when you have to deal with people?" cries Dr. Stadler throughout the novel. At first, it is the bewildered cry of a great intellect who feels himself caught in a swamp of mediocrity; at the end, it is the vicious rationalization of an evader who has acquired a vested interest in men's evil—as a sanction and excuse for his own.

James Taggart is a villain of a different order. Whereas Stadler is a man of better premises, who commits treason to his values, Taggart has no better premises and no values to betray. From his first introduction in the story—" 'Don't bother me, don't bother me, don't bother me,' said James Taggart"— he is shown as a whim-worshipper, a resentful and pretentious mediocrity moved by terror, a hatred for ability and an insatiable craving for power. This is the theme and the leitmotif of all his crucial actions, and this is the aspect from which he is presented. A real-life James Taggart may have his evil concealed beneath many confusing and contradictory surface attributes; but that precisely is the virtue of art—that it penetrates the smoke screen of the superficial, the irrelevant and the accidental, and shows the essence that lies beneath.

The same mentality that complains of Galt's characterization because Galt is given no flaws, complains of Taggart's characterization because Taggart is given no virtues. It is not a literary issue at all, but a moral and psychological one. It is two sides of the same coin and the same psychological confession: to insist that there is some bad in the best of us, and to plead that there is some good in the worst of us. An apparent good that will be sold out and betrayed every time it clashes with a basic evil, is not an actual good; it is morally irrelevant to a man's character. That a concentration-camp sadist may bring his mother flowers every Sunday, does not mean that he is less than totally evil; that a James Taggart may have his moments of remorse, does not mean that *he* is less than totally evil.

If one wishes to understand the motives of those who are made uncomfortable by such moral absolutism and who prefer to assert that *no one* can be wholly good or wholly bad, consider this: a John Galt has nothing to gain by such a doctrine—but a concentration-camp sadist and a James Taggart *have*.

Once, after having delivered an address to members of the publishing profession, Ayn Rand was asked: "What are the three most important elements in a novel?" She answered: "Plot—plot—and plot." The most beautifully written novel that lacks a plot, she has remarked, is like a superbly outfitted automobile that lacks a motor.

Plot, as stated previously, is central and basic to the Romantic novel; it proceeds from the concept of man as a being of free will who must choose his values and struggle to achieve them. The logical progression is: *choice*—therefore, *values*—therefore, the necessity of *action* to achieve them—therefore, the possiblity of *conflict*—therefore, *plot*. *Action* and *effort* are necessities of survival, of the achievement of *any* values; they are inherent in the nature of human life. *Conflict* results from the fact that (a) a man's values may clash with one another, and (b) a man's values may clash with the values and purposes of others; both (a) and (b) are possible since men are neither infallible nor omniscient. Either a man achieves his values and goals or he is defeated; in a novel, the manner in which this issue is resolved constitutes the *climax*. Thus, plot is not, as the Naturalists have contended, an "artificial contrivance" that belies the actual facts of reality and the nature of human life. Plot is *the abstraction of man's relation to existence*.

"A plot," writes Ayn Rand, "is a purposeful progression of events. A plot-structure is a series of integrated, logically connected events, moved by a central purpose, leading to the resolution of a climax. A plot-structure is the dramatization of man's free will; it is the physical form of his spiritual sovereignty—of his power to deal with existence."

Purpose is the ruling principle in her novels, in two basic respects. First, all the characters are motivated by their purposes, by the goals they are seeking to achieve, and the events of the novel dramatize the conflicts of these purposes. Second, the *author* is purposeful, that is, every event, every character and every adjective is selected by the standard of the logical requirements of the novel; nothing is accidental and nothing is included for reasons extrinsic to the needs of the plot and the theme.

Every novel, by the nature of art, carries an *implicit* philosophical meaning. But Ayn Rand's plots dramatize an *explicit* philosophical theme. In *We the Living,* the abstract theme is: "the individual against the state; the supreme value of a human life and the evil of the totalitarian state that claims the right to sacrifice it." In *Anthem,* it is: "the meaning of man's ego." In *The Fountainhead,* it is: "individualism versus collectivism, not in politics, but in man's soul; the psychological motivations and the basic premises that produce the character of an individualist or a collectivist." In *Atlas Shrugged,* it is: "the role of the mind in man's existence—and, as corollary, the demonstration of a new moral philosophy: the morality of rational self-interest."

Ayn Rand defines a "plot-theme" as the central situation that expresses and dramatizes a novel's abstract theme. Thus, the plot-theme of *We the Living* is: the struggle of three young and talented people to achieve life and happiness in Soviet Russia, and the manner in which the system destroys all three of them, not in spite of, but because of, their virtues. In *Anthem,* it is: the struggle of a young scientist to discover the concept of "ego," in a totally collectivized society of the future, from which the word "I" has vanished. In *The Fountainhead,* it is: the battle of a great innovator—an architect of genius—against a society geared and committed to mediocrity. In *Atlas Shrugged,* it is: the mind on strike.

In contradistinction to the typical philosophical novel, such as, for instance, Thomas Mann's *The Magic Mountain,* the characters in Ayn Rand's books who hold opposing views do not merely sit on verandas or on mountain tops and debate or argue their theoretical convictions, while all action is suspended. Every idea, every issue and every intellectual conflict in these novels is *dramatized*—that is, presented in terms of *action,* in terms of the practical consequences to which it leads.

"I am interested in philosophical principles," Ayn Rand

has written, "only as they affect the actual existence of men; and in men, only as they reflect philosophical principles. An abstract theory that has no relation to reality is worse than nonsense; and men who act without relation to principles are less than animals. Those who say that theory and practice are two unrelated realms are fools in one and scoundrels in the other. I wanted to present my abstract theory where it belongs—in concrete reality—in the actions of men."

The ingenuity and artistry of Ayn Rand as a plot-writer lie in the nature of the situations she creates, in her sense of drama and conflict, and in her matchless integration of philosophy and action.

Consider the basic plot-situation in *We the Living*. In order to obtain money to send Leo Kovalensky, the man she loves, to a tuberculosis sanitarium, Kira Argounova becomes the mistress of Andrei Taganov, an idealistic communist. Neither man knows of Kira's relationship with the other; and both men hate each other; Leo is an aristocrat—Andrei, a member of the Soviet secret police.

Now, the situation of a woman forced to sleep with a man she does not love, in order to save the life of the man she does love, is not new; that is the situation in *Tosca*, for instance, and in many other stories. The originality of Ayn Rand's treatment of the subject—from the point of view of plot—is in the way she intensifies the conflict and makes it more complex. In *Tosca* and in stories like it, the man to whom the woman sells herself is an unequivocal villain whom the woman despises; he *knows* that she is selling herself for the sake of another man and it is he, the villain, who has forced the action upon her. But in *We the Living*, Andrei is *not* a villain; he is profoundly in love with Kira and believes that she is in love with him; he does not know of her love for Leo. And Kira does *not* despise him; increasingly she comes to respect him. At the start of their affair, she had acted in desperation, knowing this was her only chance to save Leo and knowing that Andrei had helped to establish the system that forced such an action upon her; but as their relationship progresses, as Andrei finds the first happiness he has ever known, he begins to understand the importance of an individual life—and begins to doubt the ideals for which he has fought. And thus the conflicts involved—and the suspense about what will happen when the two men find out about each other—are brought to the highest intensity. One of the most brilliantly dramatic scenes occurs at the climax of the novel when, arriving to arrest Leo for illegal activities, Andrei finds Kira's dresses in the closet of Leo's apartment—and learns the truth of Kira's and Leo's relationship, at the moment when he holds Leo's life in his hands.

In presenting the evil of dictatorship, Ayn Rand does not focus primarily on the aspect of physical brutality and horror —on the concentration camps, the executions without trial, the firing squads and the torture chambers. These elements are present in *We the Living* only in the background. Had these horrors been the *primary* focus, the impact would be less profound—because violence and bloodshed necessarily suggest a state of *emergency*, of the *temporary*. Ayn Rand achieves a far more devastating indictment of dictatorship by focusing on the "normal" *daily* conditions of existence: the spectacle of men reduced to a chronic, intense, humiliating preoccupation with the barest physical necessities—the spectacle of endless posters and endless speeches proclaiming man's duty to the State, in a world where a private life is forbidden, where one's "leisure" hours are drained away in public meetings, parades, social-activity conferences and "voluntary" demonstrations—the spectacle of squirming mediocrities scrambling for power, the power to rule a nation or to control a committee or to dispossess one's neighbor—the spectacle of a system where servility and treachery are the currency of survival, and virtue and ability are one's passport to destruction—the spectacle of a world where lives, careers, aspirations and futures are throttled by a mindless, impersonal machine controlled by hysterical thugs, the profiteers of the doctrine that man has no right to exist for his own sake.

In the course of the novel, Leo is arrested twice—and Kira does not know if he is to be tortured, executed or if she is ever to see him again. In the end he is released, physically unharmed—to go on living in a world where such threats are the constant *and the normal*. The impact is far worse than if he *had* been executed. Leo is destroyed spiritually.

Another crucial element contributing to the power of Ayn Rand's indictment of collectivism is the fact that she presents Andrei *sympathetically;* he is not the worst representative of the system, but the best—the most idealistic and sincere. And that is why—as the events of the novel demonstrate with inexorable logic—he is as inevitably doomed to destruction as Kira and Leo. It is his *virtues* that make his survival impossible.

In her Foreword to *We the Living*, Ayn Rand writes: "The rapid epistemological degeneration of our present age— when men are being brought down to the level of concrete-bound animals who are incapable of perceiving abstractions, when men are taught that they must look at trees, but never at forests—makes it necessary for me to give the following warning to my readers: do not be misled by those who might tell you that *We the Living* is 'dated' or no longer relevant to the present, since it deals with Soviet Russia in the nineteen-twenties. Such a criticism is applicable only to the writers of the Naturalist school, and represents the viewpoint of those who, having never discovered that any other school of literature can or did exist, are unable to distinguish the function of a novel from that of a Sunday supplement article. . . . *We the Living* is not a story about Soviet Russia in 1925. It is a story about Dictatorship, any dictatorship, anywhere, at any time, whether it be Soviet Russia, Nazi Germany, or—which this novel might do its share in helping to prevent—a socialist America. What the rule of brute force does to men and how it destroys the best, will be the same in 1925, in 1955 or in 1975—whether the secret police is called G.P.U. or N.K.V.D., whether men eat millet or bread, whether they live in hovels or in housing projects, whether the rulers wear red shirts or brown ones, whether the head butcher kisses a Cambodian witch doctor or an American pianist."

During World War II, the fate of *We the Living* in fascist Italy offered a dramatic illustration of the power of Romantic art, of writing by means of *essentials*. The Italian government expropriated the literary properties of foreign authors, and a "pirated" film was made of *We the Living*. The Italian officials allowed the picture to be produced because they thought it would be effective propaganda, since the story is anti-communist. Alida Valli and Rossano Brazzi played the parts of Kira and Leo, and it was they who, years later, in Hollywood, related to Ayn Rand the following story: When the picture first appeared in the theatres, it was an instantaneous success. People flocked to see it with an interest and enthusiasm far in excess of what the government had expected. Within a few months, the government ordered the picture withdrawn from circulation and forbade its further exhibition. Some official finally had gotten the point and had grasped that which the public had grasped immediately: every scene in that picture was fully as much an indictment of fascism as of communism; it was an indictment of *all* dictatorships; it was not a Naturalistic presentation applicable only to one country and one *version* of totalitarianism; it attacked the base, it dealt in terms of *universals*, of *principles*. The Nazi government in Germany displayed greater philosophical and esthetic acuity: it would not allow the picture into the country.

In *Anthem,* this same ability to perceive issues in terms of essentials led Ayn Rand to one of her most original and inspired literary-philosophical ideas. The "I" is the root of all evil, the altruist-collectivists declare? In *Anthem's* world of the future, the word "I" has disappeared from men's language. An individual man refers to himself as "we" and to another individual as "they." And the reader is shown the nature of a world from which the concept of "ego" has vanished.

In length, *Anthem* is closer to a novelette than to a novel; in style and form, it is closer to poetry than to prose. It is by far the most abstract of her works, in its method of stylization; it is a projection of the issue of individualism versus collectivism dramatized in its purest and starkest essence.

In the world of *Anthem,* men are permitted no "selfishness"—their thoughts, their occupations, their actions are dictated by the needs of their "brothers." All the scientific and industrial achievements of the past "Unmentionable Times" have been lost; men live by candlelight, bleed the sick to cure them of their ailments, and believe that the earth is flat and the sun revolves around it. Having destroyed the independent mind, this totally collectivized society has no power to keep that which only the independent mind can create and maintain. But out of this swamp, one man of rebellious and intransigent spirit arises, who is tortured and threatened with death for the crime of pursuing knowledge for his own pleasure and purpose; he had been ordered by the Council of Vocations to be a street sweeper, as his life's occupation. Working alone, at night and in secret, he has rediscovered the electric light. The rulers of his community order the light to be destroyed—and he is forced to escape with his discovery into an uncharted wilderness.

One of the most beautiful scenes in the book (which is written in the form of his diary) occurs when the young girl whom he loves and who has followed him into the the wilderness, struggles to communicate her love for him, without the use or knowledge of personal pronouns:

"Today, the Golden One stopped suddenly and said:

" 'We love you.'

"But then they frowned and shook their head and looked at us helplessly.

" 'No,' they whispered, 'that is not what we wished to say.'

"They were silent, then they spoke slowly, and their words were halting, like the words of a child learning to speak for the first time:

" 'We are one . . . alone . . . and only . . . and we love you who are one . . . alone . . . and only.'

"We looked into each other's eyes and we knew that the breath of a miracle had touched us, and fled, and left us groping vainly.

"And we felt torn, torn for some word we could not find."

The hero's struggle to identify and name the concept of "I" is developed with such tension that when, after pages of "we," one sees the opening line of the climactic chapter, the emotional experience is one of unsurpassable violence and power: "I am. I think. I will."

It is illuminating to note, in passing, a crucial difference between Ayn Rand's projection of a totally collectivized society and the projection of such a society in Orwell's *1984*, written some years later. In *1984*, what is presented is a super-industrialized, super-scientific civilization. Orwell (and many authors who have since written similar books) may believe that totalitarianism is immoral, but they do consider it *practical;* they share the premises of those they denounce at least to this extent: they believe that it is possible to enslave man, to rule him by brute force, to forbid independent thought—and yet, *somehow,* to keep and continue all that which is the achievement of a free mind. Ayn Rand knew better. And, years later, in *Atlas Shrugged,* she showed fully what industrial civilization depends on, and what happens when human intelligence ceases to function.

One of the most impressive examples of Ayn Rand's power as a plot-writer is the climax of *The Fountainhead*. To appreciate the ingenuity of the climax, consider the personal contexts of the leading characters and their relationships to one another; consider the conflicts and problems which the plot has set up—and the manner in which the climax integrates and resolves all of them.

The first note of the coming climax is sounded when Peter Keating asks Howard Roark to design the government housing project, Cortlandt Homes, and let him, Keating, take the credit. The project involves enormous architectural difficulties—and neither Keating nor any other architect has been able to solve them. Years earlier, Keating had graduated from architectural school with honors, on the day when Roark was expelled. In school, Keating had often gone to Roark for help with his assignments. Later, when they were both in practice—Roark, struggling desperately, Keating, rising to the top of his profession—Keating had gone to Roark again and again for help with his work. Keating is the second-hander, the man without independent values or judgment, the man who lives through and by others, the borrower, who originates or creates nothing. Roark, the independent innovator, the egoist, the man who lives for his own sake and by his own mind, the man who refuses to compromise his convictions, has fought a battle of eighteen years against the society around him. Now his architectural ideas are beginning to win; he is still denounced and opposed, but clients are coming to him in increasing numbers. Keating, having ridden for years on a prestige he had not earned, is now slipping; another fashion is replacing him; and he is terrified.

Roark agrees to design Cortlandt Homes for Keating on one condition: that it be built exactly as Roark designs it.

It is Ellsworth Toohey, the architectural critic, who secures the government commission for Keating. Toohey is a second-hander moved solely by a lust for power. He preaches altruism and collectivism. He hates Roark and has been seeking to destroy him. He has worked to build up the careers of mediocrities like Keating in order to close the field to the Roarks. Now, after years of plotting and scheming, Toohey is at the height of his fame and influence; his specific goal at present is control of the Wynand newspaper chain, for which he works as a columnist.

Gail Wynand is the great tragic figure in *The Fountainhead*. He has risen out of Hell's Kitchen, by his own prodigious effort, to the position of owner of a publishing empire. Having succumbed, in his youth, to the belief that virtue and integrity have no chance in human society, that life among men is inescapably evil, he concluded that one's only choice is to rule or be ruled—and chose to rule. He has poured his energy and genius into the creation of a vast newspaper chain that does not express his own values or convictions, but panders to the worst and lowest values and tastes of the mob; this, Wynand believes, is the path to power. With the exception of the *Banner*, his New York paper, Wynand has found only two passions in life: Dominique Francon, whom he marries—and Howard Roark, whom he first attempts to corrupt and whom he now virtually worships. Roark is that which Wynand had thought impossible: a man of integrity. But the realization toward which Wynand is moving is that if a Roark can be *practical* and can succeed on his own moral terms, then there is no justification for his, Wynand's, life.

Wynand does not know that Dominique and Roark are in love with each other. Dominique had left Roark years earlier because she could not bear to witness the destruction to which, she felt certain, he was doomed. A passionate idealist, she, like Wynand, believes that the good has no chance among men. But she does not commit Wynand's treason: she does not seek any values from a world she despises. She married Wynand, whom she took as her symbol of the world's evil, in a deliberate act of intended self-destruction, seeking to kill her own ecstatic sense of life that made the world unbearable to her. Now she knows that her sense of life cannot be killed. She witnesses Keating's disintegration, she sees Roark winning his battle, she observes Wynand's helplessness before him, and she begins to understand the nature of her error—to grasp the impotence of evil.

Such is the context at the time of the climax.

When the first building of Cortlandt Homes is completed, Roark discovers that it has been totally disfigured. The bureaucrats have kept Roark's structural and engineering plans, without which the project would not have been possible; but —in defiance of their contract with Keating, which guaranteed that there would be no changes in the design—they have had the design of the building drastically altered. Keating has no legal recourse; the government bureau cannot be sued or forced to honor its contract.

Roark dynamites Cortlandt. Then he waits at the scene of the explosion to be arrested. He will talk at the trial, he states. He has decided to make this a test case.

There is a storm of public indignation against him, led by Ellsworth Toohey. Everyone is convinced that Roark is guilty; no one knows his motive; but they do not have to; Cortlandt is a *housing project*—a home for the poor; Roark has no right to a motive.

Now observe what this climax accomplishes, dramatically and philosophically. Roark's dynamiting of Cortlandt, and the events to which this leads, integrate the conflicts of the leading characters into a final focus of violent intensity, maximizing the philosophical values and issues at stake. The climax involves each of these characters intimately and, in accordance with the logic of the basic course the characters have chosen, brings each of them to victory or defeat.

Philosophically, the climax dramatizes the central theme of the book: individualism versus collectivism—the rights of the individual versus the claims of the collective. It dramatizes the role of the creator in human society and the manner in which the morality of altruism victimizes him. It dramatizes the fact that human survival is made possible by the men who think and produce, not by those who imitate and borrow —by the creators, not the second-handers—by the Roarks, not the Keatings.

95

Peter Keating, who has attempted all his life to exist as a parasite off the minds of others, makes a final, desperate effort to save his entire career by such an act of parasitism—and is brought to disaster: to public disgrace and to the full realization of his own emptiness and mediocrity.

Gail Wynand attempts to defend Roark; he thinks that he will have his one great chance: to use the *Banner*, for the first time in his life, for a cause in which he believes; this will vindicate his past and justify his pursuit of power. But the public rises in fury against Wynand for his defense of Roark; his readers desert him; and Wynand learns that it is not he who had directed public opinion, but public opinion that had controlled and directed him. He learns that a corrupt instrument, such as the *Banner*, cannot be used to serve a noble purpose. To save the *Banner*, he joins the voices denouncing Roark. But in the end—recognizing the futility of his career, recognizing that his pursuit of power has only delivered him into slavery—he closes the *Banner*. He sees that a man cannot sacrifice his values all his life and expect to escape the consequences: that if Roark and Dominique were Wynand's highest values, it is precisely *they* whom he would inevitably betray. " 'You were a ruler of men,' " he tells himself. " 'You held a leash. A leash is only a rope with a noose at both ends.' "

With the closing of the *Banner*, Toohey is left to start his struggle for power all over again; his years of scheming and plotting have brought him nothing. His fate dramatizes the fact that evil has the power to destroy, but not the power to create; that evil is blindness, emptiness and impotence; Toohey, because of Wynand's own errors, is able to destroy the *Banner*—but he is not able to take it over.

Prior to the Cortlandt explosion, Dominique had been coming to understand that she did not have to fear that her values were caught in a malevolent universe where they were doomed to destruction. The dynamiting of Cortlandt puts her to the severest test possible: her highest value—Roark—is in far worse danger than any he had faced before. But she is not afraid for him; she knows that he is right, that he has won, that it is he who belongs on earth—no matter what happens. And thus she finds her way back to him.

At his trial, Roark's statement to the jury is a summation of the philosophy which the events of the novel—and of Roark's own life—have illustrated; that all progress and achievement come from the independent mind; that altruism is the second-handers' weapon of exploitation, their device for enslaving the creator; that man is not a sacrificial animal, but has the right to exist for his own sake; that society depends on the work of the creators and has a right to that work only on the creators' terms. " 'Now you know why I dynamited Cortlandt. . . . It is said that I have destroyed the home of the destitute. It is forgotten that but for me the destitute could not have had this particular home. . . . It is believed that the poverty of the future tenants gave them a right to my work. That their need constituted a claim on my life. That it was my duty to contribute anything demanded of me. This is the second-hander's credo now swallowing the world. . . . I came here to say that I do not recognize anyone's right to one minute of my life. Nor to any part of my energy. Nor to any achievement of mine. No matter who makes the claim, how large their number or how great their need. . . . I wished to come here and say that I am a man who does not exist for others. . . . I wished to come here and state my terms. I do not care to exist on any others.' "

Roark is acquitted. His dynamiting of Cortlandt and his subsequent vindication are the final expression of his unyielding integrity—and the confirmation of his conviction that the moral *is* the practical.

Just as the events of the climax integrate and focus the conflicts and values of the various characters, so those events are themselves integrated with all the past events of the plot, and grow logically out of them—like the final, concluding statement of a long progression of syllogisms.

When one reads Ayn Rand's novels in the order in which they were written, one is struck by the enormous artistic and philosophical growth from novel to novel. All the basic elements of her literary method are present from the beginning in *We the Living*, as are, implicitly, the basic elements of her philosophy. But each work is a richer and fuller expression of those elements, a more accomplished implementation, in a startlingly new and different form.

Just as, within each novel, the climax sums up and dramatizes the meaning of all the preceding events, raised to the highest peak of emotional and intellectual intensity—so, as a total work, *Atlas Shrugged* is the artistic and philosophical climax of *all* of Ayn Rand's novels, bringing the full of her dramatic, stylistic and intellectual power to its most consummate expression.

Ayn Rand has proudly referred to *Atlas Shrugged* as a "stunt novel"—proudly, because she has made the word "stunt" applicable on so high a level. By the standard of sheer originality, the idea of a novel about the minds of the world going on strike is as magnificent a plot-theme as any that could be conceived. If Ayn Rand has scorned the Naturalists who write about the people and events next door, if she has declared that the purpose of art is to project, not the usual, but the *unusual,* not the boring and the conventional, but the exciting, the dramatic, the unexpected, the rationally desirable yet the astonishingly new—then she is, pre-eminently, a writer who practices what she preaches.

Atlas Shrugged is a mystery story, "not about the murder of a man's body, but about the murder—and rebirth—of man's spirit." The reader is presented with a series of events that, in the beginning, appear incomprehensible: the world seems to be moving toward destruction, in a manner no one can identify, and for reasons no one can understand. A brilliant industrialist—Francisco d'Anconia—appears suddenly to have abandoned all purpose and to have become a worthless playboy. A great composer—Richard Halley—renounces his career, after years of struggle, on the night of his triumph. Businessmen who have been single-tracked in their devotion to their work—such as Midas Mulligan, Ellis Wyatt and Ken Danagger—retire without explanation, and disappear. A pirate —Ragnar Danneskjöld—is loose on the high seas, attacking and robbing government relief ships. The world's most distinguished philosopher—Hugh Akston—leaves his university position and chooses to work as a cook in a diner. The abandoned remnant of a new type of motor that could have revolutionized industry, is found on a scrap heap in the ruins of a factory. And in the growing darkness of a crumbling civilization, in moments of hopelessness, bewilderment and despair, people are crying: "Who is John Galt?"—without knowing exactly what the question means or where it came from or why they cry it.

There are no "red herrings" in the story, no false clues. But the mystery is to be solved by *philosophical* detection— by identifying the philosophical implications of the evidence that is presented. When the reader is finally led to the solution, the meaning and inescapable necessity of all the things he has been shown seems, in retrospect, simple and self-evident.

It is epistemologically significant that *Atlas Shrugged* is written in the form of a mystery. This is consistent with the philosophy it propounds. The reader is not given arbitrary assertions to be taken on faith. He is given the facts and the evidence; his own mind is challenged to interpret that evidence; he is placed, in effect, in the position of the people in the novel, who observe the events around them, struggle to understand their cause and meaning, and are told the full truth only when they have seen sufficient evidence to form a reasoned judgment.

The most impressive feature of *Atlas Shrugged* is its integration. The novel presents the essentials of an entire philosophical system: epistemology, metaphysics, ethics, politics (and psychology). It shows the interrelation of these subjects in business, in a man's attitude toward his work, in love, in family relationships, in the press, in the universities, in economics, in art, in foreign relations, in science, in government, in sex. It presents a unified and comprehensive view of man and of man's relationship to existence. If one were to consider the ideas alone, apart from the novel in which they appear, the integration of so complex a philosophical system would be an extraordinarily impressive achievement. But when one considers that all of these philosophical issues are dramatized through a logically connected series of events involving a whole society, the feat of integration is breathtaking.

If one were told that an author proposed to dramatize, in a novel, the importance of recognizing the ontological status of the law of identity—one could not be blamed for being skeptical. But it is of such startling dramatizations that the virtuosity of *Atlas Shrugged* is made.

The philosophical speeches in the novel are not arbitrarily superimposed on the story, but are an integral and necessary part of the plot. They are essential to the dramatic action and to the story's final resolution. Francisco d'Anconia's speech on the nature of money, at James Taggart's wedding party, is part of Francisco's effort to liberate Rearden, to give him the intellectual ammunition he needs and ultimately to bring him to go on strike. The speech made by the tramp, who had once been a worker at the Twentieth Century Motor Company, is not merely an abstract discourse on the evil of the slogan, "From each according to his ability, to each according to his need," but is an explanation, torn from the lips of a man who can no longer bear to remain silent, of the crucial event that started all the subsequent events of the story. John Galt's radio speech is necessary to explain to the world the nature and cause of the disaster that has befallen it, and to set the conditions of the strikers' return. Observe that there is not a single idea in Galt's speech—or in any of the preceding speeches—that is not illustrated by the events of the story.

Tremendously complex in its structure, presenting the collapse of an entire society, the novel involves the lives, actions and goals of dozens of characters—from industrialists to bureaucrats to scientists to engineers to artists to intellectuals

99

to farmers to labor leaders to the lowest worker in the underground tunnels of Taggart Transcontinental. Yet every character, action and event has a dramatic and philosophical purpose; all are tied to the central situation and all are integrated with one another; nothing is superfluous, nothing is arbitrary and nothing is accidental; as the story moves forward, it projects, above all, the quality of the implacably, the irresistibly logical.

Consider, as an example of the book's unified purposefulness, the presentation of Eddie Willers in the first chapter of *Atlas Shrugged* and in the final chapter. Eddie Willers is Dagny Taggart's personal assistant on the railroad. He represents the best of the average man: the honest, conscientious person of limited ability. At the end of the story, his fate is deliberately left indeterminate; we do not know whether he will live or die; if someone comes along to save him, he will survive; if not, he will perish. The meaning of his fate is that men such as Eddie can function productively and happily in a world in which the Hank Reardens and the Dagny Taggarts are left free, but men such as Eddie have no chance in a world ruled by the collectivists. Eddie is introduced in Chapter I as he is walking toward the Taggart terminal; to him, the railroad is the symbol of civilization, of everything he loves, and he senses that it is in some inexplicable danger; he feels that something is ominously wrong with the world, but he is unable to identify it. Suddenly and unaccountably, he finds himself thinking of his childhood and of a conversation he had held with Dagny when he was ten years old: "That day, in a clearing of the woods, the one precious companion of his childhood told him what they would do when they grew up. The words were harsh and glowing, like the sunlight. He listened in admiration and in wonder. When he was asked what he would want to do, he answered at once, 'Whatever is right,' and added, 'You ought to do something great . . . I mean, the two of us together.' 'What?' she asked. He said, 'I don't know. That's what we ought to find out. Not just what you said. Not just business and earning a living. Things like winning battles, or saving people out of fires, or climbing mountains.' 'What for?' she asked. He said, 'The minister said last Sunday that we must always reach for the best within us. What do you suppose is the best within us?' 'I don't know.' 'We'll have to find out.' She did not answer; she was looking away, up the railroad track." In the last chapter of the novel, Eddie Willers is alone in the midst of a desolate prairie, aboard a stalled and stranded Taggart train, which the crew and passengers have deserted; they have gone off in covered wagons. But Eddie will not leave the train, the symbol of the civilized world he has lost. As he desperately pushes the levers of the dead engine, in a vain effort to make it start, the words of his childhood conversation with Dagny come back to him. It is like the opening theme in a great symphony, that is stated, then developed, then brought to completion in the final movement: "He was pulling at coils of wire, he was linking them and tearing them apart—while the sudden sense of sunrays and pine trees kept pulling at the corners of his mind. Dagny!—he heard himself crying soundlessly—Dagny, in the name of the best within us! . . . He was jerking at futile levers and at a throttle that had nothing to move. . . . Dagny!—he was crying to a twelve-year-old girl in a sunlit clearing of the woods—in the name of the best within us, I must now start this train! . . . Dagny, *that* is what it was . . . and you knew it, then, but I didn't . . . you knew it when you turned to look at the rails. . . . I said, 'not business or earning a living' . . . but, Dagny, business and earning a living and that in man which makes it possible—*that* is the best within us, *that* was the thing to defend . . ."

John Galt—the man who has set in motion all the events of the story—does not appear until the last third of the novel. Yet it is he who dominates the book. It is with the question, "Who is John Galt?"—asked by some nameless bum—that the novel opens. The question is a slang expression in prevalent use. By the context in which it appears, one gradually grasps its emotional meaning: it is a cry of despair—and a plea for help. It reflects the ominousness that permeates the atmosphere, the sense of impending doom.

As the story progresses, Dagny Taggart begins to suspect that there is a conscious conspiracy behind the events she is witnessing, that some destroyer is deliberately draining the brains of the world. It is not until late in the book—shortly before Galt enters the story—that she finally learns the origin of the expression, "Who is John Galt?" She meets a worker who, years before, had been employed at the Twentieth Century Motor Company—the factory, now long out of business, where Dagny had discovered the remnant of the abandoned motor. The worker tells her of the plans which the company had adopted and which led to the company's destruction: " 'The plan was that everybody in the factory would work according to his ability, but would be paid according to his need.' " Dagny observes that the worker shares her resentment of the question, "Who is John Galt?"—and worse: that it fills him with terror. And then the worker tells her: " 'It was . . . something that happened at that first meeting at the Twentieth

Century factory. Maybe that was the start of it, maybe not. I don't know . . . The meeting was held on a spring night, twelve years ago. The six thousand of us were crowded on bleachers built way up to the rafters of the plant's largest hangar. We had just voted for the new plan and we were in an edgy sort of mood, making too much noise, cheering the people's victory, threatening some kind of unknown enemies and spoiling for a fight, like bullies with an uneasy conscience. There were white arclights beating down on us and we felt kind of touchy and raw, and we were an ugly, dangerous mob in that moment. Gerald Starnes, who was chairman, kept hammering his gavel for order, and we quieted down some, but not much, and you could see the whole place moving restlessly from side to side, like water in a pan that's being rocked. "This is a crucial moment in the history of mankind!" Gerald Starnes yelled through the noise. "Remember that none of us may now leave this place, for each of us belongs to all the others by the moral law which we all accept!" "I don't," said one man and stood up. He was one of the young engineers. Nobody knew much about him. He'd always kept mostly by himself. When he stood up, we suddenly turned dead-still. It was the way he held his head. He was tall and slim—and I remember thinking that any two of us could have broken his neck without trouble—but what we all felt was fear. He stood like a man who knew that he was right. "I will put an end to this, once and for all," he said. His voice was clear and without any feeling. That was all he said and started to walk out. He walked down the length of the place, in the white light, not hurrying and not noticing any of us. Nobody moved to stop him. Gerald Starnes cried suddenly after him, "How?" He turned and answered, "I will stop the motor of the world." Then he walked out. We never saw him again. We never heard what became of him. But years later, when we saw the lights going out, one after another, in the great factories that had stood solid like mountains for generations, when we saw the gates closing and the conveyor belts turning still, when we saw the roads growing empty and the stream of cars draining off, when it began to look as if some silent power were stopping the generators of the world and the world was crumbling quietly, like a body when its spirit is gone—then we began to wonder and to ask questions about him. We began to ask it of one another, those of us who had heard him say it. We began to think that he had kept his word, that he, who had seen and known the truth we refused to know, was the retribution we had called upon our heads, the avenger, the man of that justice which we had defied. We began to think that he had damned us and there was no escape from his verdict and we would never be able to get away from him—and this was the more terrible because he was not pursuing us, it was we who were suddenly looking for him and he had merely gone without a trace. We found no answer about him anywhere. We wondered by what sort of impossible power he could have done what he had promised to do. There was no answer to that. We began to think of him whenever we saw another collapse in the world, which nobody could explain, whenever we took another blow, whenever we lost another hope, whenever we felt caught in this dead, gray fog that's descending all over the earth. Perhaps people heard us crying that question and they did not know what we meant, but they knew too well the feeling that made us cry it. They, too, felt that something had gone from the world. Perhaps this was why they began to say it, whenever they felt that there was no hope. I'd like to think that I am wrong, that those words mean nothing, that there's no conscious intention and no avenger behind the ending of the human race. But when I hear them repeating that question, I feel afraid. I think of the man who said that he would stop the motor of the world. You see, his name was John Galt.' "

No hero in fiction has received the build-up—or overture —that the author gives John Galt in the first two-thirds of *Atlas Shrugged*. But what is more remarkable still, the overture is justified: when John Galt does appear, he lives up to it.

The climax of *Atlas Shrugged* is singularly typical of the spirit of the novel as a whole: the integration of the unexpected and the utterly logical—of that which starts by appearing shocking and ends by appearing self-evident. One reader has described *Atlas Shrugged* as having the quality of "cosmic humor." It is written from the perspective of a mind that has discarded the conventional categories, standards and frame of reference—and has looked at reality with a fresh glance.

The nature of its climax was the first thing I learned about *Atlas Shrugged*—when I met Ayn Rand in 1950, while she was writing the book. She had told me nothing about the story except that the hero was an inventor. "Can you tell me what is to be the climax?" I asked. She answered: "A scene in which the hero is being tortured by the villains." "Oh," I said, faintly disappointed at what seemed a rather standard device. I saw that there was the hint of a smile in her glance. "Do they want to force him to reveal the secret of some invention of his?" I asked. "No," she said. "They want to force him to become the dictator of the country."

That is the genius of the Ayn Rand imagination—literarily and philosophically.

No other climax could sum up so eloquently the thesis and the meaning of *Atlas Shrugged*. The men of ability have all gone on strike, the world is in ruins, and the government officials make a last grotesque effort to preserve their system: they torture Galt to force him to join them and save their system *somehow*. They order him to *think*. They *command* him to take control. Naked force—seeking to compel a mind to function. And then the ultimate absurdity of their position is thrown in the torturers' faces: they are using an electric machine to torture Galt, and its generator breaks down; the brute who is operating the machine does not know how to repair it; neither do the officials; Galt lifts his head and contemptuously tells them how to repair it.

The brute runs away in horror—at the realization that they need Galt's help even to torture him. The officials flee the cellar also—"the cellar where the living generator was left tied by the side of the dead one."

Ayn Rand's novels cannot be read as most other novels are read. They cannot be skipped, skimmed or read approximately; to attempt to do so, is to fail to read them at all. Many of Ayn Rand's readers have noted this fact. She has often received letters from admirers who tell her that they had begun to read one of her novels in the casual and cursory manner which they usually found quite adequate for fiction —but then, after a short while, stopped and saw that they had to begin reading her book again, from the beginning, because they realized that in every line she is *saying something* and their customary method of reading caused them to miss too much.

Her novels are written with the purposefulness and precision of a mind that functions in full intellectual focus—and demands the same of the reader. *Atlas Shrugged* is nearly seven hundred thousand words long—and there is not one superfluous paragraph and not one extraneous word. When one considers the scope of what it covers, its economy is one of its most remarkable features. The reader who would assert that the book is too long or repetitious, imagines—because he perceives things only in the most crudely primitive and generalized manner—that he has understood the book instantly; in fact, he has not understood it at all.

If one studies the descriptive passages in Ayn Rand's novels, one will observe how frequently they serve several different purposes simultaneously, aside from the re-creating of the physical setting. For instance, in the opening pages of

Atlas Shrugged, the reader must be introduced to a New York City that is disturbingly unlike the New York City of the present, a mood of ominousness must be established, the scene must be set for the presentation of a disintegrating society. Now observe what is communicated—and by what means it is communicated—in a description of the buildings of the city, on the second page of the first chapter:

"The clouds and the shafts of skyscrapers against them were turning brown, like an old painting in oil, the color of a fading masterpiece. Long streaks of grime ran from under the pinnacles down the slender, soot-eaten walls. High on the side of a tower there was a crack in the shape of a motionless lightning, the length of ten stories. A jagged object cut the sky above the roofs; it was half a spire, still holding the glow of the sunset; the gold leaf had long since peeled off the other half. The glow was red and still, like the reflection of a fire: not an active fire, but a dying one which it is too late to stop."

In reading such a passage, one may not be fully aware of how it is happening, but—in answer to such lines as *"like an old painting in oil, the color of a fading masterpiece,"* or *"not an active fire, but a dying one which it is too late to stop"*—one's emotions will be responding, one will find oneself slowly being carried into the atmosphere of a collapsing civilization—because every line of description, every adjective and metaphor has been calculated to produce the exact effect the author intends.

It is her sensitivity to the subtlest connotations and implications of each word and image that makes the evocative power of her writing. For example:

"The telegraph poles went racing past the window, but the train seemed lost in a void, between a brown stretch of prairie and a solid spread of rusty, graying clouds. The twilight was draining the sky without the wound of a sunset; it looked more like the fading of an anemic body in the process of exhausting its last drops of blood and light. The train was going west, as if it, too, were pulled to follow the sinking rays and quietly to vanish from the earth. She sat still, feeling no desire to resist it."

There are persons to whom clarity and precision are the enemies of poetry and emotion; they equate the artistic with the fuzzy, the vague and the diffuse. Seeking in art the reflection and confirmation of their sense of life, they are psychologically and esthetically at home only with the blurred and the indeterminate: that which is sharply in focus, clashes with their own mental state. In such persons, Ayn Rand's literary style will invoke a feeling of disquietude and resentment; Ayn Rand's use of language is best characterized by a line concerning Dagny Taggert: "she had regarded language as a tool of honor, always to be used as if one were under oath—an oath of allegiance to reality and to respect for human beings." Because her writing is lucid, such persons will tell themselves that it is crude; because her writing conveys an unequivocal meaning, and does not suggest a "mobile" to be interpreted by the subjective whim of any reader, they will tell themselves that it lacks poetry; because her writing demands that they be conscious when they read it, they will tell themselves that it is not art.

But the specific trademark of her literary style is its power vividly to re-create sensory reality and inner psychological states, to induce the most intense emotions—and to accomplish this by means of the most calculated selection of words, images and events, giving to logic a poetry it had never had before, and to poetry a logic it had never had before.

Consider the sequence in *Atlas Shrugged* that describes the first train ride on the new line Dagny Taggart has built in Colorado. The literary assignment in this sequence is extremely complex: to convey the sensory reality of motion in a speeding train, as experienced by Dagny and Rearden, who are riding in the cab of the engine—to convey the exaltation of a great achievement: the creation of this railroad line against overwhelming obstacles—to illustrate the philosophical meaning of that achievement—to project that sense of life which is peculiarly Dagny's and Rearden's—and to show the start of their love affair as the inexorable climax toward which the triumphant sweep of that train ride carries them. A writer who is familiar with the technical problems involved in communicating the sensation of motion and in projecting complex emotional states, can read this sequence only with awe.

The sense of motion is caught from the opening paragraph:

"The green-blue rails ran to meet them, like two jets shot out of a single point beyond the curve of the earth. The crossties melted, as they approached, into a smooth stream rolling down under the wheels. A blurred streak clung to the side of the engine, low over the ground. Trees and telegraph poles sprang into sight abruptly and went by as if jerked back. The green plains stretched past, in a leisurely flow. At the edge of the sky, a long wave of mountains reversed the movement and seemed to follow the train."

Then, several paragraphs later:

"Things streaked past—a water tank, a tree, a shanty, a

grain silo. They had a windshield-wiper motion: they were rising, describing a curve and dropping back. The telegraph wires ran a race with the train, rising and falling from pole to pole, in an even rhythm, like the cardiograph record of a steady heartbeat written across the sky. . . .

"The glass sheets of the cab's windows made the spread of the fields seem vaster: the earth looked as open to movement as it was to sight. Yet nothing was distant and nothing was out of reach. She had barely grasped the sparkle of a lake ahead—and in the next instant she was beside it, then past.

"It was a strange foreshortening between sight and touch, she thought, between wish and fulfillment, between—the words clicked sharply in her mind after a startled stop—between spirit and body. First, the vision—then the physical shape to express it. First, the thought—then the purposeful motion down the straight line of a single track to a chosen goal. Could one have any meaning without the other? Wasn't it evil to wish without moving—or to move without aim?"

Observe, in the following paragraph, as the train enters and then passes through a city, in what manner the reader is given the essentials of the sensory perceptions experienced by Dagny and Rearden—and how the specific images selected, the rhythm and the very structure of the sentences, together convey the sense of the speed of the train and the emotional mood of the occasion:

"It was a succession of minutes, but it hit them as a single whole. First, they saw the lone shapes, which were factories, rolling across their windowpanes—then the shapes fused into the blur of streets—then a delta of rails spread out before them, like the mouth of a funnel sucking them into the Taggart station, with nothing to protect them but the small green beads of lights scattered over the ground—from the height of the cab, they saw boxcars on sidings streak past as flat ribbons of roof tops—the black hole of the train-shed flew at their faces—they hurtled through an explosion of sound, the beating of wheels against the glass panes of a vault, and the screams of cheering from a mass that swayed like a liquid in the darkness among steel columns—they flew toward a glowing arch and the green lights hanging in the open sky beyond, the green lights that were like the doorknobs of space, throwing door after door open before them. Then, vanishing behind them, went the streets clotted with traffic, the open windows bulging with human figures, the screaming sirens, and —from the top of a distant skyscraper—a cloud of paper snowflakes shimmering on the air, flung by someone who saw the passage of a silver bullet across a city stopped still to watch it."

Then, still later, when Dagny leaves the cab to look at the motors:

"She moved slowly along the length of the motor units, down a narrow passage between the engines and the wall. She felt the immodesty of an intruder, as if she had slipped inside a living creature, under its silver skin, and were watching its life beating in gray metal cylinders, in twisted coils, in sealed tubes, in the convulsive whirl of blades in wire cages. The enormous complexity of the shape above her was drained by invisible channels, and the violence raging within it was led to fragile needles on glass dials, to green and red beads winking on panels, to tall, thin cabinets stenciled 'High Voltage.'

"Why had she always felt that joyous sense of confidence when looking at machines?—she thought. In these giant shapes, two aspects pertaining to the inhuman were radiantly absent: the causeless and the purposeless. Every part of the motors was an embodied answer to 'Why?' and 'What for?' —like the steps of a life-course chosen by the sort of mind she worshipped. The motors were a moral code cast in steel.

"They *are* alive, she thought, because they are the physical shape of the action of a living power—of the mind that had been able to grasp the whole of this complexity, to set its purpose, to give it form. For an instant, it seemed to her that the motors were transparent and she was seeing the net of their nervous system. It was a net of connections, more intricate, more crucial than all of their wires and circuits: the rational connections made by that human mind which had fashioned any one part of them for the first time.

"They *are* alive, she thought, but their soul operates them by remote control. Their soul is in every man who has the capacity to equal this achievement. Should the soul vanish from the earth, the motors would stop, because *that* is the power which keeps them going—not the oil under the floor under her feet, the oil that would then become primeval ooze again—not the steel cylinders that would become stains of rust on the walls of the caves of shivering savages—the power of a living mind—the power of thought and choice and purpose.

"She was making her way back toward the cab, feeling that she wanted to laugh, to kneel or to lift her arms, wishing she were able to release the thing she felt, knowing that it had no form of expression.

"She stopped. She saw Rearden standing by the steps of

the door to the cab. He was looking at her as if he knew why she had escaped and what she felt. They stood still, their bodies becoming a glance that met across a narrow passage. The beating within her was one with the beating of the motors—and she felt as if both came from him; the pounding rhythm wiped out her will. They went back to the cab, silently, knowing that there had been a moment which was not to be mentioned between them."

Pages later, when they stand on a balcony that night, after the train ride has ended, its mood and meaning are picked up and continued, as the emotional lead into their love affair:

"She felt a rhythm without sound or movement, a sense of beating tension, as if the wheels of the John Galt Line were still speeding on. Slowly, in answer and in resistance to an unspoken summons, she turned and looked at him."

Now consider the last two paragraphs of the sequence—and ask yourself whether you are reading the description of a sex act, or a treatise on the metaphysical relation of mind and body, or a statement of the moral purpose of man's life, or all three:

"He stood looking down at her naked body, he leaned over, she heard his voice—it was more a statement of contemptuous triumph than a question: 'You want it?' Her answer was more a gasp than a word, her eyes closed, her mouth open: 'Yes.'

"She knew that what she felt with the skin of her arms was the cloth of his shirt, she knew that the lips she felt on her mouth were his, but in the rest of her there was no distinction between his being and her own, as there was no division between body and spirit. Through all the steps of the years behind them, the steps down a course chosen in the courage of a single loyalty: their love of existence—chosen in the knowledge that nothing will be given, that one must make one's own desire and every shape of its fulfillment—through the steps of shaping metal, rails and motors—they had moved by the power of the thought that one remakes the earth for one's enjoyment, that man's spirit gives meaning to insentient matter by molding it to serve one's chosen goal. The course led them to the moment when, in answer to the highest of one's values, in an admiration not to be expressed by any other form of tribute, one's spirit makes one's body become the tribute, recasting it—as proof, as sanction, as reward—into a single sensation of such intensity of joy that no other sanction of one's existence is necessary. He heard the moan of her breath, she felt the shudder of his body, in the same instant."

The complex integrations, so characteristic of Ayn Rand's literary style, are essential to the dramatic power of her writing. By the numerous thematic and emotional strands she interweaves, and by her manner of uniting the most abstract ideas with their direct physical or psychological results, she achieves an effect of extraordinary richness and intensity—making *emotion* luminously philosophical, and *thought* radiantly passionate.

The "stunt" aspect of *Atlas Shrugged* is present, not only in its plot, but in other features of its method and style as well—for instance, in ingenious, unexpected, yet completely natural and flowing transitions. An example of this occurs at the end of the chapter entitled "The Concerto of Deliverance"—when Rearden is lying in his office, waiting to meet the unknown worker who saved his life, after the attack on his mills by the government-hired thugs:

"If it's true, he thought, that there are avengers who are working for the deliverance of men like me, let them see me now, let them tell me their secret, let them claim me, let them—'Come in!' he said aloud, in answer to the knock on his door.

"The door opened and he lay still. The man standing on the threshold, with disheveled hair, a soot-streaked face and furnace-smudged arms, dressed in scorched overalls and bloodstained shirt, standing as if he wore a cape waving behind him in the wind, was Francisco d'Anconia."

One senses, at the root of this method, the profound delight of an intelligence at the *interesting*—at the inventive and non-obvious—the delight of exercising an apparently effortless skill to create the colorful, the fresh, the benevolently startling. "Benevolent" is a key word here; it denotes a peculiar quality of Ayn Rand's writing: the subtle, underlying sense of intellectual gaiety.

Atlas Shrugged is so full—in dramatic action, in stylistic virtuosity and imaginativeness, in triple-meaning descriptions, in philosophical content—that one can return to it again and again, always to discover new values one had missed before. There is a sentence in *The Fountainhead*, describing a group of houses built by Howard Roark, that is singularly appropriate to what one feels when reading *Atlas Shrugged:* "They were like variations on a single theme, like a symphony played by an inexhaustible imagination, and one could still hear the laughter of the force that had been let loose on them, as if that force had run, unrestrained, challenging itself to be spent, but had never reached its end."

A few years ago, Ayn Rand gave a series of private lectures on the art of fiction-writing. During a discussion period, she happened to remark that there was not a single word in her novels whose purpose she could not explain. One of her students opened a copy of *Atlas Shrugged*, selected a paragraph—and asked Ayn Rand to demonstrate. What followed was as brilliant a performance of literary analysis as one could ever witness. Later, I asked her to write out the analysis.

The paragraph the student had selected was taken from the first page of Chapter 9, Part Two. The context at this point of the story is as follows: the country is collapsing in an accelerating spread of mindless destruction and passive resignation. Dagny Taggart had made a futile attempt to escape: she had quit her job, in protest against the growing outrages of collectivistic controls. But she has come back, unable passively to bear the disasters perpetrated by the reign of overbearing incompetence; she feels no hope for the future and no joy, only the determination to go on working to the end. She does not know what is destroying the world, but she senses some dim connection between the legend of Atlantis and the inexplicable disappearance of the men of ability, the men she desperately needs, misses and has given up hope of finding. It is the first night of her return; she stands at the window of her apartment, looking out at the city.

"Clouds had wrapped the sky and had descended as fog to wrap the streets below, as if the sky were engulfing the city. She could see the whole of Manhattan Island, a long, triangular shape cutting into an invisible ocean. It looked like the prow of a sinking ship; a few tall buildings still rose above it, like funnels, but the rest was disappearing under gray-blue coils, going down slowly into vapor and space. This was how they had gone—she thought—Atlantis, the city that sank into the ocean, and all the other kingdoms that vanished, leaving the same legend in all the languages of men, and the same longing."

Ayn Rand's analysis of this paragraph is as follows:

"This description had four purposes: (1) to give an image of the view from Dagny's window, namely: an image of what New York looks like on a foggy evening; (2) to suggest the meaning of the events which have been taking place, namely: the city as a symbol of greatness doomed to destruction; (3) to connect New York with the legend of Atlantis; (4) to convey Dagny's mood. So the description had to be written on four levels: literal—connotative—symbolic —emotional.

"The opening sentence of the description sets the key for all four levels: '*Clouds had wrapped the sky and had de-*

scended as fog to wrap the streets below, as if the sky were engulfing the city.' On the literal level, the sentence is exact: it describes a foggy evening. But had I said something like: 'There were clouds in the sky, and the streets were full of fog'—the sentence would have achieved nothing more. By casting the sentence into an active form, by wording it as if the clouds were pursuing some goal, I achieve the following: (1) on the literal level, a more graphic image of the view, because the sentence suggests the motion, the progressive thickening of the fog; (2) on the connotative level, it suggests the conflict of two adversaries and the grandeur of the conflict, since the adversaries are *sky* and *city*, and it suggests that the city is doomed, since it is being engulfed; (3) on the symbolic level, the word *'engulfed'* strikes the keynote for the tie to Atlantis, suggesting the act of sinking and, by connotation, blending the motion of the fog with the motion of waves; (4) on the emotional level, the use of so quiet a verb as *'to wrap,'* in the context of an ominous, *'engulfing'* conflict, establishes a mood of quiet, desolate hopelessness.

" *'She could see the whole of Manhattan Island, a long, triangular shape cutting into an invisible ocean.'* This sentence is a literal, realistic description—but by the words: *'cutting into an invisible ocean,'* I prepare the way for the comparison in the next sentence, I mention the word *'ocean,'* as another link to Atlantis, and the fact that it is an *'invisible'* ocean does two things: conveys the density of the actual fog and suggests the symbolic, legendary meaning.

" *'It looked like the prow of a sinking ship; a few tall buildings still rose above it, like funnels, but the rest was disappearing under gray-blue coils, going down slowly into vapor and space.'* Here I allow my purpose to come out into the open, but, since it is prepared for, it reads like a legitimate, unforced description of a view. Yet it accomplishes the following: (1) on the literal level, a good description of the view of New York, since it is specific enough to be sensuously real; (2) on the connotative level, *'a few tall buildings still rose above it,'* suggests the heroic, the few lone fighters holding out against that to which all the lesser elements have succumbed; (3) on the symbolic level, the tie between a *'sinking'* ship and a sinking city is obvious; *'disappearing under gray-blue coils'* applies equally to coils of fog or to the waves of an ocean— *'going down slowly into vapor and space'* is my integration of all four levels, slanted just enough to make the reader notice it: the word *'vapor'* still ties the sentence to the literal description of the fog, but the thought of *'going down slowly into space'* cannot actually apply to the view nor to a sinking

112

ship, it applies to the destruction of New York and to Atlantis, that is: to the vanishing of greatness, of the ideal; (4) the emotional mood is obvious.

" 'This was how they had gone—she thought—Atlantis, the city that sank into the ocean, and all the other kingdoms that vanished, leaving the same legend in all the languages of men, and the same longing.' This is the conclusion of the description, the 'cashing-in' sentence; it is not brought in arbitrarily, but sums up the meaning of the elements which the reader has been given in the preceding three sentences, to form, in effect, the following impression in the reader's mind: 'Yes, I see why she would feel that way.'

"The above are merely the main considerations that went into the writing of this paragraph. There were many, many other considerations, directing the choice and placement of every single word; it would take pages to list them all.

"As an example, let us take the last sentence and try to re-write it. Suppose I changed it to: 'This was how Atlantis had gone, she thought.' This would have been jarring and artificial—since it would have picked up Dagny's thoughts too conveniently and directly on the subject of *Atlantis*, in the form of a full, pat sentence. The words with which I actually begin the sentence: *'This was how they had gone, she thought,'* serve as a bridge from the description of the view to intro-spection, to Dagny's thoughts—and suggest that the thought of Atlantis came to her suddenly, involuntarily, by emotional association rather than by conscious deliberation.

"Suppose I reduced that sentence to a mere mention of Atlantis and of nothing else. This would have left the real meaning of the whole paragraph to implication—a vague, optional implication which the reader would not necessarily notice. By saying *'and all the other kingdoms that vanished,'* I made my main purpose explicitly clear: that the paragraph refers to that lost ideal which mankind had always been pur-suing, struggling for, seeking and never finding.

"Suppose I had ended the sentence on *'leaving the same legend in all the languages of men.'* This would have made it merely a thought of an historical nature, with no emotional meaning for Dagny and no indication of the emotional cause that brought this particular thought to her mind. The inter-pretation of her emotional reaction would then have been left at the mercy of any particular reader's subjective inclina-tions: it could have been sadness, fear, anger, hopelessness or nothing in particular. By adding the words *'and the same longing,'* I indicated her specific mood and the essence of her emotional reaction to her present situation in the world: a desperate longing for an ideal that has become unattainable.

"Suppose I rewrote the end of the sentence in a different order, thus: 'and all the other kingdoms that vanished, leaving the same legend and the same longing in all the languages of men.' This would have placed the emphasis on the universality of the quest for the ideal, on the fact that it is shared by all mankind. But what I wanted to emphasize was the quest for the ideal, not its universality—therefore, the words *'and the same longing'* had to be featured, had to come last, almost as a painfully reluctant confession and a climax.

"No, I do not expect the reader of that paragraph to grasp consciously all the specific considerations listed above. I expect him to get a general impression, an emotional sum—the particular sum I intended. A reader has to be concerned only with the end result; unless he chooses to analyze it, he does not have to know by what means that result was achieved—but it is *my* job to know.

"No, I did not calculate all this by a conscious process of thought while writing that paragraph. I will not attempt here to explain the whole psychological complexity of the process of writing; I will merely indicate its essence: it consists of giving one's subconscious the right orders in advance, or of setting the right premises. One must hold all the basic elements of the book's theme, plot and main characters so firmly in one's mind that they become automatic and almost 'instinctual.' Then, as one approaches the actual writing of any given scene or paragraph, one has a sense or 'feel' of what it has to be by the logic of the context—and one's subconscious makes the right selections to express it. Later, one checks and improves the result by means of conscious editing."

Such is the artistic genius of Ayn Rand.

In *Atlas Shrugged,* Ayn Rand has created more than a great novel. By any rational, objective literary standard—from the standpoint of plot-structure, suspense, drama, imaginativeness, characterization, evocative and communicative use of language, originality, scope of theme and subject, psychological profundity and philosophical richness—*Atlas Shrugged* is the climax of the novel form, carrying that form to unprecedented heights of intellectual and artistic power.

Atlas Shrugged has inspired the most passionate admiration—and the most violent antagonism. Neither response is difficult to understand, if one considers everything which, literarily and philosophically, the novel represents—and challenges. Contrast the nature of the story in *Atlas Shrugged* with the stories, currently hailed as great literature, concerning sensitive homosexuals in search of personal identity, smiling old ladies with irresistible compulsions to strangle birds and cats, mothers engaged in incestuous relationships with their sons, dope addicts who find spiritual fulfillment in Zen Buddhism, undistinguished mediocrities whose claim to importance is the adulteries or murders they suddenly commit for no reason known to anyone, least of all to their authors. Contrast the sense of life and the view of man projected in *Atlas Shrugged* with that projected by all the fashionable voices now wailing that life is sordid and futile, that human nature is a sewer, that man's mind is impotent, that man is metaphysically helpless, that terror is man's natural state. And then remember that every esthetic response is a psychological confession.

In an age when one of the most demanding aspects of writing a novel, the construction of a plot, is solved by the declaration that plot is "vulgar" and "artificial"—when pretentious little stories about nothing whatever are hailed as the expression of a "superior sophistication" *because* they are about nothing whatever—when ponderous, unwieldy sentences are taken, not as evidence of an author's ineptitude, but as proof of his "sincerity"—when unintelligibility is viewed as the hallmark of "profundity"—when the projection of any emotional mood except boredom or hysteria is regarded as "unreal"—when purposefulness, clarity or any other manifestation of intellect is treated as an artistic liability—when, in a word, literature is dominated by the worship of unconsciousness—it is not startling that the supporters of such a trend should be disinclined to understand or identify the nature of Ayn Rand's artistic achievement. If they apprehend in *Atlas Shrugged* the presence of that which is irrevocably inimical to their view of life and of art, if they sense that to acknowledge *Atlas Shrugged* as great literature is to set a standard devastating and terrifying in its implications for their own products and values, if they feel that it is *Atlas Shrugged* or them—can one say that they are mistaken?

Just as in philosophy Ayn Rand has challenged the modern doctrines of neo-mysticism and epistemological agnosticism, so in literature she has challenged the view of man as an impotent zombie without intellect, efficacy or self-esteem. Just as she has opposed the fashionable philosophical dogmas of fatalism, determinism and man's metaphysical passivity, so she has opposed the fashionable literary projections of man as a stuporous puppet manipulated by instinct and socio-economic status. Just as she has rejected the mystics' theories of Original Sin, of man's depravity and the misery of life on earth, so she has rejected the presentations of unfocused, whim-worshipping neurotics staggering along a trail of hysterical destruction to the abyss of whimpering defeat. Just as she has rescued philosophy from the cult of the anti-mind and the anti-man, so she has rescued literature from the cult of the anti-novel and the anti-hero. As an artist, she has brought men a new sense of life. As a philosopher, she has brought them the intellectual implementation of that sense of life: she has shown what it depends upon and how it is to be earned.

When one considers the quality of enraptured idealism that dominates her work, and the affirmative view of the human potential that she projects, the most morally corrupt of the attacks leveled against her—and the most psychologically revealing—is the assertion that she is "motivated by a hatred of humanity."

It is culturally significant that writers who present dope addicts and psychopaths as their image of human nature, are *not* accused of "hatred for humanity"—but a writer who presents men of integrity and genius as her image of human nature, *is*.

In Ayn Rand's novels, the heroes, the men of outstanding moral character and intellectual ability, are exalted; the men of conscientious honesty and average ability are treated with respect and sympathy—a far more profound respect and sympathy, it is worth adding, than they have ever been accorded in any "humanitarian" novel. There is only one class of men who receive moral condemnation: the men who demand any form of the unearned, in matter or in spirit; who propose to treat other men as sacrificial animals; who claim the right to rule others by physical force. Is it her implacable sense of justice—her loyalty to those who are *not* evil—her concern for the morally innocent and her contempt for the morally guilty—that makes Ayn Rand a "hater of humanity?" If those who charge Ayn Rand with "hatred," feeling themselves to be its object, choose to identify and classify themselves with the men she condemns—doubtless they know best. But then it is not Ayn Rand—or humanity—whom they have damned.

In presenting the struggle of an innovator against the society of his time, in *The Fountainhead,* Ayn Rand wrote many passages that were to prove prophetic of her own future. One such passage, especially relevant here, occurs at a trial where Howard Roark is being sued by a client who had commissioned him to build a "Temple of the Human Spirit" and who subsequently claimed that Roark's temple was sacrilegious. The following is from Dominique Francon's testimony at that trial:

" 'Howard Roark built a temple to the human spirit. He saw man as strong, proud, clean, wise and fearless. He saw man as a heroic being. And he built a temple to that. A temple is a place where man is to experience exaltation. He thought that exaltation comes from the consciousness of being guiltless, of seeing the truth and achieving it, of living up to one's highest possibility, of knowing no shame and having no cause for shame, of being able to stand naked in full sunlight. He thought that exaltation means joy and that joy is man's birthright. He thought that a place built as a setting for man is a sacred place. That is what Howard Roark thought of man and of exaltation. But Ellsworth Toohey said that this temple was a monument to a profound hatred of humanity. Ellsworth Toohey said that the essence of exaltation was to be scared out of your wits, to fall down and to grovel. Ellsworth Toohey said that man's highest act was to realize his own worthlessness and to beg forgiveness. . . . Ellsworth Toohey is a lover of mankind. . . . The Stoddard Temple is a threat to many things. If it were allowed to exist, nobody would dare to look at himself in the mirror. And that is a cruel thing to do to men. Ask anything of men. Ask them to achieve wealth, fame, love, brutality, murder, self-sacrifice. But don't ask them to achieve self-respect. They will hate your soul. . . . They won't say, of course, that they hate you. They will say that you hate them. It's near enough, I suppose. They know the emotion involved.' "

This passage was written twenty years ago.

The most tragic victims of the man-degrading nature of contemporary literature are the young. They have watched the progression from the boredom of conventional Naturalism to the horror of nightmare Symbolism—the progression from stories about the folks next door to stories about the dipsomaniac next door, the crippled dwarf next door, the axe-murderer next door, the psychotic next door. *This,* they are now informed, is what life is *"really"* like.

In projecting the artist's view of man's metaphysical relationship to existence, art explicitly or implicitly holds up to man the value-goals of life: it shows him what is possible and what is worth striving for. It can tell him that he is doomed and that *nothing* is worth striving for—or it can show him the life of a Howard Roark or a John Galt. It is particularly when one is young, when one is still forming one's soul, that one desperately needs—as example, as inspiration, as fuel, as antidote to the sight of the world around

117

one—the vision of life as it might and ought to be, the vision of heroes fighting for values worth achieving in a universe where achievement is possible. It is not *descriptions* of the people next door that a young person requires, but an *escape* from the people next door—to a wider view of the human potentiality. This is what the young have found in the novels of Ayn Rand—and that is the key to the enormous popularity of her novels.

Speaking before a group of university students, Ayn Rand has stated:

"Art is an expression of one's sense of life. *Where*, in today's culture, do we find any remnant of the joyous, the benevolent, the confident, the beautiful, the exciting? . . . Why are the higher reaches of artistic skill devoted exclusively to the colors of festering wounds and the sounds of cosmic wailing? . . .

"In the field of esthetics, those of you who are sick of the neo-savages of non-objective art, should rebel against their dogma that the garbage can is a symbol of man's soul. Take them at their word. Grant them their right to reveal *their* souls in the appropriate form they have chosen. But do not grant them the right to speak for *your* soul nor for the soul of man nor for his sense of life. . . . In the face of their maudlin whining that they have given up, flaunt the fact that *you* have not. To the motto 'We who are *not* about to die,' add: 'We who are *not* impotent, we who are *not* hopeless, we who are *not* depraved, we whose lives are *not* "banal" nor "gritty" nor irrational.'

"The correction of a disaster has to begin with the correction of its cause. It is philosophy that has brought us to this state—it is only philosophy that can lead us out. *Not* the philosophy of the neo-mystics, which has run its course—but the rebirth of a philosophy of reason, that is: a reassertion of man's self-esteem, with its three consequences: a rational morality, a rational esthetics and a Romantic renaissance in art."

In her own novels, that renaissance has found the greatest and most inspiring of beginnings.

A Biographical Essay

by Barbara Branden

IV
Who Is Ayn Rand?

"To hold an unchanging youth is to reach, at the end, the vision with which one started."

It was a world of irresistible gaiety. It was made of the music that tinkled arrogantly against crystal ovals of brilliance strung across the vast solemnity of the ceiling—music that danced defiantly on the soft, faded elegance of velvet drapery and on the stern white marble of glistening walls—music that surged upward through the stately grandeur of the opera house, carrying, in its rise, the laughter of a weightless exultation. It was made of graceful bodies whirling in effortless motion on a stage held in light rays, of silk gowns and radiant smiles and gleaming top hats—against the backdrop of a huge window which framed the painted image of lighted streets and the skyscrapers of a foreign city, sparkling and beckoning in the distance.

Beyond the walls of the theater—beyond the reach of the operetta—was a city of unending grayness: the grayness of crumbling buildings and crumbling souls, of stooped shoulders and bread lines and ration cards, of chronic hunger and chronic despair and the odor of disinfectants, of steel bayonets and barbed wire, and marching feet moving in a grim parade of death to sudden arrests in the night, of weary men crushed to their knees under waving flags and clenched fists. Only the flags and the fists relieved the grayness: the fists were stained, by a different dye, the same red as the flags. The city was Petrograd. The year was 1922.

A slender young girl with large eyes sat high in the last balcony of the opera house, leaning forward tensely, listening to the meaning of the most ecstatic sounds she had ever heard. The bright notes sparkling and leaping in the air around her and the reckless gaiety of the scene spread out on the stage below, were carrying a message to her, and a promise. They told her there was a sunlit, carefree world —a world of unobstructed action, of unobstructed fulfillment —somewhere beyond the dark night and the darker horrors, and it waited only for her to claim it. She listened with grave solemnity to the promise—and she gave a promise in return: that if she could not be the physical citizen of that glittering world, she would be its spiritual citizen. She took her oath of allegiance, with passionate dedication—with the gay score of an operetta as the holy bible on which she swore—an oath never to let the reality of her true homeland be dimmed by the gray exhaustion of a life lived under the alien weight of the ugly, the sordid, the tragic; to hold the worship of joy as her shield against the sunless murk around her; to keep burning within her that fuel which alone could carry her to the world she had to reach, the fuel which had kept her moving through her seventeen years: the sense of life as an exalted, demanding, triumphant adventure.

Thirty-five years later, and more than five thousand miles away, the young girl was to erect a monument to that music, and to the sense of life she had never lost or betrayed. The monument was *Atlas Shrugged*. The girl was Ayn Rand.

* * *

Ayn Rand was born on February 2, 1905, in the city of St. Petersburg (later called Petrograd, and finally, Leningrad). For the future writer of *Atlas Shrugged*, no country could have been more inimical a background than Russia—prerevolutionary Russia no less than communist Russia. From her earliest years, she felt a profound antipathy to the philosophical and psychological atmosphere around her: to the dark, almost Oriental mysticism that permeates the Russian mentality—to the blind, primitive worship of brooding emotions—to the unquestioning belief that suffering is man's inevitable fate on earth, which must be accepted in patient resignation.

Against this dismal background, Ayn's favorite word was *"Why?"* In a photograph taken when she was five years old, she sits straight in her chair, hands folded in her lap, gazing curiously into the camera; her eyes are large, dominating her face, and one is struck with the unusual perceptiveness of the eyes, with the look of calm self-confidence and of an active, eager intelligence.

She was not an "introspective" or "introverted" child, as

those terms are normally used. Her mental focus was directed outward, not inward. She wanted to perceive, she wanted to learn, she wanted to understand the world around her, she demanded the answers to countless questions. When she was confronted with any new aspect of reality, her first thought was: What is it?

She was six years old—two years before Russian children began school—when she decided to teach herself to read and write. By asking her parents to show her how one word was written, then another, she mastered the alphabet in a few months. Before she entered school, she read and wrote easily.

An outstanding student, she achieved her grades effortlessly, without needing to study outside of school hours. But classes soon became a monotonous duty: she grasped, on first reading, the content of her textbooks, then restlessly endured the teacher's laborious explanation of material already clear to her. The single great pleasure of her school years was mathematics; in its rigorous, demanding clarity she found a constant and exhilarating intellectual challenge.

Despite a keenly active mind, she had at first little interest in reading. Her mother—insisting that she become accomplished in French—subscribed to a French children's magazine. Ayn was drearily bored with the stories it contained: sentimental, rambling tales of helpless orphans and cruel stepmothers and gray-haired, kindly godmothers. She could not understand why she was expected to enjoy reading them. She would not be interested in such people, she told one of her sisters indignantly, if she met them in real life; *why* should she find them interesting in fiction?

She was eight years old when she read a story that she *could* like—and fell in love with fiction. It was a detective story, in which the leading character, in a series of exciting and dangerous adventures, pursues and ultimately captures a notorious jewel thief. It was not the concrete events of the story as such, nor the specific characters, that intrigued her: it was the *abstraction*, and the delighted realization that one could write about people and events immeasurably more interesting than the people and events around one.

She began inventing her own stories. She thought about them constantly. Sitting in classrooms, barricaded behind a stack of textbooks—the boredom of her lessons swept away —she scribbled happily and intently. The motive impelling her to invent stories was the sense that it was not right to wait passively for others to provide her with what she wanted. If—with the growing rebellion of a sovereign consciousness against the trite and the ready-made—she longed

121

to see the imaginative, the unusual, the purposeful, then it seemed self-evident that she must create them herself.

One of her stories concerned a heroine whose husband is captured by the enemy during a war. He awaits imminent execution. Determined to save him, and with only hours left, the heroine devises an ingenious method of rescue. She has just begun to carry out her plan when she receives word that their child is gravely ill and needs her. She must choose between abandoning her child and leaving her husband to certain death. She makes her choice: she will not desert the greatest of her values—her husband. The story does not end with disaster: she is successful in freeing him, and their child recovers.

It would be unusual to find so firm and so unconventional a moral stand in a person of any age. But one would surely expect a young girl to identify herself with the helpless child and to take its side in opposition to the romantic loyalties of adults. Ayn was eight years old when she wrote this story.

In the spring of 1914, an event occurred which was of profound intellectual and emotional significance for her, and which helped her to identify the values and ideals slowly forming in her mind. The event was the discovery of a hero.

He was tall and slender; a strand of fair hair fell over his forehead; he wore an open shirt, and soldier's leggings over long legs. He was a man of arrogant self-confidence, of relentless purposefulness, of proudly flaunted self-esteem. His name was Cyrus. He was the leading character in a children's story.

The story—a magazine serial entitled *The Mysterious Valley*—was about British officers stationed in India; they are threatened by an evil rajah, who plots to destroy them and to overthrow British rule. Cyrus, their leader, is captured with his men and brought in chains to the rajah's hidden valley; he laughs at threats of torture, defying the rajah and his warriors; armed only with his daring and his ingenuity, he vanquishes his captors and leads his men to freedom.

There are many children who respond eagerly to the excitement of adventure stories—only to be told, by adults, that when they grow up they will learn that "Life is not like that," that the romantic and the benevolent are not to be lived, but to be forgotten in the "serious concerns" of human existence. And the children *do* forget—then, in their turn, pass on the same injunction.

Ayn, age nine, saw in the person of Cyrus that which those children—and adults—failed to see. She knew that his meaning was not merely a soldier who defeats a rajah. She knew that he represented an ideal against which she would measure all other men. She knew—not in the form of a consciously identified concept, but as the implication of her emotional reaction—that the intensity of her feeling was her response to a symbol of man at his highest potential: man in control of reality, supremely confident and efficacious, able to choose great purposes, to struggle against terrible odds, and to win.

From that time on, she knew that *she* would *never* forget the promise of human greatness which Cyrus represented, and that nothing less could ever interest her. Concretized and real on the pages before her was everything she wanted of life. She turned from those pages to find that their after-image stood as a barrier between her and the values held by those around her. The after-image made her childhood easier than it had been—and more difficult. Easier, because she now understood what she wanted and what she loved. She had seen what was possible. She would wait—not unhappily, but with a tense, impatient expectancy—to grow up to the future that would be hers, the future in which the possible would become the real.

It made her childhood more difficult, because it intensified her feeling of spiritual isolation. She had known, for as long as she could remember, that her interests differed from those of other children; she had thought: *I* am interested in *serious* things; they are not. From adults, she consistently received admiration for her intelligence, for her grades and accomplishments at school—together with the uneasy sense that something in their attitude toward her was alien and wrong. Like a leitmotif running through her days, she heard the reproach: "You take things too seriously"—"You're too self-centered"—"You're too intense." She had felt no resentment toward her schoolmates or toward the adults, only a faintly puzzled indifference; and she felt no resentment now. But the gulf had widened: she knew there was no Cyrus in *their lives*—no value that meant to them what his image meant to her.

In the summer of that year, she chose her future profession. She was vacationing in Western Europe with her parents and younger sisters. War was declared while they were in Paris, and they hurried to London, hoping to board any ship that would take them across the North Sea—the only route to Russia which was still open. One evening during the anxious days of waiting, Ayn was alone in their London hotel room; she was inventing a story about the group of girls whose blond heads and gay, mocking smiles she had seen on a poster advertising a musical revue; the poster had given her the happy

123

sense of really being abroad, in a world untouched by the oppressive gloom of Russia. As she marched up and down the room, devising adventures and dangers and romantic escapes for her heroines, it became suddenly, startlingly real to her— as a completed thought fully formed in her consciousness —that the mental activity in which she was engaged was a *writer's* activity, that this was what it *meant* to be a writer. The thought was followed by another, which seemed simple, self-evident and very solemn: I'm going to be a writer.

While the boat which took her home to Russia crossed a North Sea treacherous with German mines, this was the single thought at the forefront of her mind: her decision to be a writer—and the sense that it was a decision of enormous importance.

In a deliberate process of training for her future career, she began to write short novels. Because she wanted to see people she could admire, the characters she invented were independent and daringly adventurous; because she wanted to witness events that were interesting and important, she showed her characters overcoming obstacles in the pursuit of demanding goals; because plotless stories bored her, she carefully structured the events of her stories to build to a dramatic climax; because she believed that tragedy was not what mattered in life, her stories had a sunlit, benevolent quality and culminated in the success of her heroes.

With the self-sufficiency of a child intent on her own mental concerns, she remained peacefully at odds with the immediate reality around her. Her relationship with her schoolmates was polite, but distant, and she took little part in their activities. Her sisters were younger than she, and could not share the interests that absorbed her. She had few clashes with her parents, who regarded her as exceptionally gifted, but she did not feel particularly close to them, intellectually or emotionally.

Her father owned a prosperous small business in St. Petersburg. The family lived comfortably in a large apartment. Their summers were spent in a country resort, where Ayn's greatest pleasure was listening to the light foreign tunes played by a military band in the park.

Although she was engrossed in writing stories, Ayn was not, by inclination, a sedentary child. If she rarely joined in the games of her schoolmates, it was not because she disliked physical activity, but because she disliked the dull and the purposeless in *any* activity. One of her happiest memories was of two weeks in Switzerland during her vacation abroad: her family had stayed in a hotel high in the mountains, and

Ayn spent her days exploring the mountains and caves with a young Swiss boy, leaping perilously from rock to rock, her dress torn and her legs scratched, in the purest, most joyous sense of physical adventure she had ever experienced, and with the excited knowledge of a higher cliff always ahead to be scaled.

She could not have known, that summer, that political events in Russia were building slowly and ominously toward an explosion—an explosion which would blast every life in the country and would leave, as its debris, fear, privation and death.

She witnessed the first portent of what was to come, on a cold winter day early in 1917. Standing at the window of her room, which overlooked a public square, she saw a large crowd gathering; they were waving banners and shouting anti-Tsarist slogans. Soldiers appeared, ordering them to disperse. The crowd refused, the soldiers raised their rifles—and Ayn heard the first shots of the Russian Revolution.

Eleven months later, from the same window, she watched the last rites of that revolution: the funeral procession of the delegates to the Constituent Assembly—chosen in the first free and general election in Russian history—who had been shot down by the communists at the Assembly's first meeting. As the open coffins moved slowly by, the twelve-year-old girl looked down at the body of a beautiful young woman whose white face and black hair were vivid against a scarlet pillow.

In the streets of Petrograd, as the weeks passed, the funeral procession was replaced by its cause: soldiers with bayonets and a loose, hooligan manner—and by its effect: the sense of being helplessly in the power of something brutal, savage and mindless. Crudely lettered posters appeared on the buildings and back fences of the city, announcing the slogans of the new rulers. Stories were whispered about former government officials vanishing in the mounting wave of arrests, about industrialists and newspaper editors shot without trial. Private property was confiscated. One day, Ayn watched in shocked indignation as soldiers burst into her father's place of business, stamped a red seal on the door, and declared the business nationalized in the name of the people. The people shivered in bread lines; there was no food to buy, no money and no work.

Ayn was startled by the fact that while everyone complained indignantly about the physical hardships created by the communists, no one seemed equally indignant about their ideology. When—at the age of twelve—she first heard the communist slogan that man must live for the state, she knew,

125

consciously and clearly, that this was the horror at the root of all the other horrors taking place around her. Her feeling was one of incredulous contempt: incredulity that such a statement could be uttered in human society, and a cold, unforgiving contempt for anyone who could accept it. She saw, in that slogan, the vision of a hero on a sacrificial altar, immolated in the name of mediocrity—she heard the statement that the purpose of *her* life was not her own to choose, that her life must be given in selfless servitude to others—she saw the life of any man of intelligence, of ambition, of independence, claimed as the property of some shapeless mob. It was the demand for the sacrifice of the best among men, and for the enshrinement of the commonplace—who were granted all rights *because* they were commonplace—that she held as the unspeakable evil of communism. Her answer to the slogan was that *nothing* could be higher or more important than an individual's right to his own life, that it was a right beyond the claim of any other individual or group or collective or state or the whole population of the globe.

As hunger and terror engulfed Petrograd, she watched— and endured—the practical consequences of the communist ideology. Her family lived meagerly and precariously on her father's savings. The savings began to wither away; the state did not.

It was against the background of these events that she discovered the novels of Victor Hugo. She first read *The Man Who Laughs*. Then she read *Les Miserables;* then all the rest of Hugo's novels. It was the discovery of a world of unprecedented scope and grandeur, of magnificently ingenious plots, of inexhaustible imaginativeness, of an exalted sense of life, of man seen as a hero. It was a world swept free of the commonplace and the trite—a world dedicated to the exciting, the dramatic, the *important*. There were many of Hugo's specific ideas and values with which she knew, even then, that she could not agree. But what she felt, without the words to name it fully, was that *this* was literature "as it might be and ought to be."

Among Hugo's characters, she found her favorite in *Les Miserables*. It was not Jean Valjean, the leading character, nor Marius, the younger hero. It was Enjolras, the young leader of the insurrectionists, who dies fighting on the barricades in one of the most exalted and dramatically powerful scenes in all of Hugo's novels. She regarded Marius as a weak, sentimental young man. But in Enjolras, the austere, implacable rebel—whom Hugo describes as "the marble lover of liberty," who "had but one passion, the right; but one thought, to remove all obstacles"—she saw the dedicated purposefulness and the intransigent love of rectitude that was the essence of her concept of human greatness.

This, she felt, is what matters—Hugo's novels and the figure of Enjolras—not the dismal, tortured existence to which she and all those around her were condemned. This, she felt, is what one lives for—this sense of life and this view of man.

Desperately seeking refuge from the growing tyranny of the communist regime, Ayn's family left Petrograd for the Crimea, which was in the hands of the White Army. They spent three years there—years during which they felt themselves camped hazardously on a battlefield, as the Crimea was taken by the Reds, then retaken by the Whites. The despotism of the conquerors was crushing, whichever side was temporarily in power. By 1921, when the battered area had again fallen to the Red Army, it was evident that this time the communist occupation would be final and that no refuge could be found anywhere in Russia.

In the midst of the violent changes occurring in her life and throughout the country, a change was occurring in Ayn's approach to ideas and method of thinking—a change which fascinated and absorbed her. She called her new method: thinking in principles. She had held definite convictions before, but now—in a major step toward adulthood—she began to formulate her ideas in conscious, conceptual terms; she began to construct abstract logical chains of "Why's," to identify the deepest reasons of her convictions, to ask herself, about all the issues of her concern, *what* she believed, and *why*. One result of this change was a greater sense of intellectual control, and the knowledge that she was better able to prove and defend her convictions. A second result was an unaccustomed loneliness—a loneliness for someone with whom she could talk, someone to whom ideas would be as important as they were to her.

She was not unsocial by basic attitude or premises, but she felt a sense of strain with her schoolmates at the Crimean gymnasium. Her manner toward them switched between intensity and shyness—a passionate intensity when discussing intellectual issues, a helpless, shy reserve in purely social situations. The intensity came from her conviction of the crucial value of ideas; the reserve came from the fact that she did not know what to talk about when one was not supposed to talk about anything of importance.

She had not before taken the initiative in approaching any of her classmates, but she became interested in one of them, a girl whom she knew only slightly. The girl appeared to have

127

many of the qualities Ayn admired: she seemed intelligent, self-confident and independent—although, Ayn observed dubiously, she was popular and comfortably at ease with the other girls. Deciding to learn if she really did have unconventional ideas and values, Ayn walked over to her one day and asked gravely, without context or explanation: "Would you tell me what is the most important thing in life to you?" The girl looked startled, but she thought for a moment, then answered solemnly: "My mother." After an instant, Ayn said, "Oh, I see," and walked away. She felt a crushing, painful sense of disappointment, and lost all interest in the girl.

The single person with whom she could talk about ideas, was her father. He discovered, to his astonishment, her active interest in political theory; to her delight, she learned that he shared many of her convictions. A warm, intellectual friendship formed between them.

These were the years of Ayn's adolescence, and she flew through her days, impatient with the present, her eyes fixed on the future. While her mother, shaking her head reproachfully at Ayn's torn, unpressed dresses and tangled hair, reminded her that she would soon be a young lady, she shrugged indifferently and searched for more of Hugo's novels. While her classmates began to whisper excitedly of dates, she wondered how they could be interested in "just boys," and decided that *she* could care only for a hero. While the adults around her doubted that there would be a future for any Russian, she planned the novels she would write some day.

Between 1918, when Ayn left for the Crimea, and 1921, when she returned to Petrograd, three incidents stand out in sharp relief, eloquently revealing the nature of her character and psychology, and the direction in which her values were developing.

The first incident occurred during the journey to the Crimea. The train on which the family was traveling stopped suddenly in the gathering dusk, in the midst of an empty countryside, miles from Odessa, the nearest city; the track ahead had been blown up—perhaps by Reds, perhaps by Whites, perhaps by roving bandit gangs. Some of the passengers, Ayn's family among them, hired peasants with horse-drawn carts to take them to Odessa. It was night before they left, the carts bumping jerkily over the frozen ground. As they moved fearfully through uninhabited plains, a shot rang out and a voice ordered: "Halt!" A group of armed, ragged men emerged from the darkness, commanding the terrified passengers to step down from the carts and hand over their money. A woman screamed that they would all be shot. Ayn was thirteen years old, and the possibility of death had never before been real to her; it was real now. Standing with the other passengers, her back to the bandits' guns, the Russian night stretching bleakly around her, she wondered if she would die. If it *is* the end— she thought—still, I have had something great in my life. I have had the image of Enjolras. If I'm going to be shot, I'll think of him at the last. I'll think of how *he* faced death. I want to be worthy of him. I want to die in *my* kind of world.

The passengers were released to continue their journey; it was early morning when they saw the buildings of Odessa in the distance.

The second incident occurred when Ayn was not yet fourteen. It consisted of an entry in her dairy: "Today, I decided that I am an atheist."

There had never been a time when she was willing to accept an idea without proof, nor when she failed to give reasons for her convictions, in whatever terms her age and knowledge permitted. If she asked "Why?" about an adult's statement and was told that she must not expect to understand, that she must "just believe" or "just feel it" or "have faith"—her response was an astonished contempt. She would not enter into discussions with anyone who rejected reason; in her mind, such a person was either stupid or dishonest. When told, as an accusation, that she lacked faith, she would proudly reply: "I haven't any faith at all."

Her parents, who were Jewish, were not particularly religious, and had given her no formal religious training. The question of the existence of God had not interested her before. But now, attempting to formulate her convictions on a number of fundamental issues, she considered the question scrupulously—and concluded that there was no God. She wrote the causes of her conclusion in her diary: first, that there are no *reasons* to believe in God, there is no *proof* of the belief; and second, that the concept of God is insulting and degrading to man—it implies that the highest possible is not to be reached by man, that he is an inferior being who can only worship an ideal he will never achieve. By her view, there could be no breach between conceiving of the best possible and deciding to attain it. She rejected the concept of God as *morally* evil.

The third incident was her reaction to her teacher's suggestion that she become a mathematician. It was the spring of 1921; she was sixteen, and had just graduated from the gymnasium. Mathematics was the one subject of which she had never tired; the more difficult the problems, the greater her interest and enthusiasm. She showed such a talent for it

129

that her teacher told her it would be a tragedy if she chose any other career. Her answer, despite her love of the subject, was: "No, it's not enough." Mathematics, she thought, was a *method*. Like logic, it was an invaluable tool, but it was a means to an end, not an end in itself. She wanted an activity that, while drawing on her theoretical capacity, would *unite* theory and its practical application. Significantly, the only career which had ever tempted her—apart from fiction —was engineering.

She could not yet have stated it in philosophical terms, but the desire for the union of the theoretical and the practical was an essential element in the appeal that fiction held for her: fiction made possible the integration of the widest abstract principles and their direct expression in and application to man's life. It was *man* who stood at the center of her intellectual universe; all the circuits of her consciousness led, as her primary mental focus, to the realm of values, of human action, of man's life on earth. By her deepest premises, she was a *moralist*, in her desire to define a moral ideal; and an *artist*, in her desire to project, through fiction, the living reality of that ideal. She wanted to project it, using as her tool the precise, unsentimental mind of a mathematician.

Ayn had left Petrograd still a child. When she returned at the age of sixteen, she was not yet an adult, but no longer a child. In the midst of the terrors of civil war, she had thought about the supreme importance of the human mind; waiting wearily in ever-growing queues for ever-diminishing rations of food, she had struggled to grasp the meaning of good and evil; trudging to school through mud puddles against the piercing Crimean winds, wearing thin, patched shoes and her mother's cut-down summer coat, she had formulated her concept of individualism. Caught in the chaos of a vast country screaming in its final agony, she had forged the essence of her value-system and her character.

To name the essence of her character and psychology as they could be seen emerging from the questions and gropings of childhood, is to name a combination of two qualities usually held to be impossible in combination. Most men experience their concern with facts, on the one hand, and their concern with values, on the other, as deriving from two separate allegiances in their soul. The two allegiances, it is held, are often inimical; man, it is maintained, must choose between his perception of reality, and loyalty to his ideals— between the practical and the moral. Failing to question the validity of this dichotomy, most men fight a constant inner

130

battle between their intellect and their moral integrity—and, choosing one side or the other, become non-valuing "realists," contemptuous of any ideals, or helpless "idealists," unable to cope with the reality they have chosen not to perceive.

What is remarkable in Ayn's development is the complete absence of any such inner dichotomy. She experienced no conflict—and would not have understood how a conflict could exist—between her mind and her values. She thought that one chose values by perceiving reality; she knew that many people did not seem to do this; she did not know why, nor what it was that they did instead. She could not understand why anyone would choose values not intended to be achieved in reality; the phenomenon was incomprehensible to her. It was this untroubled integration of the rational and the moral, that was the key to her unique outlook. It was the primary focus on *understanding*—whether the subject was a mathematical equation or the nature of love or the justice of a social system—that was the motive power of her psychology.

Ayn entered the University of Petrograd in the fall of 1921. Because the central focus of her intellectual interests was man, and because she wanted a factual knowledge of the past for her future novels, she majored in history. She made detailed outlines of stories to be written in the future, but she did no writing during her college years: she felt herself too young to deal satisfactorily with the complex themes she was projecting—and she could not write political or philosophical novels in Soviet Russia. One of her outlines, originally conceived as a play, became, years later, the novelette *Anthem*.

In her first year at the university, she took a course in the history of ancient philosophy, which consisted of a detailed study of Plato and Aristotle. She was profoundly impressed with Aristotle's theory of knowledge and his definition of the laws of logic; she rejected completely the mysticism and collectivism of Plato. Her teacher, Professor N. O. Lossky, was a confirmed Platonist and a distinguished international authority on Plato's philosophy; he was a stern, exacting man, contemptuous of all students—particularly of women, who, he believed, had no business in philosophy; it was said that he failed most students the first time they took his examination. At the end of the course, a line of students waited their turn outside his study for his oral examination, nervously wondering which of three possible grades they would receive: Perfect, Passing or Failure. When Ayn's turn came, he questioned her gruffly about Plato's system. She would have preferred questions about Aristotle's philosophy, but she answered easily, precisely and impersonally. After a while, although she had not stated any estimate, Professor Lossky remarked sardonically: "You don't seem to agree with Plato, do you?" "No, I don't," she answered. "Tell me why," he said. She replied: "My philosophical views are not part of the history of philosophy yet. But they will be." "Give me your examination book," he ordered. He wrote in the book and handed it back to her silently. He had written: Perfect.

In her readings in philosophy, she discovered Nietzsche's *Thus Spake Zarathustra.* Because Nietzsche revered the heroic in man, because he defended individualism and despised altruism, she thought that she had found a spiritual ally. But she was made uneasy by the implication that a great man would seek power, not over nature, but over other men; to rule, she thought, was an unworthy occupation for a hero; a hero would not degrade himself by spending his life enslaving others.

As she read further in Nietzsche's writings, her hope gradually changed to disappointment. And when she discovered, in *The Birth of Tragedy,* an open denunciation of reason, she knew that any value she might find in his works could be only partial and selective; she saw that in their basic premises, Nietzsche and she were philosophical opposites.

Her two great literary discoveries of this period were Schiller and Dostoyevsky. What she admired in Schiller's plays was their combination of wide ideological issues with vivid romantic drama; she admired the fact that Schiller's characters are motivated by specific goals or values which they seek to achieve, and the plays dramatize the clash of those values—the fact that the characters are highly conscious of the convictions that activate them and of the philosophical principles involved in their conflicts, and that, as a result, the emotional violence of the stories is infused with a tone of intellectuality.

Her interest in Dostoyevsky was of a more narrowly literary and technical nature. She was profoundly in disagreement with the mysticism and altruism of his philosophy; his work, to her, was a fascinating intellectual discovery, but not a personal emotional experience. She admired him, above all, as a master of plot-construction, who expertly integrated abstract themes and dramatic action, making the events of his stories carry and illustrate his philosophical themes—and as a brilliant psychological observer. Of Dostoyevsky's novels, her favorite was *The Possessed,* because of the complex ingenuity of its plot and its unmasking of the mentality of Russian revolutionaries.

During Ayn's first year at the university, it became increasingly dangerous for students to express their opposition to communism. But at times her revulsion against the evils she saw made it impossible for her to be silent. One night, she lay awake in terror, expecting at any moment to hear soldiers' fists pounding on the door; she knew that she had gone too far that day: she had told a communist student that he and his comrades would ultimately hang from the lampposts of the city. Several months later, such a statement would have been more than dangerous: it would have been a sentence of death.

Her family lived in dreary squalor, crowded into a small apartment in a building her father had once owned. Constant employment was a luxury available only to a few; her mother taught in the city schools when she could; her father worked at whatever he could find. When there was no work, they starved. One evening, after a dinner consisting of a handful of dried peas, Ayn felt her legs sagging under her, and she sank to the floor, too weakened by hunger to stand; she remained there until the weakness passed.

As if to place a final unendurable burden on the exhausted city, epidemics of typhus swept Petrograd. One ventured into the streets at the risk of one's life. People smelled of carnation oil and kerosene—their sole defense against the typhus-carrying lice.

As the communist stranglehold continued to tighten, a persistent, gnawing fear of arrest was added to the panic of hunger and the horror of disease. No former bourgeois could be certain of living beyond the moment. Ayn would arrive at the university to learn that a student had disappeared suddenly, unaccountably and irrevocably—or that another, accused of counter-revolutionary activities, had been condemned to the slow death of Siberia. She met a young man, a fellow student, who still dared to speak against communism with defiant bluntness; she felt the first beginnings of a romantic interest in him, but he was arrested and sent to Siberia and she never saw or heard from him again.

The barrage of propaganda which poured forth on the city seemed endless. Every hour of every day, men were told that their lives belonged to the dictatorship of the proletariat, that each breath, each thought, each action and each dream must be consecrated to the state; the terror and the agony remained their own.

For Ayn, the worst torture of these years was not the

133

periods of acute suffering, but the chronically sordid, ugly bleakness of life—the colorlessness of a world where the highest achievement men dreamed of was to obtain a half pound of butter through a doctor's prescription, where men's souls grew shabbier and pettier with each dreary year, as if to match their material existence, where men dragged themselves from day to empty day, with nothing to desire because there was nothing to hope for.

Such was the entry into young womanhood of a girl who believed that joy is the meaning and purpose of human existence.

But she found a life line, thrown to her from the world abroad. It was the music of foreign operettas—of Lehar, of Kalman, of Millöcker, of Offenbach—brought to Russia for the first time since the revolution. She saw Millöcker's *The Beggar Student* eleven times; she saw Lehar's *Where the Lark Sings* eight times—and could not take her eyes from the backdrop on the stage, which showed the lighted street of a modern foreign city. She obtained the money for tickets by walking three miles to the university every day, to save her carfare. Every Saturday morning, she was standing outside the opera house by six o'clock, whatever the weather, waiting for the box office to open four hours later, so as to be certain of obtaining a seat in the last balcony, the only one she could afford.

No symphony or grand opera could give her what the operettas offered. With a few rare exceptions, the best of the world's serious music is touched by tragedy. Only these operettas—like the staccato sounds of military marches and the syncopated rhythms of popular foreign tunes she had heard and loved in childhood—could offer her the life-giving reality of a world untouched by pain. She listened, feeling a still, inviolate happiness almost unbearable in its intensity.

She saw the people around her slowly beginning to adapt and adjust themselves to the conditions of Soviet life, and to lose the awareness that those conditions were evil. She saw them come to accept the brutality to which they were subjected as the *normal*. She knew that she was witnessing an act of surrender and of self-destruction more terrible than any the communists could enforce. And she knew that that which she heard in the music of the operettas was a possession to be guarded with her life. Years later, she would describe Hank Rearden's attitude toward pain in words that equally described her own: "In moments of suffering, he had never let pain win its one permanent victory: he had never allowed it to make him lose the desire for joy."

134

In her final year of university, she found another window into her kind of world—through foreign movies. It was the great romantic period of the German silent movies—the period of Fritz Lang and Ernst Lubitsch, of Conrad Veidt and Mia May and Hans Albers, of *Siegfried* and *The Indian Tomb* and *The Oyster Princess*. These were her favorites, and they seemed to glow from the screens of the theater like the glow of the first sunrise over a darkened earth.

American movies began appearing in Petrograd. She hurried eagerly to see, not the popular Mary Pickford or Charlie Chaplin pictures, which she disliked, but movies such as *The Island of Lost Ships* and *The Mark of Zorro*. She felt that she was seeing the universe she had glimpsed, years ago, in its abstract essence in *The Mysterious Valley*—a world of free, joyously purposeful, active men. She knew that the stories she would write would be more philosophical, the heroes she would create more intellectual, than those she watched on the screen; but part of what fascinated her was precisely that these movies were *not* philosophical, as if all problems had been solved and all questions answered, and men were free simply to act and to achieve. Once in a while, she would see a long shot of New York City—of slender buildings shimmering with light, streaking upward into the sky; she would sit through two shows for the sake of a single brief glimpse, before returning to the darkened streets of Petrograd.

She believed that the communist regime could not last. If it were overthrown, she would be free to write her novels; if it were not, she would find a way to leave Russia—she would *have to* find a way.

She graduated from the university in the spring of 1924. She was nineteen years old. She was able to obtain a job as guide in a historical museum, where she lectured to apathetic groups whom she steered through the exhibits. The tours meant nothing to them but a boring duty they had to perform. The job meant nothing to her but a senseless ritual which was a means of getting food rations.

Early in 1925, her mother received an unexpected letter from relatives in America, who had left Russia many years before. It was a voice from a distant planet. Her mother entered into a correspondence, and in one of her letters, she wrote that Ayn would like to visit America. Ayn and her mother had grown closer during the past years; understanding that Ayn was suffocating in Russia, that no adjustment was possible, her mother was willing to allow her to travel alone across the world. Her father, afraid for her safety, was hesitant, but her mother insisted that Ayn must be allowed to go.

Mail service between Russia and the rest of the world was slow. A month passed. Ayn felt as if she were suspended in space, waiting in a kind of limbo. Then the answer came. It contained the affidavit required of visitors by the American authorities.

She filled out her application for a Russian passport. She waited. There was nothing to do but wait, and try to survive the waiting. Somewhere, someone was deciding her future; there was no way to know who or why or by what standard. During certain periods, Soviet citizens, particularly students, were granted passports relatively freely; during other periods, the gates of Russia slammed shut, and permission to leave the country was impossible to obtain. No one could predict what the policy would be from moment to moment.

Six months crawled by. She continued to instruct visitors to the museum on the horrors of slavery and imprisonment and tyranny under the Tsar. She continued to hope that the bars encircling the recipients of the communist beneficence would lift for an instant to let her escape.

Her passport was granted in the fall of 1925. It permitted her to visit the United States for six months. Her parents arranged for her to travel across Europe by train, and to sail from Le Havre.

Shortly before her departure, her mother gave a small farewell party. One of the guests, a man whom Ayn knew only slightly, said to her, with the sudden, tense earnestness of desperation: "If they ask you, in America—tell them that Russia is a huge cemetery and that we are all dying slowly." "I'll tell them," she promised.

When she said good-bye to her family at the railroad station, she believed that she would see them before long. Either the Soviets would collapse, or she would earn enough money to bring her family to America. It was not until many years later that she realized she had seen them for the last time.

She looked out the window as the train approached the Russian border. Then the border was behind her. Russia was no longer the present. It was the past. The years of dismal grayness fell away. She felt that she was separated from those years by a distance not of miles but of centuries. An unobstructed world lay ahead.

One final problem remained: to secure a visitor's visa from the American consul in Riga, Latvia. When he told her that she was free to go to America, she walked out of the consulate into the cold of a bitter winter day. She did not feel the cold. There was a thin sheet of ice over the cobblestones of the street. She moved over the ice with swift certainty, steadied by the conviction that nothing could harm her now.

She stopped for a few days in Berlin. She celebrated her twenty-first birthday there; she went to a musical revue; she bought photographs of her favorite movie actors. In Paris, walking through the Louvre, then through the shops of the city, where she bought her first foreign dresses, she felt an almost drunken exhilaration. She had reached a civilized world at last—and she was going to the most civilized country of all, the one country on earth where men were completely free, where collectivism had no foothold and no chance.

At nine-thirty one evening, early in 1926, she boarded her boat at Le Havre. As the boat pulled away from the shore, she stood on deck. She watched the coast recede into the darkness. She could see the shoreline and a few lights. It was her last salute to Europe.

Eight days later, she stood on a pier at the Hudson River, tears running down her face, looking through the lightly falling snow at the skyscrapers of New York City.

* * *

At the age of twenty-one, Ayn Rand was slender, slightly under medium height, with dark hair cut short and swept back impatiently from a high forehead, and large, intensely perceptive eyes. Her eyes and face were animated, conveying an impression at once of intransigent intellectuality and of an almost childlike eagerness, as though she constantly expected something interesting and exciting to happen.

She arrived in New York with fifty dollars in her purse—and the outlines of seventeen plays and novels in her mind. She spent two days looking at the buildings and the glittering electric signs of the greatest city in the world, the city that was her symbol of everything she admired in life.

When she reached Chicago, where her relatives lived, she began writing movie scenarios. She was determined to make a name for herself as a writer, and to earn her living. She had studied English briefly in Russia; she knew that she was not yet ready to write a novel in English, but she could write stories for the silent screen. She worked with a feeling of a race against time, of having no right to relax because the future was so uncertain.

There was one absolute in her mind: she would never return to Russia. She would find a way to remain in America, even if it meant spending years in Canada or Mexico, waiting to be readmitted under the permanent quota.

In the summer, having been granted an extension of her visitor's visa, she set out for Hollywood. She took with her a hundred dollars she had borrowed, a letter of introduction from a Chicago movie distributor to an official of the Cecil B. de Mille Studio, and four original scenarios.

Had the events of her first weeks in Hollywood been presented in a movie scenario as fiction, Naturalists would have accused their writer of glamorizing reality.

The day after her arrival, she left the Hollywood Studio Club, where she had taken a room, and went to the de Mille Studio. She gave her letter of introduction to the studio official; she was told, as she had expected, that there was no job available for her at present. She was walking toward the studio gate when she saw an open roadster parked at the side of the road—and de Mille at the wheel. She stopped, stunned, to look at her favorite American director. After a moment, realizing that she was staring, she walked on. To her amazement, his car drew up beside her, and he asked pleasantly: "Why were you looking at me?" She had just come from Russia, she answered, and she was very happy to see him. He opened the car door and said: "Get in." As they drove—she did not know and did not care where they were driving—she told him who she was, why she had come to the studio, and that she wanted to be a movie writer. He drove to the outdoor set where scenes for *The King of Kings* were being shot; if she planned to write for the movies, he said, then she must learn how movies were made. At his invitation, she came to the set daily to watch the shooting. At the end of a week, he suggested that if she needed a job, she could work as an extra.

To have met de Mille in this manner, to find herself working on a movie set, to see actors and actresses she had watched on the screens of Petrograd, gave her the incredulous, exhilarated sense of moving through an adventurous reality that felt totally and impossibly natural.

Each morning, in the dimness of predawn, she hurried from the Studio Club in order to be on the set by six o'clock. One morning, she boarded a streetcar as usual for the long ride to the studio in Culver City. She looked out the window for a few minutes. Then she glanced across the aisle.

He was tall and slender; a strand of fair hair fell over his forehead; he wore an open shirt, and slacks over long legs.

138

The skin of his face was taut against high cheekbones. His mouth was long and thin. His eyes were a cold, clear blue. He was half-dozing, his body relaxed with the boneless elegance of a cat.

She felt a shock of astonishment—a sense almost of recognition—and an emotion of such intensity that she could not know if it was pleasure or pain. She knew that if she were a painter and were asked to put on canvas her own private vision of the perfect human face and figure, it would be this face and this figure that she would struggle to create. She felt as if she were chained to her seat—or chained to him—unable to move.

Then she felt the jolt of a sudden terror: he would get off the streetcar, and she would never learn who he was. Desperately, she tried to think of an excuse to speak to him.

The streetcar reached Culver City. She saw him rise, get off—and walk toward the studio gate. She dashed to the dressing rooms to change into her costume. He was the first person she saw when she reached the set. He wore a short tunic and sandals, and a Roman scarf over his hair; he was an actor playing a bit part in *The King of Kings*.

She watched him all that day as he moved through the crowded set. Perhaps he would talk to someone, she thought —someone whom she knew, who could introduce her. But he spoke to no one. Between takes, he sat alone. His manner was aloof, suggesting a serene, confident self-sufficiency. Once, she sat beside him for a moment on a flight of stairs. She thought of nothing but of how she could meet him— and that she *had* to meet him.

One afternoon, a few days later, during the rehearsals of a mob scene, the extras were told to mill about the set— which represented a street in Jerusalem—while the actors were given specific assignments and a pattern of action to follow. She watched carefully as he was given his instructions. During the shooting of the scene, she made her way toward him—and stepped directly into his path. He stumbled over her foot. He apologized, and they began talking. Afterward, she could not remember what they had said, only that his name was Frank O'Connor.

When she arrived on the set the next day, he was not there. She learned that the scenes in which he was working had been completed. She did not know where he lived; his name was not listed in the telephone book; the casting office refused to release the addresses of actors; the few people with whom she was acquainted could not help her. He had vanished, and she knew of no way to find him.

There were times, in the months that followed, when she felt, despairingly, that she would never see him again. But beyond the reach of any painful emotion was a quiet, steady source of serenity: the conviction that she would discover some way to find him, even if she did not yet know how.

In these months, she was engaged in her first professional struggle as a writer. Soon after meeting de Mille, she had submitted her four scenarios to him; they had been rejected. When *The King of Kings* was completed, she submitted a fifth, written in Hollywood. De Mille liked this one; he considered buying it, then wavered—then, on the advice of his scenario department, it, too, was rejected. In the report from the scenario department, Ayn Rand heard for the first time the objection she was to hear again and again through the coming years, the objection deriving from literary standards and a view of life diametrically opposite to her own: the story, the report said, was unrealistic, improbable, too romantic; the characters were "not human enough." Her reaction to such criticisms was, then, as it would be in the future: contempt. She was not insensitive to the fact that she had a great deal to learn as a writer; but she knew—by the nature of the criticisms she received and the nature of the screenplays that *were* produced—that it was not for such flaws as they might possess that her scenarios had been rejected: her extravagantly imaginative romanticism was totally out of style with the type of stories that were then being filmed. Several years later, she wrote a stage play about an unconventional movie actress whose goal, spirit and personality clashed totally with the "folks next door" style of Hollywood movies—just as Ayn Rand's scenarios clashed totally with that style. The actress's press agent, in a mood of drunken despair, gives the following release to the press—and if one understands the spirit of the release and considers the novels Ayn Rand was to write, one will appreciate the nature of the conflict between her approach to art and that represented by the prevailing Hollywood standards: "Kay Gonda does not cook her own meals or knit her own underwear. She does not play golf, adopt babies or endow hospitals for homeless horses. She is not kind to her dear old mother—she *has* no dear old mother. She is not just like you and me. She never was like you and me. She's like nothing you bastards ever dreamed of!"

Notwithstanding his scenario department's rejection of her scripts, de Mille offered Ayn Rand the job she had wanted. She became a junior screen writer. Her work consisted of writing brief outlines of screen treatments for stories owned by the studio. Her salary—twenty-five dollars a week—seemed to her an incredible fortune. When she received her first check, she thought of the evenings she had spent in the theaters of Petrograd, watching American movies; she had not known she would be earning her living, two years later, as a screen writer for Cecil B. de Mille.

In her free time, she went to the movies and read a great deal of current and representative American literature. She had read the stories of O. Henry; she had been fascinated by the cheerfully inexhaustible ingenuity of his plots—the ingenuity of a mind that never settled for the obvious, but skillfully devised and made credible the totally unexpected and unusual—and by the light-hearted, benevolent gaiety that was his trademark. She found few other American writers whom she could like. One day, she asked a librarian: "Don't you have any novels with good plots and serious themes?" The librarian answered, almost wistfully: "They don't write them any more." I will, thought Ayn Rand.

She did discover one novel, that is her favorite to this day: *Calumet "K."* Its authors, Merwin and Webster, were popular writers of the turn of the century. *Calumet "K"* is the story of a man's struggle to build a giant grain elevator, of the powerful forces that oppose him, and of the ingenuity with which he conquers one obstacle after another to reach his goal.

On a summer day in 1927, she went to interview the superintendent of a construction job on Hollywood Boulevard, as research for a story de Mille had assigned to her. The superintendent had been detained, and she decided to wait in a nearby public library. She entered the library—and stood motionless. Sitting at a table, reading, was Frank O'Connor. She had not seen him for nine months. He looked up, and smiled in recognition.

He led her outside into the summer afternoon. They walked aimlessly—and talked purposefully. They discussed movies and writing and acting and what they intended to do in the future; they talked eagerly, without strain and with no sense of being strangers. By the end of the day, she knew that what she had seen in his face, that first morning on the streetcar, she now had found in his character. She had found the man of first-hand values, of independent judgment—of unborrowed soul. She had found her spiritual ally, who saw the world as she saw it.

Frank O'Connor was born twenty-nine years earlier in Lorain, Ohio, where his father was a foreman in a steel mill.

At the age of six, he already manifested the intellectual independence and rationality that was to be the crucial bond between him and the girl who would be born a year later halfway across the world. When he was taken to church one Sunday morning, he was told that according to the dogma of religion, all babies are born in sin, and must be cleansed of their evil. He was shocked at such an idea, and rejected it indignantly. Sin meant lying and stealing; how could a newborn baby lie and steal?—he protested. If this was what religion taught, he decided, then it didn't make sense. There was something wrong—something *bad*—in a dogma that unjustly condemned the innocent.

When Frank was ten years old, the first primitive, experimental—and immensely thrilling—moving pictures came to Lorain. With the first two-reeler that he watched, he was fascinated by the medium. His favorite movies were stories of adventure, of daring and courage and heroism. His favorite actor was Wallace Reed. But it was not acting or writing or any other single aspect of the movies as such that held him; it was the total phenomenon, the art form itself. *This,* he decided, was his future.

He and his elder brother organized the neighborhood children into an acting company, and put on plays in an unused basement. Frank was interested in every part of the activity; sometimes he was director, sometimes actor—or playwright or set designer or business manager. These productions—presented to parents and friends of the company; price of admission, one pin—were his first training ground.

He was fifteen when he decided to go to New York, where the major movie studios were located. As a step toward financing the trip, he obtained a job in a steel mill. He left Lorain a year later. Taking whatever jobs he could find, he gradually worked his way from city to city toward his destination. It was three years before he reached New York.

He had not decided which aspect of movie-making he wanted as a permanent career; but he thought his most likely means of entry into the movie world would be as an actor. Despite his startling good looks, parts were difficult to obtain for a young man without professional experience or contacts. He lived precariously, struggling to earn enough money for food and rent while making the rounds of the studios.

One July day in Central Park, he helped a truck driver to change a leaking tire. What could he do in return?—the driver asked. "Take me *there*," Frank said, pointing to the name printed on the side of the truck: D. W. Griffith Studio.

By the end of the day, he was helping an assistant director to repair a boat at the Griffith studio in Mamaroneck; by the end of the week, he was an extra on the set of *Orphans of the Storm.* During the filming of the picture, he worked in almost every department of the studio: he worked in the wardrobe, he designed costumes, he painted sets, he assisted the director, he was an extra in mob scenes, he had a bit part in the movie's opening scene.

When Griffith left to make a movie in Europe, Frank remained in Mamaroneck, working for a department store, delivering furniture and decorating windows until Griffith returned and the studio reopened. This was the pattern of the next several years: while a movie was in production, Frank worked at the studio; in the intervals between productions, he took whatever jobs he could find.

In 1925, Griffith left permanently for Hollywood, where the studios were moving. Frank decided to follow the studios. Once again, he worked his way to his destination, on a freighter going through the Panama Canal. His first movie job in Hollywood was as a bit player in *The King of Kings.*

Today, thirty-five years after he glanced up from his book in the library to see Ayn Rand looking at him, he speaks of his earliest memories and impressions of her with the tone of a man who has just fallen in love. When they talked on the set of *The King of Kings,* he explains, he had the sense that he was confronting an absolutely unique personality. It was not simply her obvious intelligence; it was something he could not then name, something that set her apart from anyone he had known before. In the months following their encounter in the library, as they began to meet with ever-increasing frequency, the causes of that initial impression became clear to him.

"One of the most striking things about her," he remarks, "was her complete openness—the absence of any trace of deviousness. The total honesty. You knew that it would be inconceivable for her ever to act against her own principles. Other people professed so many things that bore no relation to what they actually did. But you knew that anything Ayn said, she *meant.* . . . She had a tremendous capacity for enjoyment. Whether it was a piece of music she liked or a story or some present I brought her that cost a dollar—she was so expressively and radiantly delighted. . . . She constantly passed value judgments. If she liked something, she liked it violently. If she didn't like something, she could communicate *that* violently, too. . . . When we were with other people, she was reserved, even shy—until they began dis-

143

cussing ideas. Then all the shyness vanished. She was as confident then, in her early twenties, as she is now. . . . The people we knew all talked about the things they were going to do in the future, *if* they got 'the breaks.' Ayn never spoke that way. She never thought about 'breaks.' She was convinced that it was up to her—and she was absolutely determined that she would get where she wanted to go. It didn't matter how difficult it was, or what hell she had to go through. She never wondered if she was going to succeed. The only question was how long it would take."

The period following their meeting was one of the happiest of Ayn Rand's life. It was also—in a different respect—one of the hardest. De Mille closed his studio, moving to Metro-Goldwyn-Mayer as an independent producer—and she was out of a job. For the next year and a half, she had to take whatever odd jobs she could find. She stuffed envelopes, she sold subscriptions to *The Hollywood Citizen*, she worked as a waitress in a roadside diner. There was one month during which she lived on thirty cents a day. She had never believed that anything was owed to her by others, and she did not believe it now. She would have to find a way out, and by her own efforts.

During this year and a half, one principle governed her attitude toward Frank O'Connor: that no pain was to touch their relationship. A passage describing Hank Rearden's thoughts as he faces Dagny Taggart, equally describes Ayn Rand's attitude of that time: "He grasped a feeling that he had always experienced, but never identified because it had always been absolute and immediate: a feeling that forbade him ever to face her in pain. It was much more than the pride of wishing to conceal his suffering: it was the feeling that suffering must not be granted recognition in her presence, that no form of claim between them should ever be motivated by pain and aimed at pity. It was not pity that he brought here or came here to find."

When Ayn Rand worked as a waitress, she took jobs in outlying districts of Los Angeles, in the slum areas, more than an hour's streetcar ride from Hollywood, in order to be certain Frank O'Connor would not see her there. He never knew of her financial hardships, nor the sort of work she was doing. She was not ashamed of the work—such a concept would not have occurred to her—but he, too, was struggling on an irregular income, and she was determined that he must not think she needed help. It was not help that she sought from him. The bond between them—and that which she wanted to keep untouched by the painful difficulties of her struggle—was that sense of life which was peculiarly their own.

It was not the drudgery and the worries that she was to remember later, or that were important to her at the time. It was the hours she spent with Frank. It was the moment when he came to the Studio Club for the first time, and she saw his tall figure moving across the room toward her. It was the day he brought her an impossibly extravagant bunch of golden chrysanthemums, the first flowers she had ever received, which she kept in their vase long after they had died. It was the times when she had not thought he would call, and she answered the telephone to hear the unexpected sound of his voice. It was the spring day in 1929 when they stood before a judge, listening to the words of the marriage ceremony.

That spring, they drove to Mexico together, so that she could re-enter the United States as the wife of an American citizen. When they returned, she applied for American citizenship; she felt politically secure for the first time.

In early summer, she obtained an office job in the wardrobe department of RKO Pictures. She started as a filing clerk. Within six months, she was given a raise in salary. Within a year, she was head of the office. Frank O'Connor was working at various studios with some regularity. They were able to permit themselves an occasional luxury: they bought their first radio and their first car—the latter a second-hand convertible, more expensive than they could fully afford; Frank ordered a desk to be made for Ayn—she still works at it today—and gave her a portable typewriter.

In 1930, Ayn Rand began outlining *We the Living*.

"We the Living"—she has stated*—"is *not* a novel 'about Soviet Russia.' It is a novel about Man against the State. Its basic theme is the sanctity of human life—using the word 'sanctity' not in a mystical sense, but in the sense of 'supreme value.' The essence of my theme is contained in the words of Irina, a minor character of the story, a young girl who is sentenced to imprisonment in Siberia and knows that she will never return: 'There's something I would like to understand. And I don't think anyone can explain it. . . . There's your life. You begin it, feeling that it's something so precious and rare, so beautiful that it's like a sacred treasure. Now it's over, and it doesn't make any difference to anyone, and it isn't that they are indifferent, it's just that they don't know, they don't know what it means, that treasure of mine, and

---

* In her Foreword to the 1959 Random House edition.

there's something about it that they should understand. I don't understand it myself, but there's something that should be understood by all of us. Only what is it? What?'

"At that time, I knew a little more about this question than did Irina, but not much more. I knew that this attitude toward one's own life should be, but is not, shared by all people—that it is the fundamental characteristic of the best among men—that its absence represents some enormous evil which had never been identified. I knew that *this* is the issue at the base of all dictatorships, all collectivist theories and all human evils—and that political or economic issues are merely derivatives and consequences of this basic primary. At that time, I looked at any advocates of dictatorship and collectivism with an incredulous contempt: I could not understand how any man could be so brutalized as to claim the right to dispose of the lives of others, nor how any man could be so lacking in self-esteem as to grant to others the right to dispose of *his* life. Today, the contempt has remained; the incredulity is gone, since I know the answer."

At the time of writing *We the Living,* it was apparent to her that Americans did not recognize the full nature of the evil of collectivism; she did not yet know the extent to which sympathy with the collectivist ideology was growing and spreading. She was aware of the lip service which Americans paid to altruism; she was not yet aware of the extent to which altruism was an active political and cultural influence. The political tradition of America was implicitly individualistic; she believed that that base was firm—and that the demonstration of the link between altruism and collectivism would be a major blow to altruism in the mind of any honest man.

Working at RKO, she could devote only Sundays and her yearly week's vacation to the novel. She had no way of knowing how many years would be needed to complete it. But the novel was progressing; nothing else mattered.

One of her difficulties—especially frustrating for one to whom clarity and precision are the highest of literary values —was that she was not yet fully at home in the English language. She did not permit herself an inexact phrase, an approximate metaphor, an irrelevant sentence, an awkwardly expressed thought. Sometimes, she spent an entire day struggling with a single short paragraph that dissatisfied her. She considered literary or ideological sloppiness as reprehensible for a writer as the medical sloppiness of a surgeon who would remove "something" in the approximate area of his patient's appendix.

In *Atlas Shrugged,* when Richard Halley, the composer, denounces those who claim that art represents the spontaneous outpouring of the artist's blind feelings, and tells Dagny Taggart: "I, who know what discipline, what effort, what tension of mind, what unrelenting strain upon one's power of clarity are needed to produce a work of art—I, who know that it requires a labor which makes a chain gang look like rest and a severity no army-drilling sadist could impose . . ." —he speaks for the author of *Atlas Shrugged*—and for the author of *We the Living.*

Ayn Rand briefly interrupted work on *We the Living,* late in 1931, to write a movie original, entitled *Red Pawn.* Her earlier scenarios, written while she was still learning the medium, had been an experiment and a beginning; she considered *Red Pawn* her first professional, accomplished work. She hoped to sell it for a sum that would enable her to devote all her time to the novel.

Red Pawn is the story of a beautiful and glamorous woman who comes to a bleak island off the Siberian coast of Soviet Russia, a prison for men convicted of political crimes; she is to be the mistress of the austere, dedicated prison commandant, whom she has never seen. He had asked the authorities to send him a woman—*any* woman. When, against all his principles, he falls deeply in love with her, he does not know that she had schemed to come to the island, and that her husband is one of his prisoners.

A studio story editor, who had insisted in a newspaper interview that he was seeking new young talent and original ideas, told Ayn Rand that she ought to write "realistic stories about average people." He rejected *Red Pawn.* "Write about the people you know," he advised. She did not attempt to explain that she wrote in order to create the kind of people she would *like* to know.

A woman executive of a major studio warned her that *Red Pawn* would *never* sell. "The story is too improbable," she said. "Life isn't like that." Ayn Rand did not attempt to explain that she wrote in order to project what life *should* be like.

Red Pawn was bought by Universal Pictures in 1932. Ayn Rand was paid fifteen hundred dollars for the story and for writing the screenplay. It was her first sale. Her professional career as a writer had begun.

Universal subsequently released the actress for whom they had intended the vehicle, and, later, traded *Red Pawn* to Paramount Pictures for a story that had cost Paramount twenty thousand dollars; when Ayn Rand learned of this, she did not resent it—she was delighted by the implicit compliment to her work. The story has not been produced.

The sale of *Red Pawn* permitted her to leave the wardrobe department. A three-year-long jail sentence had come to an end.

On an evening in 1933—it was one of her rare evenings away from her desk—she happened to see a play laid in a courtroom. She thought: Wouldn't it be interesting if someone wrote a courtroom drama with an indeterminate ending —one in which the jury would be drawn from the audience and would decide whether the accused is guilty or not guilty? Wouldn't it be interesting if . . . ?

Several months later, she completed her first stage play, *Penthouse Legend*—later produced under the title: *The Night of January 16th*.

The Night of January 16th is a courtroom drama in which the factual evidence of the heroine's guilt or innocence is evenly balanced, so that the verdict has to be determined by the moral philosophy of the jurors. They must judge, by the standard of their own values, the diametrically opposite characters of the woman on trial and the major witness against her. Jurors are selected, each night, from the audience; they witness the play and decide on their verdict at the end of the last act.

When the play was completed and was being submitted to producers, Ayn Rand returned to work on the final chapters of *We the Living*. Despite the pressure of her work, she began to take a more active interest in the cultural and political life around her. She watched the political scene with a growing sense of uneasiness. America was moving into the "Red decade" of the 1930's. She began to read in increasing numbers of newspapers and periodicals that the nightmare from which she had escaped was a "noble experiment." She listened to intellectuals denouncing individualism, industry and the profit motive in a manner she had not expected to hear outside of Russia. Collectivism was being advocated more and more openly. Such was the political atmosphere in America when she finished *We the Living*.

The novel was completed toward the end of 1933. It had taken her four years. She sent the manuscript to her agent in New York—and waited.

As the months passed, her agent sent word of rejections from one publishing house after another. She began to hear, for the first time, that she was too concerned with *ideas*, that readers must be appealed to through their emotions, not their intellect. How could one reach the emotions, she wondered, except through the mind?—and why would any writer care to try? She had no knowledge of how to write for mindless readers, and no wish to gain the knowledge; nor did she share the contempt for the reading public held by those who told her that her work was "too intellectual."

A number of publishing houses did not trouble to disguise the fact that the cause of their rejection was not literary, but political: they did not care to publish a novel that denounced Soviet Russia.

While waiting to learn if *We the Living* would break through the wall of unmoving resistance, she wrote a novelette: *Ideal.* (She later adapted it for the stage; it has not been produced.)

The idea of the novelette came to her in the following way. A middle-aged woman of her acquaintance, pleasant but undistinguished and conventional—a kind of *Mrs.* "Babbitt"—spoke one day of a famous actress whom she, the woman, claimed to worship. "If only I could meet her!" she declared. "I'd give my life for it!" *Would you?*—wondered Ayn Rand. What do your values actually mean to you? What if . . . ?

Ideal is the story of a movie actress whose appearance and personality suggest so unusual a beauty of spirit that her audiences see in her the embodiment of their own deepest values and ideals. She attempts to discover whether those who claim to worship her do want, in actual reality, that which she represents—or whether they want it to remain only a distant, unrealizable dream. As the story progresses, all of them betray her, in different ways and for different reasons, as they betray their own ideals—all but one: a young man who gives his life for her when he believes that her life is threatened; in so doing, he shows her that there exist on earth a few rare men who are not content merely to dream, who will live—or die if they must—for their values.

Ideal is enormously revealing of the psychology of its author. Here again, one sees the union of attitudes rarely found in combination: the union of the most passionate and exalted idealism with a profound scorn for those who are *only* "idealists," who renounce the responsibility of translating their ideals into action and reality. In the play version of the story, Kay Gonda, the heroine—who is tortured by the discovery that her alleged admirers actually hate that which she represents, because it is a reproach to them—has the following exchange with Johnnie Dawes, the young man who will soon die to save her:

KAY GONDA What do you dream of?

JOHNNIE Nothing. Of what account are dreams?

KAY GONDA Of what account is life?

JOHNNIE None. But who made it so?

KAY GONDA Those who cannot dream.

JOHNNIE No. Those who can *only* dream.

As if to underscore Ayn Rand's rejection of any split between her values and her actions, she was faced with a major decision shortly after the completion of *Ideal*. *We the Living* was not yet sold. The last of her money was running out. Then, she received two offers for *The Night of January 16th*. One was from the Broadway producer Al Woods. A contract with him would mean a Broadway production, and all that that entailed professionally and financially; it was a chance to begin her play-writing career at the top. The other was from the screen actor E. E. Clive, who produced occasional plays on a modest budget at the Hollywood Playhouse, a small local theater. In terms of professional advancement and monetary reward, there was no comparison and no contest between the two offers.

It was with E. E. Clive that she signed a contract. Al Woods insisted that he be granted the right to make changes in the script. She would not grant it.

The play opened at the Hollywood Playhouse in October, 1934, under the title: *Woman on Trial*. Arriving at the theater on opening night, standing on the pavement before the brilliantly illuminated entrance, she looked up at her name and the title of her play sparkling on the marquee.

The reviews, next day, were highly complimentary—and shockingly disappointing to her. The play was praised for aspects which she considered of secondary importance; that which she considered most original and ingenious was ignored or mentioned only in passing. She had the sense that her play had not been *seen*. To be praised by standards other than her own, meant nothing to her.

The play had a reasonably successful run, and when it closed, Al Woods renewed his offer. He agreed to a new wording of the clause in the contract which had been under dispute. Her authority was not defined to her full satisfaction, but she decided that she was justified in taking a calculated risk. Woods planned immediate production, and asked her to come to New York at once.

Ayn Rand and her husband set out across the country by automobile. There was nothing to hold Frank O'Connor in Hollywood. He had become progressively disillusioned by the state of the movie industry, by the trend toward naturalistic, "folksy" pictures, and by the parts that were offered to him. As he obtained bigger parts, he grew more, rather than less, skeptical of the possibilities of achieving what he wanted in the movies. In *As Husbands Go,* he was cast in the comedy role of an awkward, ungainly juvenile, and make-up men struggled vainly to disguise his striking appearance and aristocratic manner so as to make him convincing in the part of a fool. The potential he had seen in the movie art form was still real to him, but he saw no way to realize that potential under the present conditions.

When they arrived in New York, they learned that production had been postponed. Al Woods had not obtained the necessary financial backing, and did not know how long he would require to do so. Apart from a small monthly option paid for the play, they had no money whatever. Frank O'Connor spent his days desperately searching for work, but it was the height of the depression, and no jobs were to be found. Ayn Rand did free-lance reading for movie studios—first RKO, then M-G-M. Her job consisted of reading books and manuscripts submitted to the studio, synopsizing them and evaluating their screen potentiality. Her income was irregular, sometimes falling to as low as eleven dollars a week. They lived in a small furnished room, budgeting themselves with ruthless severity; one day, they had fifty cents between them, and their only food was the remains of a box of oatmeal. Month by month, she waited for word that Al Woods had obtained his backing; by late winter, he told her that he would not be ready to go into production until the next fall.

Rehearsals for *The Night of January 16th* finally began in the late summer of 1935. Ayn Rand emerged from the following month with the sense of having escaped a medieval torture chamber. She and Al Woods clashed constantly; he kept asking for cuts and changes in the script that clashed with the play's theme; he insisted on toning down or eliminating many of the play's philosophical elements, the very elements which alone made a jury verdict possible or intelligible. The play opened for a tryout week in Philadelphia. The audiences were enthusiastic and the reviews favorable, but it was a week of constant, hectic rewriting, of arguing against suggestions that she include irrelevant, meaningless bits of dialogue which she was asked to remove the next night.

On opening night in New York, she felt neither excitement nor pleasure nor fear; the play was no longer in a form that satisfied her. But *The Night of January 16th* was a success. The audience was most enthusiastic about the "stunt" aspect

151

of the play: the device of an ending that was determined by a jury drawn from the audience. This device was the aspect that Ayn Rand herself was most pleased with and proud of. It was also the aspect which had most frightened producers, who feared that it would destroy the illusion of realism.

The play ran for seven months. Two road companies went on highly successful tours. It was produced in Britain and other foreign countries. That summer, it was performed in stock theaters all over the country. Today, twenty-six years later, it is virtually a classic of the summer stock repertoire.

The most memorable event of the Philadelphia tryout week was not the response of the audiences, nor the packed houses, nor the praise of the critics, nor the disputes with Al Woods, but the letter from her agent informing Ayn Rand that The Macmillan Company wanted to publish *We the Living*. She signed the contract when she returned to New York.

The novel was published in March of 1936.

"Tell them that Russia is a huge cemetery and that we are all dying slowly." She had kept her promise.

"Her novel suffers from aristocratic bias," charged one review. "Definitely prejudiced in tone," declared another. A third announced: "God is too frequently on the side of the non-Soviets." "The author pours out her hatred for a collectivist world," was one reviewer's summary. Another informed the public: "The tale is good reading, but bad pleading. It is not a valuable document concerning the Russian experiment."

Such praise as the book did receive omitted mention of its ideological content. The novel was advertised scarcely at all. Sales trickled in slowly. There was no way for its potential public to learn of its real nature or value except through the individual, private recommendations of those who had discovered it on their own.

A year after publication, sales suddenly began to climb; the dramatic power of the book was breaking through the barrier of opposition and noncommittal indifference; the novel was becoming talked about and known. But it was too late. The Macmillan Company—after issuing a first edition of three thousand copies—had destroyed the type. The book which dared denounce collectivism appeared to have been killed by critics who were *not* "prejudiced" against dictatorship, but only against its enemies.

In 1959, *We the Living* was re-issued by Random House. In 1960, New American Library published a paperback edition—and printed more than 400,000 copies within one year, twenty-four years after the novel's original publication.

*   *   *

Ever since childhood, Ayn Rand's thinking and mental development were dominated by the concept of the ideal man. That concept was, in a fundamental sense, the focus of both her philosophical and literary interests. By her basic premises, she was a *moralist*—that is, her primary intellectual concern was with *values*, with defining the actions and goals proper to man.

In childhood and adolescence, when she was initially forming her philosophical values, her concept of the type of man who would embody her values was, necessarily, highly generalized. As her thinking matured, her moral abstractions attained increasing specificity, and, accordingly, her concept of the human ideal became fuller and more detailed. But the essence remained unchanged. "I have held the same philosophy I now hold, for as far back as ˌ can remember," she writes. "I have learned a great deal through the years and expanded my knowledge of details, of specific issues, of definitions, of applications—and I intend to continue expanding it—but I have never had to change any of my fundamentals. My philosophy, in essence, is the concept of man as a heroic being, with his own happiness as the moral purpose of his life, with productive achievement as his noblest activity, and reason as his only absolute."

At the time of writing *We the Living*, she did not consider herself ready, in philosophical knowledge or literary experience, to attempt a full portrait of her concept of the ideal man. The ideal is only suggested, in that which Kira sees in Leo, in that potential which he would have reached had he lived in a free country. In the last scene of the novel, as Kira, desperately wounded, struggles across a snow-covered plain toward the border, toward the world that exists beyond Soviet Russia, she is kept moving by the vision of life as it could be abroad and of Leo as he might have been. She dies before reaching the border. Ayn Rand lived to cross that border, to give reality to her concept of life and of man as he might be—in *The Fountainhead* and in the person of Howard Roark.

The theme of *The Fountainhead* was born on the day that Ayn Rand grasped the distinction between two basic types of human motivation.

She identified the theme as "individualism versus collectivism, not in politics, but in man's soul." Her first notes, dated December 4, 1935, begin with the statement: "The first pur-

153

pose of this book is a *defense of egoism in its real meaning*."

She conceived the idea of the novel when she was still living in Hollywood. She was acquainted with a girl whose psychology puzzled her. The girl had an executive position with a major studio, and was struggling—with a desperate, amoral ferocity, scheming, manipulating and conniving—to advance her own career. The girl was passionately ambitious; so was Ayn Rand. The girl was enormously hard-working; so was Ayn Rand. Yet, Ayn Rand sensed, there was a basic difference in the nature of their ambition—a difference of profound moral and psychological importance. Seeking a clue to the principle involved, she asked the girl: "Can you tell me what it is that you want? What is your goal in life?" The girl answered immediately, as if the answer had long been clear in her mind: "I'll tell you what I want. If nobody had an automobile, then *I* would want to have *one* automobile. If some people have *one*, then *I* want to have *two*." Ayn Rand replied only: "I see." What she felt was incredulity, indignation, contempt. Her mind raced with the implications she saw in the girl's statement; in a few brief sentences, she had been provided with the key to answer the question she had wondered about for years, the question about people whose values and actions seemed incomprehensibly irrational: "But how *can* they?"

It was typical of Ayn Rand's "psycho-epistemology"—of her method of using her consciousness and considering intellectual issues—that she was not content with what would ordinarily be taken as an explanation of the girl's motivation; she was not content to dismiss it with some superficial bromide such as "She's a social climber," or "All she cares about is material possessions," or "She just wants to feel superior." She looked for a fundamental principle that would make the girl's attitude intelligible.

The girl, she thought, would conventionally be called "selfish." But wasn't a *self*—that which thinks, judges, values and chooses—precisely what she lacked? *I* want to achieve things that are important—important objectively, in reality, in fact—thought Ayn Rand; *she* wants only to make an impression on others. I choose my own goals, I decided *that* I wanted to write, and *what* I wanted to write; she struggles to imitate the goals chosen by others. I set my own standards; her desires are dictated by the standards of others. *Why?* What is the concept that will name the essence of the difference involved . . . ?

She was led to define two different ways of facing life—two antagonists—two types of man. The man of self-suffi-

154

cient ego, of first-hand, independent judgment—and the spiritual satellite, the dependent who evades the responsibility of judging. The man whose convictions, values and purposes are the product of his own mind—and the parasite who is molded and directed by other men. The man who lives for his own sake—and the collectivist of the spirit, who places others above self. The creator—and the second-hander. Howard Roark—and Peter Keating.

In her notes, dated February 9, 1936, one finds an interesting insight into her early thinking about Roark's characterization: "How he feels is entirely a matter of his own, which cannot be influenced by anything or anyone on the outside. His feeling is a steady, unruffled flame . . . a profound joy of living and of knowing his power, a joy that is not even conscious of being joy, because it is so steady, natural and unchangeable. If outside life brings him disappointment—well, it is merely a detail of the battle. He will have to struggle harder—that's all. . . . He is in conflict with the world in every possible way—and at complete peace with himself."

The characters of Roark and Keating came into being with the first definition of the novel's theme. The characters of Gail Wynand and Ellsworth Toohey were conceived as variants of spiritual collectivism—Wynand, who could have been great, but who makes the disastrous error of seeking greatness through ruling others, and finds that he has surrendered himself to them and is not their ruler, but their slave; Toohey, the complete antithesis of Roark, the man whose only passion is power-lust, the man who can live only by, through and for others.

The method by which Ayn Rand arrived at the concept of the novel's heroine, Dominique Francon, is an illuminating illustration of how a writer may employ the process of abstraction in the creation of a character.

Psychologically, Dominique Francon and Ayn Rand are very different. Dominique is motivated by the bitter conviction that values and greatness have no chance among men and are doomed to destruction. Ayn Rand's basic conviction is that evil, by its nature, is impotent, that only the good—the rational—can ultimately triumph. Yet she arrived at the essence of Dominique's character by means of introspection. "Dominique," she has remarked, "is myself in a bad mood."

Thinking about the contempt that she had felt for depravity, the passionate rebellion against the rule of mediocrity, the indignation against injustice—she asked herself what the consequences would be if that were her *permanent* inner state and view of life. And thus she projected the psychology of a woman who is stopped and paralyzed by contempt—a woman who withdraws from the world because of the intensity of her idealism—a woman who fights against the man she loves in order to make him renounce his career before he is destroyed.

One of the most famous incidents in *The Fountainhead* is the first meeting of Roark and Dominique and the start of their love affair. The idea for that incident arose out of the following experience.

In the fall of 1934, when Ayn Rand and her husband were driving through Virginia on their way to New York, she happened to notice a chain-gang of convicts working on a road under construction. A little later, she noticed an old and very beautiful Southern mansion, with graceful white columns and weathered, dark-red brick walls, that had the air of a feudal castle. The two images suddenly united in her mind, and she had the essence of the quarry scene in *The Fountainhead:* Dominique, fragile, delicately austere, aristocratic, the chatelaine of the surrounding countryside, walks from her estate to the granite quarry owned by her father—to see Howard Roark, a nameless worker drilling granite under the broiling sun, his face streaked with stone dust, his shirt clinging to his gaunt body, looking up at her with a glance that is an act of ownership.

Ayn Rand chose architecture as Roark's profession and as the background of the novel, for two reasons. She wanted to show the essence of a creative man's attitude toward his work, an attitude that would apply to *any* profession; architecture —because it is, simultaneously, an art, a science and a business—was an excellent vehicle for that purpose. But she had another, personal reason. During her college days in Russia, she had seen photographs of American skyscrapers; she had thought that some day she would write about those symbols of man's achievement and pay them the tribute which they deserved. When, standing on the Hudson River pier, she had looked at the buildings of New York for the first time, that thought had become a firm decision.

After the publication of *The Fountainhead*, she would be asked if Roark was patterned after Frank Lloyd Wright. He was not. She has stated: "The only resemblance between Howard Roark and Frank Lloyd Wright is in their basic architectural principles and in the fact that Wright was an innovator fighting for modern architecture against tradition. There is no similarity in their respective characters, nor in their philosophical convictions, nor in the events of their lives."

Having selected architecture as Roark's profession, she plunged into two years of intensive research. She had always liked modern buildings, but she had never studied architecture and had no formal knowledge of the field. Throughout 1936 and 1937, she read widely on the history of architecture, on its esthetics, on architectural engineering; she read professional journals, in order to learn the specific and immediate problems with which architects had to deal; she read the few available biographies of architects. By the fall of 1937, she was sufficiently familiar with the theoretical aspects of the profession. In order to gain practical experience, she decided to work in an architect's office for a few months. Eli Jacques Kahn, a famous New York architect, gave her a job as typist. He was the only one in the office who knew that her real purpose in working there was research for a novel.

During these years, she was outlining the plot of *The Fountainhead*. Devising the concrete events of the story, presenting the theme in terms of action, was the most difficult literary assignment she had ever undertaken. The story had to span Roark's whole career, covering a period of eighteen years—yet it had to maintain a unified, tightly integrated progression. In her early notes, she described her assignment as follows: "The story is the story of Howard Roark's triumph. . . . It has to show every conceivable hardship and obstacle on his way—and how he triumphs over them, why he *has to* triumph. These obstacles, of course, can come from only one source: other men. It is *Society*, with all its boggled chaos of selflessness, compromise, servility and lies, that stands in the way of Howard Roark. As he goes on, it is every conceivable form of 'second-hand living' that comes to fight him, that tries to crush him in every possible manner . . . and fails in the attempt. To every second-hand creature he stands as a contrast, a reproach and a lesson."

Ayn Rand had set herself a unique literary and philosophical goal. Historically, the originators of moral philosophies presented their theories in the form of treatises, as non-fiction. The writers of fiction who *dramatized* moral concepts, were not philosophical originators; writers of the Romantic school, such as Hugo, Schiller, Dostoyevsky, Rostand, took as their base the moral code of the culture of their time, which the majority of their readers accepted. Like the philosophers, Ayn Rand was presenting a *new* moral theory. Like the fiction writers, she was *dramatizing* it in a novel. She had rejected the common context, the conventional view of morality, and was presenting an unprecedented concept of good and evil, a new definition of egoism, a radical view of man—not in the form of a treatise, but concretized and illustrated in human action, in the character of Howard Roark, in the events of a story.

It was more than three years after the original idea for *The Fountainhead* that the plot structure was completed, and she began the writing of the novel. With the words that open the story: "Howard Roark laughed"—the ideal man was born.

At intervals, because she knew that *The Fountainhead* would be the work of many years, she interrupted it for shorter assignments. In 1937, she was spending the summer in Connecticut, where her husband was acting in a stock theater; she "rested" by writing the novelette *Anthem*—the story she had conceived while still in college in Petrograd. (*Anthem* was first published in England in 1938; it was not published in America until 1946.) In 1939, her stage adaptation of *We the Living* was produced on Broadway, under the title *The Unconquered;* it was not successful. That same year, she wrote a play, a philosophical murder mystery (as yet unproduced) entitled *Think Twice*.

The opening chapters of *The Fountainhead* were rewritten again and again, until she was fully satisfied with them. By the early part of 1940, she had completed one-third of the novel. At the suggestion of her agent, the book was submitted for publication.

During the next two years, *The Fountainhead* was rejected by twelve publishing houses.

The intellectual world of the period was dominated by collectivism in politics and by naturalism in literature. The rejections were based on one or the other—or both—of these two allegiances. The reports declared that the novel was too controversial—that it went against the prevailing political climate of opinion—that it was too intellectual—that the story was improbable—that the hero was unsympathetic—that no one could identify himself with Roark. *The Fountainhead* had no commercial possibilities, was the verdict.

Ayn Rand had been living on her earnings from *The Night of January 16th*. Her money was running out. She continued to write steadily, burdened by the knowledge that her savings would probably not last long enough for her to finish the book. By the fall of 1940, she had only seven hundred dollars left.

It was under these circumstances that she took three months

off from writing, using the last of her savings, to work for the election of Wendell Willkie.

She had realized, for some time, the nature of the political situation in America, and that the New Deal policies of the Roosevelt Administration were leading the country deeper and deeper into collectivism. She was appalled by the ineffectuality of those who spoke in defense of capitalism; she saw that their moral uncertainty and constant compromising were disastrous. When Willkie—representing himself as a crusading, intellectual, *uncompromising* defender of free enterprise—appeared on the political scene and was nominated as the Republican presidential candidate, she was convinced that his election was of the most crucial and immediate importance.

She and her husband offered their services to the New York headquarters of the Willkie Clubs. They worked fulltime, and without pay. She formed an "intellectual ammunition" bureau, preparing factual and theoretical material for use by Republican speakers and writers. She spoke on street corners, often to vocally hostile crowds. Once, a heckler demanded: "Who are you to talk about America? You're a foreigner!" Calmly, she answered: "That's right. I *chose* to be an American. What did *you* do, besides having been born?" The crowd laughed and applauded—and the heckler was silent.

A theater on Fourteenth Street, near Union Square, a strongly pro-Roosevelt district, was showing Willkie campaign movies and requested speakers to answer the audiences' questions. Seven times a day for two weeks, Ayn Rand answered questions from the stage of the theater. It was an experience she enjoyed immensely, and it further confirmed her in her respect for the American public, in her conviction that the so-called "common man" is singularly *un*common. The most intelligent and rational political questions she heard anywhere were asked by the audiences from the working-class area of the theater. She was delighted, too, by her own ability to make complex political principles clear and to establish communication even with antagonistic audiences.

The alleged intellectual and political leaders were a shocking contrast to those they were expected to lead. For the first time, Ayn Rand met and dealt with large numbers of "conservatives," who professed their devotion to the defense of free enterprise—and whose devotion consisted of compromise, timidity, fence-sitting and an aggressive non-intellectuality. The worst disappointment was the disintegration of Willkie throughout the campaign, as "me, too" became his unstated

159

motto: the moral fire and integrity that had won him the nomination and the enthusiastic support of millions gradually disappeared.

On the night of the election, when Willkie made his concession speech, Ayn Rand had the desolate feeling of having fought in a battle that had been doomed—and worse: in a battle that had been betrayed by its own generals.

The fall and winter of that year were among the most difficult periods of Ayn Rand's life. Three months and seven hundred dollars had been lost. She was not financially able to return to writing. She got a job as a reader for Paramount Pictures.

She had been working for several months when Richard Mealand, the Paramount story editor, learned that she had left her agent and that *The Fountainhead* was no longer being submitted to publishing houses. He had read the completed portion of the book. It was a great novel, he said, and offered to recommend it to any publisher of her choice. It was one of the rare occasions when an admirer of her work was eager to express his estimate in action.

She chose a publishing house with a reputation for good salesmanship of serious novels.

Six weeks later, the editor notified her that he was rejecting the manuscript. He asked her to come to his office. Against normal publishing procedure, he showed her a report written by a member of the firm's editorial board. The report said: "This is a work of almost genius—'genius' in the power of its expression—'almost' in the sense of its enormous bitterness. . . . I wish there were an audience for a book of this kind. But there isn't." This was typical, the editor told her, of the other reports he had received. All had praised the novel—all had predicted commercial failure.

Listening to him, Ayn Rand's feeling of shocked revulsion was not directed at the decision, but at the reasons for it. She had not known that there was something much worse than men who rejected a good book because, by their literary standards, they thought it was bad. Such men were merely stupid or dishonest. They had not reached the moral degradation of men who rejected greatness *because* it was greatness, who rejected a book not because it was bad but because it was *too good*—who *consciously* preferred mediocrity.

When Richard Mealand offered to recommend the book to another publisher, she selected the Bobbs-Merrill Company, which had recently issued a strongly anti-communist book. Mealand arranged a meeting with the editor, Archibald G. Ogden.

160

Knowing that publishing houses usually required a month or more before reaching a decision on a manuscript, she was startled to receive a telephone call from Archibald Ogden less than a week after she had submitted the book to him. He had called, he said, to tell her that *The Fountainhead* was magnificent. If the decision were his, he would draw up a contract immediately. But the final decision had to be made by the company's head office in Indianapolis. He was sending the manuscript to the head office, with a strong recommendation.

While she waited for word from Indianapolis, she continued reading for Paramount—reading one undistinguished book after another and thinking of the book that had found no publisher. "You're casting pearls," Frank O'Connor told her one day, "without getting even a pork chop in return." (Readers of *The Fountainhead* will recognize in what form this remark found its way into the novel.)

Six weeks passed. Early one morning, as she was wearily completing a rush assignment on which she had worked through the night, the telephone rang. It was Archibald Ogden. He was ready to draw up a contract for the publication of *The Fountainhead*.

Later, she learned the story behind the acceptance. On the strength of two reports on the novel from Indianapolis editors—one that called it a great book but said it would not sell, a second that said it was a bad book but *would* sell—D. L. Chambers, the head of Bobbs-Merrill, had returned the manuscript to Ogden, telling him to reject it. Ogden was a young editor in an important position which he had held for only a few months. He staked his job on *The Fountainhead*. He wrote Chambers: "If this is not the book for you, then I am not the editor for you." The return wire said: "Far be it from me to dampen such enthusiasm. Sign the contract."

The contract was signed in December, 1941. Ayn Rand had one year in which to complete the manuscript. Her deadline was January 1, 1943.

Almost two-thirds of the novel remained to be written. She worked day and night, with intense concentration and unlimited energy—in a state of cheerfully agonized tension. As the days and months went by, she measured time by the distance from January first, and by the mounting stack of manuscript pages on her desk.

Once, when she was depressed because of minor interruptions that had prevented her from working, her husband told her, jokingly: "It's nothing that a little writing won't cure." He was to repeat it often during the years to come.

They both knew that it was true—that no negative emotion could withstand the sense of achievement that writing gave her.

Early in December, she worked through a single unbroken stretch of thirty hours. For two nights and a day, she wrote steadily, without sleep, stopping only to eat, as one refuels a motor, so that she could continue to write. She felt exultantly clear-headed, as if she could work indefinitely without tiring.

As the novel neared completion, the days before her deadline were running out. She began the final typing of the manuscript, working around the clock, sleeping only for a few hours at long intervals—while Frank O'Connor and his brother worked in twelve-hour shifts, proofreading the manuscript and collating pages.

In *The Fountainhead,* Gail Wynand asks Roark: "Howard, when you look back, does it seem to you as if all your days had rolled forward evenly, like a sort of typing exercise, all alike? Or were there stops—points reached—and then the typing rolled on again?" "There were stops," answers Roark. "Did you know them at the time—did you know that that's what they were?" asks Wynand. "Yes," says Roark. As she walked toward the Bobbs-Merrill office in the brilliant crispness of a winter morning, Ayn Rand knew that *this* was a stop for *her*—a point reached. It was December 31. She was carrying the completed manuscript. A few hours earlier, she had typed the final sentence of *The Fountainhead:* "Then there was only the ocean and the sky and the figure of Howard Roark."

Ayn Rand had always been opposed to the idea, held by many writers, that a writer must inevitably feel some sense of dissatisfaction with his work, that he can never perfectly express what he wishes to say. While writing *We the Living,* she had still been in the process of mastering her technique and of developing her own unique style, and she had had the added difficulty of writing in a language which was not yet fully natural to her. But with *The Fountainhead*—which was far more complex in theme, plot and characterization—she felt fully in control and fully satisfied with her means of expression; the means were perfectly matched to her end; she had achieved exactly what she wanted, in precisely the form she had intended.

The advance payment on royalties that she had received for *The Fountainhead* had provided only enough money to enable her to finish the novel. Now, the advance was gone. She returned to work at Paramount. She did not mind it. Her main assignment was completed.

Frank O'Connor had been struggling to break into the theater, but jobs were scarce. To carry them over this period, he took a job as clerk in a cigar store.

Discussing the novel one day with Isabel Paterson, a prominent author and book reviewer for the New York *Herald-Tribune*, Ayn Rand said: "If *The Fountainhead* does not make me famous, I'll continue to write, but I will not expect any recognition in my lifetime. I know the nature of this novel. I do not care to become famous for any other." "What sale would you consider a success?" asked Isabel Paterson. "One hundred thousand copies," answered Ayn Rand. Isabel Paterson gasped: "Do you realize how few books *ever* sell that many copies?" "If it sells a a hundred thousand copies," said Ayn Rand, "then it will be a known widely enough for my kind of readers to discover it."

In the weeks preceding publication, Archibald Ogden reported that the book was already causing a stir: he was receiving enthusiastic telephone calls from booksellers and editors of publications to whom advance copies had been sent.

On the day before publication, Frank O'Connor told her, with happy confidence: "We've made it, this time."

The Fountainhead was published in May, 1943.

One of the first reviews called it an interesting book about architecture, and said its message was that we ought to do something about the people in the slums; another announced that the ideas it presents are selfish and reactionary; another described Roark as a selfless architect; a "liberal" reviewer attacked it ferociously. None of the reviewers stated the theme of the novel. The one fact—more than any other—that Ayn Rand had wanted the public to know, was that this was a book about *individualism*. For all practical purposes, it was as if the press were under censorship; "individualism" seemed to be the forbidden, the terrifying word.

There was an exception. Lorine Pruette, who reviewed the novel for the Sunday *New York Times Book Review*, wrote: "Ayn Rand is a writer of great power. She has a subtle and ingenious mind and the capacity of writing brilliantly, beautifully, bitterly." The review made explicitly clear that the theme of the book was individualism versus collectivism. "Good novels of ideas," Lorine Pruette stated, "are rare at any time. This is the only novel of ideas written by an American woman that I can recall. . . . You will not be able to read this masterful work without thinking through some of the basic concepts of our times."

The advertisements were, for the most part, vague, noncommittal and meaningless. There was no way for any reader of the advertisements to distinguish *The Fountainhead* from all the other allegedly "big" and "challenging" books offered to them daily by means of the same routine bromides.

Throughout the spring and summer months, sales trickled in with ominous slowness. Then, in the fall—when *The Fountainhead* appeared to be following the pattern of *We the Living*—the sales began to rise. By November, 18,000 copies had been sold.

It was in November that Warner Brothers expressed interest in purchasing the movie rights and inquired about the price.

Ayn Rand told her agent, Alan C. Collins of Curtis Brown, Ltd., that she would not sell the movie rights for less than $50,000. She knew that this was a dangerously high demand, since no other companies were bidding for the book. She explained: "One day, the rights to *The Fountainhead* will be worth much more than that. But if I sell it for fifty thousand dollars, I will not regret it. If I sell it for less, I *will* regret it."

She waited for word of the studio's decision. One afternoon, ten days later, she came home from lunch feeling weary and discouraged. Frank O'Connor was waiting for her, an odd look on his face. "Well, darling," he said, "while you were out to lunch, you've become fifty thousand dollars richer." Alan C. Collins had telephoned a few minutes earlier. Warner Brothers had accepted the price and was buying *The Fountainhead*.

That evening, she and her husband went for dinner, as usual, to a neighborhood cafeteria. The cafeteria offered two types of meals: one cost forty-five cents, the other sixty-five cents. They had always ordered the former. They glanced at the menu, automatically ignoring the more expensive dishes, then looked at each other, startled, and began to laugh. They had suddenly realized that *tonight* they could afford a sixty-five-cent dinner.

At her husband's firm insistence, she went shopping for a fur coat. "Buy any kind of fur you like," he told her, "so long as it's mink." Slightly shocked by the idea of such extravagance, she obeyed: it *was* mink.

In December, they left for Hollywood. Her contract with Warner Brothers called for her to write a screenplay of *The Fountainhead*. On her first trip to Hollywood, seventeen years earlier, she had traveled by day coach; Frank O'Connor had worked his way on a freighter. Now, they took the Twentieth Century to Chicago, then a stateroom on the Chief, happily and incredulously reveling in a luxury that had never before been possible to them.

Ayn Rand had worked in Hollywood as an extra in mob scenes; she had seen the bottom of that world. She had left with the sense that the movies were an unfinished issue in her life. Now, she was returning at the top, the author of a best-selling novel, with all the doors of the movie world thrown open to her.

The first person she met when she arrived was Henry Blanke, who was to be the producer of *The Fountainhead*. Blanke was enthusiastic about the project and was anxious that her screenplay be as faithful to the book as possible. Due to the shortage of materials for the many sets which a film such as *The Fountainhead* would require, production could not be planned until after the war.

She completed the screenplay within six months. She was offered a screenwriter's contract by Hal Wallis, a Warner Brothers producer who was planning to establish his own production company in affiliation with Paramount Pictures. The contract she obtained was unusual, by the standards of conventional studio policy: it committed her to work only six months out of every year; the other six months, she would be free for her own writing.

She and her husband bought a small ranch in the San Fernando Valley, twenty miles from Hollywood—thirteen acres of land, and a modern house of steel and glass designed by Richard Neutra. She worked in a sunlit study facing the austere blue shapes of hills in the distance. The chief pleasure the house gave her was the sense of privacy.

Frank O'Connor managed the ranch. He reconditioned the land, landscaped the grounds and grew acres of flowers for commercial sale. Through the years, as he had seen the types of movies and plays that were being produced, he had grown progressively less interested in the career of an actor. Simultaneously, he had been developing an interest in the direction of the visual arts. His first step toward a new career was the decision to have a business of his own, which the ranch provided.

Thrown into the midst of unaccustomed luxury after years of struggle, Ayn Rand often found herself thinking of a line quoted in Victor Hugo's *The Man Who Laughs:* "No man can pass abruptly from Siberia to Senegal without fainting" —only she had no time to faint. In the two years following their arrival in Hollywood, she and her husband worked harder than ever. She worked under the pressure of constant studio deadlines; he worked on the ranch eighteen hours a day; there were days when they had no time to see each other except at the dinner table. Typical of this period is the fact that, on her first vacation after two years, Ayn Rand drove into Beverly Hills to make two purchases: the complete works of Aristotle and three suits by Adrian.

The sales of *The Fountainhead* continued to rise. Most novels reach their peak sales during the first few months after publication, and then decline. But *The Fountainhead* rose to its highest sales two *years* after publication: during 1945, 100,000 copies were sold. (At about that time, another studio offered Warner Brothers $450,000 for the screen rights, but Warner Brothers refused to sell.)

The success of the book was made by word-of-mouth recommendations. Some years later, referring to this period, Ayn Rand wrote: "I did not know that I was predicting my own future when I described the process of Roark's success: 'It was as if an underground stream flowed through the country and broke out in sudden springs that shot to the surface at random, in unpredictable places.' "

By 1948, sales had exceeded 400,000 copies. When the movie was released in 1949, the book reappeared on the best-seller lists—an unprecedented six years after publication—and 50,000 copies were sold within six months. In 1952, the New American Library published it in paperback.

Today, the "non-commercial" book for which there was no audience has sold over 500,000 copies in hard-cover editions and over a million copies in paper-back. The book that was "too intellectual" is read by truck drivers and farmers. The book that was "too controversial" is studied in university classrooms. *The Fountainhead* has achieved the status of a modern classic.

Almost from the beginning, Ayn Rand was deluged with mail from her readers. Publishers have said that they know of no other writer who has inspired an equivalent response. The letters came—and still come—from professors and unskilled workers, from students and soldiers, from Americans and Europeans and Asiatics and Africans, from housewives and scientists and businessmen and artists. They write that they have found in Roark's moral intransigence a personal ideal—that the image of Roark has given them a greater courage to stand by their own convictions and to fight for their own achievements—that *The Fountainhead* has liberated them from the guilt they had experienced for their failure to live by the altruist ethics—that it has taught them to feel proud of their work—that after reading it, they gave up meaningless jobs which they had accepted as second-best, and returned to the careers for which they had longed—

that it has given them the sense of what is possible in life, what is possible to man, what is possible to *them*. During the war, a group of fliers wrote that after every mission they gathered around a candle while one of them read passages from the novel to the others. A young soldier wrote that he would feel better about the war if he could think it was being fought for the ideals of *The Fountainhead*.

Discussing the book's unusual career, Ayn Rand has said: "The success of *The Fountainhead* has demonstrated its own thesis . . . the success of *The Fountainhead* was made by the public. Not the public as an organized *collective*—but by single, individual readers who discovered it of their own choice, read it on their own initiative and recommended it on their own judgment."

* * *

The idea for her next novel arose out of Ayn Rand's refusal to be an altruist.

It was a few months after the publication of *The Fountainhead*, when the book was selling slowly and no one could predict its future spectacular success. One evening, during a telephone conversation, an acquaintance of Ayn Rand said that the moral philosophy of *The Fountainhead* was of crucial importance to men's enlightenment, but that they were unable to accept it in fiction form. "You must write a non-fiction treatise on your morality," the acquaintance insisted. Ayn Rand replied that she had no desire to do so, since she considered the case presented in the novel fully clear and understandable to any rational mind. "If they don't respond to *The Fountainhead*," she said, "why should I wish to enlighten or help them further?" The acquaintance continued to press her, arguing that it was her *duty* to write a non-fiction treatise, because people *needed* it. "Oh, they do?" answered Ayn Rand. "What if I went on strike? What if *all* the creative minds of the world went on strike?" She added, in passing: "That would make a good novel"—and they went on to discuss other matters. When she hung up the telephone, Frank O'Connor, who had been in the room, remarked: "It *would* make a good novel."

She and her husband talked all through that night. By morning, she had decided that "the mind on strike" was to be the theme of her next novel. She had not yet decided that its title was to be *Atlas Shrugged*.

As the first step in a project that was to encompass fourteen years, she began studying the problems and the history of heavy industry, of railroads, steel, oil, copper. For particular sequences which demanded highly specialized knowledge, she did more detailed research: in order to describe the break-out of a blast furnace at Rearden's mills, she struggled through the complex instructions contained in a technical manual for furnace foremen. She interviewed railroad and steel executives, and visited plants on both coasts. One summer, returning to Los Angeles from New York, she drove along the exact route she had chosen for the first run of the John Galt Line: diagonally across Colorado from Cheyenne, Wyoming through Denver, then on southwest. She interviewed the Vice-President in Charge of Operations of the New York Central Railroad—a dignified, white-haired gentleman who was to retire the following year; she wondered what his reaction would be if he had known he was to become a beautiful young woman of thirty-four.

She obtained the railroad's permission to ride in the engine of the Twentieth Century Limited. In a letter to Isabel Paterson, describing the experience, she wrote: "The most thrilling moment was when the engine started moving, and the ride through the underground tunnel out of Grand Central. Everything I thought of as heroic about man's technological achievements, was there concretely for me to feel for the first time in my life. . . . I was not afraid at all. It was the feeling of being in front and of knowing where I was going, instead of being dependent on some unknown power. . . . All I felt was a wonderful sense of excitement and complete security. . . . At Harmon they changed the engine, and I got into my first Diesel . . . the engine rides as if it were floating. It actually seems to glide; you don't feel the wheels under you at all. . . . The next morning, I had to get up at six o'clock, and got into the engine again at Elkhart, Indiana. During the night they had their first snowstorm. It was still dark when we started riding through the snow. . . . They put me into the engineer's seat and let me drive the engine myself. . . . I have now driven the Twentieth Century Limited. They let me start the engine from a small station, and of course, there were three men standing behind me watching, but still nobody touched a lever except me, and I started the train and accelerated it to eighty miles per hour . . . the signal lights seemed to be coming along every few seconds. . . . An old railroad man . . . was riding on the cowcatcher of a switch engine on a siding; when he looked up, as our train came along with me in the engineer's seat, the look on his face was something I have never seen on any human face before. It was like an exaggerated close-up in a movie farce. *There* was a man who was staring,

168

stunned and stupefied. . . . I am completely ruined now as a train passenger. I was bored all the way out of Chicago, riding in a compartment. That's much too tame. I would love to travel across the whole continent in the engine."

The many aspects of her research had to be done during the six months of each year that she was free to work on *Atlas Shrugged*. The other six were spent as a screenwriter for Hal Wallis Productions; her work consisted of adapting the stories of other authors for the screen; it included the highly successful *Love Letters* and *You Came Along*.

As to her social life, she found that the only interest she had in common with the people she met in Hollywood was political: there was a growing concern over the communist influence on the motion picture industry and a growing anti-communist movement. She became known in Hollywood as an active and vocal opponent of collectivism. In a pamphlet entitled *Screen Guide for Americans* (written for the Motion Picture Alliance for the Preservation of American Ideals, an anti-communist organization) she stated: "The purpose of the Communists in Hollywood is *not* the production of political cal movies openly advocating Communism. Their purpose is *to corrupt our moral premises by corrupting non-political movies*—by introducing small, casual bits of propaganda into innocent stories—thus making people absorb the basic principles of Collectivism *by indirection and implication*."

In the summer of 1947, the House Committee on Un-American Activities began an investigation of communist penetration of the movie industry. A group of writers and directors—subsequently known as "The Hollywood Ten"—were subpoenaed by the Committee; at the hearings in Washington, their Communist Party membership cards were produced. The Committee also requested a group of anti-communist actors, writers and producers—subsequently called "The Friendly Witnesses"—to testify about the communist influence in Hollywood. Ayn Rand was included in this group. She was to testify as an expert on communist propaganda. During the long weeks of the hearings, she was given a chance to analyze only one movie, but a number of newspapers across the country printed excerpts from her *Screen Guide for Americans*. As a consquence of the hearings, and, to a significant extent, as a consequence of the *Screen Guide*, the types of propaganda that the pamphlet exposed began to disappear from the screen.

Considerable pressure had been brought to bear upon the anti-communist witnesses, to prevent them from testifying; many of them were told, subtly or openly, that their co-operation with the Committee would be professionally dangerous to them. When an acquaintance congratulated Ayn Rand on her courage in testifying, she answered: "I'm not brave enough to be a coward—I see the consequences too clearly."

Perhaps the greatest philosophical and moral victory she achieved in Hollywood in her battle against collectivism, was the film version of *The Fountainhead*.

When she sold the screen rights, she knew that she was taking a calculated risk. Film studios never purchase literary material without acquiring the right to make any changes they please in adapting it to the screen. She knew that she would have no legal control over the movie script; it could be altered in any manner the studio wished, at any moment, for any reason. Her sole weapon was her own power of moral persuasion.

In the spring of 1948, *The Fountainhead* was put into production and she was called back to the Warner Brothers studio to write the final script. In the months that followed, the studio was the scene of a quietly ferocious battle. It was the kind of battle which no one ever hears about, and which is probably the hardest to fight. She was under constant pressure to disguise, dilute or tone down the philosophical theme of her novel, to turn her ideas into meaningless generalities that would shock no one. She was fighting the same battle that Roark had fought: the battle against the men who demanded compromise. Instead of being asked to destroy the integrity of a building by means of architectural bromides such as Greek ornaments, she was asked to destroy the forceful clarity and originality of her script by means of ideological bromides. In the most timid of all mediums, in an industry whose guiding principle was a quest for "the lowest common denominator"—she was fighting to present on the screen a moral code that defied the moral tradition of two and a half thousand years. She argued with studio executives, with the agents and lawyers of various stars, with the Johnson Office. (The latter, interestingly enough, objected not to the love scenes, but to certain philosophical passages of Roark's courtroom speech.) Henry Blanke, the producer, stood by her sympathetically; but intellectually, she had to fight the battle alone.

She won. Her script was shot exactly as she wrote it. In an unprecedented studio ruling, the actors were forbidden to improvise on the set. The novel's theme and meaning were preserved. She won by means of nothing but the power of rational persuasion.

When one sees the movie, one is startled to hear, coming

170

from the screen in our day, in the present intellectual climate, such dialogue as the proud statement made by Gary Cooper in the role of Howard Roark: "I came here to say that I do not recognize anyone's right to one minute of my life. Nor to any part of my energy. Nor to any achievement of mine." One may project what was required of their author to see that lines such as these were brought to the screen.

The main purpose for which Ayn Rand had originally decided to sell the screen rights—to make the novel more widely known—was achieved. The movie brought it an ever-wider readership, and continues to do so to this day, when it appears in neighborhood theaters and on television screens across the country.

Ayn Rand had remained in Hollywood to wait for the production of *The Fountainhead*. But during the waiting, she had discovered that dividing her time between *Atlas Shrugged* and screenwriting was becoming unbearable; *Atlas Shrugged* was growing into an enormous project, demanding her full time and mental energy. After several attempts, she succeeded in persuading Hal Wallis to release her from her contract—which would have brought her more than $70,-000 during the next two years. She needed her freedom to make *Atlas Shrugged* her exclusive assignment and goal.

In order to achieve full conceptual clarity before translating her theme into a plot-structure, she had made extensive notes on the ideas that were to be involved in the novel explicitly or implicitly. These notes are a treasure-house of philosophical analysis—and a key to the rigor, clarity and scope of the mind that created *Atlas Shrugged*. The notes include such issues as the meaning of "free will"—the relationship between mind and body—the nature of universals—the law of identity as the bridge between metaphysics and epistemology—the difference between a creative process and a learning process—the distinction between errors of knowledge and breaches of morality—the psychology of sex—the nature of logic—the spiritual meaning of money—the relationship between happiness and moral values—the creative man's attitude toward pain—the psychology of the parasites and why they hate the creators—the meaning of charity—the social conditions necessary for material production—the parasites' fear of self-responsibility—the industrialist and the artist as exponents of man's creative ability.

"My most important job," she wrote, "is the formulation of a rational morality of and for man, of and for his life, of and for this earth."

In these early notes—as she began to plan the novel in

specific detail and to define the philosophical issues involved —one sees the scope of the novel begin to grow and broaden. The following is typical of that process.

While projecting what would happen if the men of the mind went on strike, while defining how and why civilization would collapse, she was led to a crucial question. If it is the men of the mind who carry the world on their shoulders and make civilization possible—why have they never recognized their own power? Why have they never challenged their torturers and expropriators? When she grasped the answer, she knew it was to be one of the most important moral concepts in the novel: the concept of "the sanction of the victim." She saw that it is the *victims*, the men of virtue and ability, who make the triumph of evil possible by their willingness to let their virtues to be used against them: their willingness to bear injustice, to sacrifice their own interests, to concede moral validity to the claims of their own destroyers.

Her identification of the disastrous moral consequences of the mystics' soul-body dichotomy was another contributing element to the growth of the novel's scale. The soul-body dichotomy is one of the essential philosophical issues in *Atlas Shrugged*. In her early notes, she described the way in which this dichotomy has served as sanction and excuse for the persecution of industrialists and for the scorn directed against those who create the physical means of man's survival. She wrote, as an aside to herself: "It would be interesting to show, some day, how the same principle operates in relation to sex." She saw that just as men do not understand that the source of the production of wealth is man's mind, so they do not understand that the source of a man's sexual desires and choices is his philosophical values; both production and sex are scorned, for the same reason, as mindless, "animalistic" activities that have no relation to man's spirit. At the time of writing these notes, she did not plan to deal with the issue of sex in the novel. But as her work on the plot-structure progressed, the meaning of the soul-body dichotomy as applied to sex became a crucial part of the story. The manner in which it is tied, through the character and life of Hank Rearden, to the same dichotomy in the realm of economics and politics, constitutes one of the most brilliant feats of integration in *Atlas Shrugged*.

The following three excerpts from her notes, written in April of 1946, provide an interesting illustration of part of the process by which a philosophical novelist proceeds from wide abstractions to the concrete events of a specific story.

"The collectivists and the champions of the 'common

172

man,'" she wrote, "have screamed for so long about strikes, about the dependence of the industrialist upon his workers, about the workers supporting him, creating his wealth, making his livelihood possible, and what would happen to him if they walked out. Very well. I will now show who depends on whom, who supports whom, who creates what, who makes whose livelihood possible, and what happens to whom when who walks out." (Later, this note, intended as a personal assignment, was included almost verbatim in a statement by one of the novel's characters.)

She planned to show the gradual collapse of an entire economy, not in the form of a haphazard series of sketches of various industries, but by means of a unified and integrated story. She chose railroads as the main background of the story because they deal with all the other major industries, thus functioning as the blood system of the economy.

Another note, written later that same month, states: "Reverse the process of expansion that goes on in a society of producers: Henry Ford's automobile opened the way for [the expansion of many] industries: oil, roads, glass, rubber, plastics, etc. Now, in a society of parasites, the opposite takes place: a shrinking of industries and productive activities. A James Taggart at the head of a big concern would have exactly the opposite effect from that of a Henry Ford."

A third note states: "Since the essence of the creator's power is the ability of independent rational judgment, and since this is precisely what the parasite is incapable of—the key to every disaster in the story, to the whole disintegration of the world is, in each case (big or small), a situation where independent rational judgment is needed and cannot be provided (cannot—in the case of the parasites involved; will not—in the case of the creators)."

In devising the plot-structure of the novel, she had to call upon her full power of dramatic integration. Each key event had to carry and illustrate the philosophical theme, and, simultaneously, contribute to the economic disintegration of the country, advance the personal relationships among the characters, and heighten the element of mystery and suspense created by the disappearance of one man of ability after another. Readers of *Atlas Shrugged* will know with what skill this was accomplished.

One of her first assignments, in devising the events of the novel, was to select the characters through whom she would dramatize her theme.

In a note dated January 20, 1947, she wrote: "Show that the real sources, key spots, spark plugs of material production (the inventors and industrialists) are creators in the same way, in the same sense, with the same heroic virtues, of the same high *spiritual* order, as the men usually thought of as creators—the artists. Show that *any* original rational idea, in any sphere of man's activity, is an act of creation and creativeness. *Vindicate* the industrialist—the author of material production." Through the character of Hank Rearden, she presented the embodiment of the moral greatness she wanted to vindicate. Rearden, the industrialist, the man of action and of this earth, is the Atlas who carries the world on his shoulders and receives torture as payment. Galt speaks for Ayn Rand when he describes Rearden as "the greatest of the victims I have avenged."

Dagny Taggart is Ayn Rand's first portrait of the ideal woman. Kira was still a young girl at the end of *We the Living;* Dominique was paralyzed by a profound inner conflict. But Dagny is free of psychological conflict, serene in her basic relationship to existence, passionately ambitious and creative. She is the woman thought to be impossible by the mystics' view of life—and of sex: the woman engineer, dealing with the material world of metal rails and freight cars and Diesel engines, who is, simultaneously, a consummately feminine hero-worshipper.

Francisco d'Anconia—Galt's closest friend and the first man to join him in the strike—is one of Ayn Rand's most colorful and dramatic figures: the man of ruthless purposefulness who assumes the role of a playboy in order to destroy his fortune in plain sight of the whole world. Francisco's leitmotif is a light-hearted gaiety: he is the man with a superlative capacity for the enjoyment of life, who is an iron-disciplined worker of unsurpassed productive energy and ability. It is Dagny who names the cause-and-effect relationship between these two aspects of his character: "She heard him laughing; it was the gayest sound in the world. . . . The capacity for unclouded enjoyment, she thought, does not belong to irresponsible fools; an inviolate peace of spirit is not the achievement of a drifter; to be able to laugh like that is the end result of the most profound, most solemn thinking." "Francisco," Ayn Rand has remarked, "is the philosophical expression— the concretization in a human character—of what I heard in the operetta music I fell in love with in my childhood."

If the leitmotif of Francisco is an indestructible gaiety, the leitmotif of Ragnar Danneskjöld (the philosopher who becomes a pirate) is an implacable sense of justice. ". . . my only love," Ragnar tells Rearden, "the only value I care to live for, is that which has never been loved by the world, has never won recognition or friends or defenders: human ability. That is the love I am serving—and if I should lose my life, to what better purpose could I give it?" There are few statements in *Atlas Shrugged* that more intimately express the soul of its author.

Ayn Rand can no longer remember when the device of "Who is John Galt?" first occurred to her. The expression, everything it was to imply in the story, and the character of John Galt himself, seemed present in her mind from the earliest concept of the novel. Just as the person of Galt dominates all the events of *Atlas Shrugged,* so his spirit and image dominated the conceiving and writing of the entire novel. When she wrote *The Fountainhead,* she regarded Howard Roark as an ideal man, but she knew that his portrait was not her full and final statement on the subject. The portrait of John Galt is.

It is significant that the attributes most sharply emphasized in Galt's portrait are intransigent rationality, implacable realism, untouchable serenity, inviolate self-esteem. "Galt"— to quote a friend of Ayn Rand—"is the man whom reality fits like a glove." When one considers that the theme of *Atlas Shrugged* is the role of reason in man's existence, it is clear why Ayn Rand chose to feature *realism* as Galt's dominant psychological trait.

An essential characteristic of Galt—and of Ayn Rand— is a profound contempt for evil, a contempt based on the conviction that evil is the irrational and, therefore, the blind, the aberrated, the impotent. Evil is to be fought, when necessary, but not to be taken seriously in one's own view of life, not to be granted any metaphysical power, importance or significance; evil is to be despised, not hated or feared. One may observe this premise in the plot-structure of *Atlas Shrugged:* the central lines of dramatic conflict are not between the good and the evil, but between the good and the good—between Galt and Francisco on the one hand, and Dagny and Rearden on the other. The errors that set Dagny and Rearden in conflict with Galt and Francisco are errors of knowledge, not breaches of morality. This same basic pattern is apparent in *The Fountainhead:* the central conflict is Roark versus Dominique and Wynand. In both novels, the villains merely cash in on the consequences of the heroes' conflicts, but are not the initiators, the source or the motive power of the story's events. "In my novels, and in actual life," Ayn Rand has observed, "the alleged victories of evil are made possible only by the flaws or the errors of those who are essentially good. Evil, left to its own devices, is impotent and self-defeating. To make my central conflicts a struggle between heroes and villains, would be to grant to evil an honor it doesn't deserve."

After more than two years of preparation, she did not begin the actual writing of *Atlas Shrugged* until she had worked out a complete, chapter-by-chapter outline of the plot and knew the entire structure of the story.

The opening page of Chapter I of the manuscript is dated: September 2, 1946. She did not know, when she wrote the first line—"Who is John Galt?"—that it would take her eleven years to answer that question fully.

The enormous intensity of concentration which the novel demanded of her made it progressively more difficult, during the next three years, to switch her mental focus to her screen-writing assignments. When she obtained her release from her contract with Hal Wallis Productions, in 1949, she retired into virtual seclusion. She seldom left the ranch and had few visitors. The months passed and the pile of manuscript pages grew. In the evenings, when she was too exhausted to write, her one form of relaxation was to play her favorite records: predominantly, they belonged to the category of the so-called light-concert music, such as the operettas of Kalman and Lehar; among classical composers, the only one whose works she enjoyed fully was Rachmaninoff; of the others, she liked only those works that conveyed the exultant, non-tragic sense of life she sought in music, such as Chopin's *Butterfly Etude* or the second movement of Saint-Saens' *Concerto No. 2 in G Minor.*

In the winter of 1950, she received a fan letter from Nathaniel Branden. He was nineteen years old; he had come from Toronto eight months earlier, and was studying psychology at the University of California at Los Angeles. He had read *The Fountainhead* when he was fourteen years old; he had reread it many times since, studying its ideas, and was profoundly committed to its philosophy. He wrote to Ayn Rand, asking questions about the wider philosophical implications of her novel. As she told him later, it was the unusual perceptiveness of his questions that made her write him a lengthy and detailed reply. She concluded her letter by explaining that she could not undertake a philosophical correspondence and if he had further questions to ask, she would give him an appointment to discuss them in person. Two days later, she received a letter from him, requesting an appointment.

He came to her home on an evening in early March. He

arrived at 8:30 P.M. and did not leave until 5:30 A.M. His questions ranged from politics and economics to epistemology and psychology; he did not know if he could expect to be given a second appointment; he learned later that it was the very range and scale of his questions that guaranteed it. When he was leaving, Ayn Rand told him that he was welcome to come again, or to telephone her if he wanted further discussion. "Do you mean it?" he asked. "Of course." "May I call you tomorrow?" She smiled. "Certainly." He telephoned the next evening—and they talked philosophy for two hours.

Thereafter, he telephoned daily, but he did not request another appointment until a week later. He asked, "May I bring a friend with me, who is also an admirer of *The Fountainhead?*" She answered, "By all means, bring him along." He explained, "It's not a he—it's a she." It was thus that I met Ayn Rand.

Like Nathaniel, I had first read *The Fountainhead* some years earlier. I planned to be a writer; *The Fountainhead* was to me what the novels of Victor Hugo had been to Ayn Rand: it was literature as it might be and ought to be. It was through *The Fountainhead* that Nathaniel and I had met. Two years before we came to U.C.L.A., where I was studying philosophy, I had met him in Winnipeg, which was then my home; a mutual acquaintance had brought us together, on the grounds of our common admiration for *The Fountainhead*.

When I asked Nathaniel his impression of Ayn Rand, after his first meeting with her, he answered, "Mrs. Logic." Within an hour of arriving at her home, I knew why he had said it. I had never encountered a human being in whom the psychological attribute of rationality was so pronounced; one grasped it almost as a visible presence. It was conveyed by the complete openness of her manner—by the precision and clarity of her speech—by the directness of her answers and the fact that she gave reasons for her every statement—by the intense perceptiveness of her glance—by the natural, effortless delight she projected in the act of intellectual analysis. One sensed that here was a person incapable of being motivated or influenced by emotion rather than reason—a person who did not allow her judgment to be affected by any concern other than the truth or falsehood of an issue and who expected the same rigorous objectivity from her listeners.

In the months that followed, we visited Ayn Rand and her husband at least once a week; the conversation seldom ended before five or six in the morning. Sometimes, when classwork kept me away and Nathaniel came alone, he

177

would go to sleep, at dawn, on the couch in Ayn Rand's study —then, a few hours later, they would resume the discussion of the preceding night. Of the four of us, Ayn Rand proved to be the closest to inexhaustible: when she discussed ideas, her sense of time vanished, she had unlimited energy and the kind of intellectual enthusiasm which is commonly ascribed to youth, but we had never seen a remote equivalent of it in any of our contemporaries. She was a person to whom ideas *mattered,* as they did not matter to anyone else we knew. Often, when we arrived in the evening, she would come out of her study, having had no time for dinner; she would look one step away from collapsing—then Nathaniel or I would mention some philosophical issue or problem that had, perhaps, arisen in class, and the lines of exhaustion would vanish from her expression, she would begin to ask questions and to talk, and we would see the face of a forty-five-year-old woman become the face of a twenty-year-old girl within the span of ten minutes.

Both Nathaniel and I had been seeking, since adolescence, to acquire a consistent view of life; we were interested in philosophy, not merely as a theoretical, academic discipline, but as a set of principles to guide one's actions in practice. The attitudes of the adults with whom we had attempted to discuss our quest, had ranged from indifference to resentful condemnation, and could best be summed up by the standard formula: "Wait till you grow up, you'll come down to earth" —with the unstated implication that to "come down to earth" meant to abandon one's intellect. Ayn Rand was the first person we had ever met who held that the intellect is the one indispensable tool for living on earth; in her attitude toward the power and importance of ideas, she seemed closer to us than to her own contemporaries: she was like a youth who had started out on the same quest, but had never given up and had reached her goal, and could now show us the steps of that long road.

Nathaniel had always felt contempt for the people who believed that "practicality" consists of being mindless. He was the only man I had met who regarded philosophy as a practical necessity. To both of us, Ayn Rand was the living confirmation of that conviction.

We wondered, occasionally, why she was willing to give us a great deal of time and attention, particularly in a period when she had cut herself off from almost all social contacts. One evening, Nathaniel openly asked her that question. She laughed and answered, "Don't you know that the pleasure of dealing with active minds outweighs any differences in age or knowledge?"

Many of our conversations centered on politics and economics: both Nathaniel and I were indignantly opposed to any form of totalitarianism, whether communist or fascist, but in all of our schooling, we had never been offered any antidote except the mass of contradictions known as a "mixed economy," which we were observing all around us; we had never discovered capitalism. It was Ayn Rand who helped us to discover it.

From the first, we asked Ayn Rand a great many questions about her new novel. At that time, no one had read the manuscript except Frank O'Connor, to whom she read each chapter as she finished it, and Archibald Ogden, who had read part of the script during a visit to California. She did not intend to show the novel to anyone else until it was completed. She told us only that the novel was a mystery in form and that its background was railroads and the steel industry. Nathaniel asked her, somewhat skeptically: "But will the novel be philosophical? Can you make businessmen romantic or interesting?" She smiled. "Wait and see."

It took us a few months, but our constant questions about the book wore her down—and she finally agreed to let us read the first chapter. Then, as we persisted, she permitted us to read the second chapter; then the third; then all of the novel written thus far.

It was an unrepeatable intellectual and emotional experience. Coming each week to read a new section of the book, we felt as if we had gained private entry into the world that had been the dominant focus of our thought, development and concern since the age of fourteen, when we discovered *The Fountainhead*. Reading *The Fountainhead* then, neither of us could have known that we would be reading Ayn Rand's next novel in manuscript at her home. Reading *Atlas Shrugged*, we could not have known that when it was published, its dedication page would state: "To Frank O'Connor and Nathaniel Branden."

One of the most painful days of our lives came in the summer of 1951, when Nathaniel and I had to move to New York, to continue our studies at New York University. We did not expect to see Ayn and Frank for two years; she believed that it would take her at least that long to finish the novel (she was just beginning to write Part III). She disliked California, she felt a growing homesickness for New York— the first homesickness she had ever experienced for any geographical locality—but she did not want to interrupt her work and to move until the novel was finished. But early in October, Nathaniel received a long-distance telephone call: it was Ayn, announcing that they would arrive in New York in three weeks. The day after she completed the chapter called "Atlantis," she found that she could not bear to remain in California any longer; she talked it over with Frank—it was the quickest decision they ever made—and by evening they were making arrangements to move back to New York.

Once again, they drove across the country. This time, they shared the ride with a passenger: a six-week-old gray and white kitten, which a neighbor's cat had given birth to in the back seat of their car; they named the kitten "Frisco," in honor of Francisco d'Anconia. Subsequently, in acknowledgment of his omniscient expression, Frisco acquired the title of "Professor of Epistemology."

On their arrival in New York, they moved into an apartment where an eight-by-twelve-foot office replaced Ayn Rand's luxurious California study—much to her delight. The passion for New York that she projects in her novels is expressive of her own attitude. Living anywhere else, she had felt that she was a visitor, a temporary exile from her real home. In *We the Living,* Lydia, Kira's sister, looking at a stage setting, says: "How beautiful! It's almost real"—and Kira, looking at a landscape, says: "How beautiful! It's almost artificial." Like Kira, it was the *man-made* that Ayn Rand loved, the sight of man's conquest of nature; New York was its symbol.

At one time, she had wanted to build a house in the country near New York, which Frank Lloyd Wright had designed. She had met Frank Lloyd Wright, whose work she greatly admired, shortly after the publication of *The Fountainhead*. He had written to compliment her on the novel, saying: "I've read every word of *The Fountainhead*. Your thesis is *the* great one. Especially at this time. . . . Your grasp of the architectural ins and outs of a degenerate profession astonishes me. . . . Your novel is Novel. Unusual material in unusual hands and, I hope, to an unusual end." In the summer of 1945, she and her husband had visited Wright at Taliesen East, and had commissioned him to design a home for them, to be built in the future: the sketches show a beautiful, complex structure of three stories, with her study at the top. But now, after seven years of living in the country, they decided not to build the house; they decided that never again would they choose to live away from the city.

Within a few weeks of her return, the city became only a presence to be seen from the window of her study, as she resumed the task of writing. She drove herself on a ruthless schedule: she worked seven days a week, for as many hours each day as she was able to write; it was not unusual for her to eat dinner at midnight; there was one period of especially intense work when she did not step out of the apartment for thirty-three days.

Her only form of "rest" consisted of philosophical discussions. Such discussions, she explained, belonged in "the same world" as her novel, they allowed her a change of subject, but let her maintain the same intensity of intellectual concentration; she could resume her work the next morning with a sense of unbroken continuity. But a cocktail party or an evening in today's theater would paralyze her for days; it was not *thought* that she found exhausting.

As a result of Nathaniel's work, our discussions during this period became increasingly concerned with the subject of psychology. He was profoundly opposed to the dominant schools of psychological theory, such as behaviorism and psychoanalysis. In regard to psychotherapy, he was convinced that value conflicts lay at the base of neurotic conflicts, and that no method of treatment could be successful if it evaded the necessity of dealing with moral values. He realized the enormously important implications of Ayn Rand's ethical philosophy for the science of psychology. In her concept of man as a being whose basic means of survival is *reason*, and her concept of reason as a faculty to be exercised *volitionally*, he saw a key to the problem of defining the nature of mental health, the root of mental illness, the principles of psychological motivation. He wrote a series of papers on the issues he was investigating and the theories he was formulating; central to his thinking was a new concept of self-esteem. Both as a philosopher and a novelist, Ayn Rand was intensely interested in the problems of motivational psychology, and his theories became one of our chief topics of discussion.

I shall permit myself to boast that one of the few events which Ayn Rand considered important, during those years, was my marriage to Nathaniel, in January of 1953. I cannot say, however, that it was an event unrelated to philosophy: Nathaniel and I had met because of *The Fountainhead;* its author and her husband were matron of honor and best man at our wedding.

Through the years, Nathaniel and I had become acquainted with a number of young people who shared our admiration for *The Fountainhead* and who were eagerly interested in its ideas. We introduced to Ayn Rand those whose interest proved to be authentic. They joined us in meeting on Saturday eve-

181

nings, for the purpose of discussion. Ayn Rand nicknamed the group "the class of '43"—because 1943 was the year *The Fountainhead* was published. We were not a formal organization nor did she regard us as an actual class. We were an informal group of friends who met together because of our common interest in ideas; while Ayn Rand or Nathaniel frequently led the discussion, we were in no sense a "school."

Eventually, by reason of its relevance to the issues we discussed, Ayn Rand let all the members of this group read *Atlas Shrugged* in manuscript form. All of us were concerned with the application of the ideas of *Atlas Shrugged* to our respective professions or fields. The group represented diverse professions: Leonard Peikoff is a college instructor in philosophy; Alan Greenspan is an economic consultant; Allan Blumenthal is a psychiatrist; his wife, Joan Blumenthal, is a painter; Mary Ann Rukavina is an esthetician and art historian; Harry Kalberman is an account executive in a large brokerage firm; his wife, Elayne Kalberman, is a former registered nurse, and now the mother of a young daughter named Kira after the heroine of *We the Living*.

During this period, Ayn Rand discovered the writer who became her favorite contemporary novelist, from the aspects of originality, imagination, sense of drama and, above all, plot-structure: Mickey Spillane. She disagrees with some of his ideas, but she admires him for the fact that—contrary to the literati's superficial assertions—Mickey Spillane writes like a *moral crusader:* he approaches conflicts in the uncompromising terms of "black-and-white," his hero, Mike Hammer, is not an exhausted cynic but a moral avenger; Spillane's style never projects the fashionable, evasive "it seems to me," but the firmly committed *"it is."*

In the fall of 1955, a major turning point occurred in Frank O'Connor's life. Some time after arriving in New York, he had decided to go into the florist business, and had taken a job with a large firm in order to gain experience. In his first floral arrangements, he exhibited a startlingly imaginative sense of visual drama and design; one could recognize his work at a glance; it was totally unique; it projected an originality so forceful that it seemed almost incongruous to the medium it employed: one felt as if a Diesel motor were being used to pull a child's wagon. One evening in 1955, when "the class of '43" was discussing painting, Joan Blumenthal (the Joan Mitchell) remarked that any intelligent person, granted a reasonable amount of interest and effort, could learn to draw with some degree of competence. She offered to prove it by giving lessons to anyone in the group who would care to attempt the experiment. Several of us laughingly agreed to try —including Frank O'Connor.

He had never given any thought to painting or expressed any interest in the subject. But what happened when he began to work in Joan's classes had the quality of an explosion: it was as if a subterranean talent, lying dormant for years, suddenly found an outlet and burst into the open. It was obvious, almost from the first lesson, that he was in a category by himself: while the other members of the class struggled slowly (and eventually did vindicate Joan in her claim), he shot forward like a rocket. His early drawings exhibited a violent self-assertiveness, an astonishing sense of drama and composition, in spite of their technical flaws. Ever since childhood, as an integral part of his interest in the theater and the movies, he had been intensely preoccupied with the visual: with composition, with spatial tensions and relationships, with esthetic form and design: now, it was the accumulated visual observations of years that his imagination was calling on and using, filling his brain with dramatic sensory projections. He began to draw and sketch constantly. His drawings were scattered all over the apartment—and often, when one spoke to him, one saw that he had not heard, he was frowning in concentration and staring critically at some sketch halfway across the room. Soon he began working in pastels; he worked ceaselessly; he would come out of his room when Nathaniel and I arrived, his clothes smeared with chalk, in a state of quiet, ferocious rapture; he would utter a brief "Hello" and go back to his easel. He was fifty-seven years old; he did not know how long it would take him to master the technique of painting; but *this*, he knew, was the work he wanted.

It was fascinating to observe—as the months passed and he gained greater skill, and undertook ever more ambitious subjects—in what manner his painting revealed an artistic affinity to Ayn Rand's novels: in his extravagant imaginativeness, in his sense of visual drama, in the peculiar union of tension and serenity, of luminous austerity and passionate sensuousness.

Recognizing his need for technical training, he enrolled in the Art Students League. He joined the class conducted by the distinguished painter, Robert Brackman, member of the National Academy of Design. Meeting Mr. Brackman recently, Nathaniel asked him in private his opinion of Frank O'Connor's work. "It was obvious almost immediately," said Robert Brackman, "that Frank was not a student when he came to my class. He was already an artist. He had an absolutely individual way of doing things, right from the beginning. I saw that all he needed from me was technical advice—I would point out the kind of errors it would take him a long time to discover on his own—but in every other respect, I knew that he should be left free to develop in his own way. . . . With most students, one can see a dozen different historical styles reflected in their early work. There were no historical influences at all in his work. . . . I was floored at how quickly he learned. I didn't think that anyone could grow that fast. . . . Whatever subject he's given to paint, his first idea is always: What is the most dramatic way of presenting it? So far, composition is his strongest point technically. . . . Some people work at painting all their lives and never find themselves, never really find what they want to say or how they want to say it. Frank had found himself from the start."

Such were the major events of her world, while Ayn Rand was writing the final chapters of *Atlas Shrugged*.

When she was working on the chapter entitled "Their Brothers' Keepers," she encountered an unexpected difficulty: she found herself unable to formulate Francisco d'Anconia's farewell message to the world after he blows up d'Anconia Copper. The message had to contain—in the briefest possible form and in a style characteristic of Francisco—the essence of the motive behind his action. After many unsuccessful attempts, she explained her problem to Frank. "You mean," he inquired, "that it should be something like 'Brother, you asked for it'?" "Not *like* it!" she cried, delighted. "That's it!" She handed him her pen. "It's your sentence," she said. "You write it." In the manuscript, "Brother, you asked for it!" appears in Frank O'Connor's handwriting—a thing she would have allowed to no one else.

The working title of the novel had been "The Strike," but she was dissatisfied with it because it gave away the key to the mystery. It was Frank who suggested "Atlas Shrugged." She had never thought that the entire theme, meaning and spirit of the book could be summed up so eloquently in two words.

The hardest intellectual and literary assignment of Ayn Rand's career was John Galt's radio speech. She had known in advance that the speech would be difficult and that there was no way to predict how long it would take her to write it. She hopefully estimated the task at three months; it took two years.

In the events of the novel, she had given the concrete evidence from which her philosophical abstractions could be drawn. Now, her task was to make those conclusions explicit. Galt's speech is the abstract summation, of which the events of the story are the concretes and particulars. In this respect, she was consciously following the pattern of the process by which man's consciousness gains understanding: just as a man's perception of concretes must precede his abstractions, so the reader of *Atlas Shrugged* is first shown the facts, the evidence, then given the conceptual identification of their meaning. One will not find a single abstract principle in Galt's speech that is not illustrated in the events of the story.

The enormous difficulties entailed in writing the speech arose predominantly out of two factors: that the speech had to be a condensation of her entire philosophy—and that it had to be formulated with the precision of a legal document, while maintaining a style and form appropriate to a *novel*.

To achieve the necessary condensation, she had to write every section of the speech at considerable length, then reduce it to the most economic statement of its essentials. The 35,000 words of the speech represent the briefest summary of the dozen or so full-length philosophical treatises which she had to write in order to select those final words.

The speech had to contain many important philosophical definitions, it had to offer closely reasoned arguments for its conclusions, it had to refute a great many erroneous philosophical theories—but it had to have the tone and manner, not of an academic lecture or debate, but of a moral crusader's speech to a collapsing world. This method of presentation required of her that she constantly "think on a double track," as she put it—that is, that she formulate a rigorously logical progression, then adapt the style to fiction, concerning herself with such issues as literary rhythm, emotional tempo, color and drama of expression. She felt as if, in order to achieve what she wanted, she had to stretch the capacity of every brain cell in her head—but when the job was done, she knew that the hardest part of *Atlas Shrugged* was behind her. She had given John Galt a statement worthy of him.

The three concluding chapters of the novel that follow Galt's speech were among the most enjoyable for her to write, because here the task consisted predominantly of straight-line action developments; these chapters complete the climax begun by the speech and bring the story to its final resolution. The philosophical work was done; she was able to enjoy the luxury of working with a single concern: that of a dramatist and plot-writer.

About eleven years earlier, in the first chapter of *Atlas Shrugged*, she had written a description of Richard Halley's music, with the knowledge that she would repeat it verbatim in the last chapter. That description is the philosophical leitmotif of the novel; she knew that it would sound different the second time—that the same words would carry a greater meaning, a more specific conviction, a fuller reality, a deeper emotional power—and that that difference would tell a perceptive reader what it was that he had learned from the chapters between. Now, at last, she reached the day when she wrote that passage for the second time, in the opening paragraph of the novel's final sequence:

"It was a symphony of triumph. The notes flowed up, they spoke of rising and they were the rising itself, they were the essence and the form of upward motion, they seemed to embody every human act and thought that had ascent as its motive. It was a sunburst of sound, breaking out of hiding and spreading open. It had the freedom of release and the tension of purpose. It swept space clean and left nothing but the joy of an unobstructed effort. Only a faint echo within the sounds spoke of that from which the music had escaped, but spoke in laughing astonishment at the discovery that there was no ugliness or pain, and there never had had to be. It was the song of an immense deliverance."

She had come out of the most brutal dictatorship in history, she had risen past years of poverty, of struggle, of intellectual isolation, she had moved by the power of her knowledge of man and of life as they could be, by the image of John Galt and of his world—it was the world to which she had pledged herself since childhood—and now she had given to that world and to the sense of life from which it came the reality of a superlative artistic projection. *"To hold an unchanging youth,"* she had written in the novel, *"is to reach, at the end, the vision with which one started."*

On an evening in March, 1957, she wrote, on the last page of her manuscript:

" 'The road is cleared,' said Galt. 'We are going back to the world.'

"He raised his hand and over the desolate earth he traced in space the sign of the dollar."

Today, she can remember nothing of that evening, except that she stood up from her desk, walked out of her study and, in a state of dazed numbness and exultation, handed to Frank O'Connor the last page of her manuscript to let him see the words: "The End."

The end of the job of writing was the beginning of the job of fighting the worst elements of today's culture. "I know that I am challenging the cultural tradition of two and a half thousand years," she told us. She knew that she would have to stand alone against some of the most powerful and destructive pressure groups of our time.

The choice of a publisher for *Atlas Shrugged* was a difficult decision to make. Ayn Rand did not undertake it until after she had completed Galt's speech. When word got out in publishing circles that she was finishing her new novel, most of the leading publishers approached her agent, Alan C. Collins, expressing interest in it. Her main consideration was to find a publisher from whom she could expect, not necessarily agreement with her ideas—an innovator cannot expect it— but intellectual *understanding* and willingness to face the kind of antagonism her book would arouse. For various special reasons, she and her agent selected four publishers and met with them, in turn, to discuss the novel. In each case, she told them the novel's philosophical theme, and warned them that they were not to expect a single favorable review from today's intellectuals, most of whom share the premises of her villains.

Although none of the publishers seemed to be afraid of such a prospect, it was the attitude of Random House that impressed her most. Bennett Cerf understood her problem and suggested a daringly unconventional means of solving it; he suggested that she submit her novel to four or five publishers simultaneously (which is never done), with their full knowledge, for the purpose, not of a financial contest, but of an *ideological* contest, that is: for the purpose of finding out how they proposed to handle a controversial novel. Bennett Cerf won the contest by the mere suggestion of such an idea: she tried it on the other three publishers; one of them refused to participate; the other two were willing, reluctantly and disapprovingly. This made her decide that no actual contest was necessary and that *Atlas Shrugged* would be submitted to Random House first.

An additional element of great importance to her was the fact that at their first meeting, Donald Klopfer, vice-president of Random House, had grasped the implications of her novel's theme almost before she had fully stated it. "If you propose to offer a *moral* defense of capitalism," he said, "wouldn't you have to clash with the entire tradition of Judeo-Christian ethics?" She did not ask him whether he agreed or disagreed with her position: what impressed her was the acuity of his philosophical perceptiveness; he had understood an issue which, to this day, the professional defenders of capitalism fail to understand.

The rest was simple. After they had read the manuscript of

187

Atlas Shrugged, Bennett Cerf opened their next meeting with Ayn Rand by the words: "Name your own terms."

Atlas Shrugged was published on October 10, 1957.

The attacks and denunciations which she had predicted, were disgorged from newspapers and magazines with the philosophical integrity and graciousness that one expects of a lynch mob or of a modern intellectual. Sophisticated commentators expressed horrified dismay at the fact that Ayn Rand did not seem to regard the Sermon on the Mount as the final word on ethics. Some reviewers praised the book, but the intellectual level of the praise, for the most part, was not significantly above that of the attacks.

It soon became apparent that *Atlas Shrugged* was to repeat the history of *The Fountainhead*, but on a wider scale and with a more profound impact: the book became the subject of heated discussions in homes across the country; hundreds, then thousands of letters were written to Ayn Rand by her readers, expressing enthusiasm for her achievement and asking philosophical questions—but the response was, in effect, underground. No one chose publicly to identify what Ayn Rand had accomplished in *Atlas Shrugged* or why she was attracting an ever-expanding following or what was the philosophical, literary and cultural significance of so unusual a form of popularity.

In January of 1958, in response to the requests for a detailed, systematic presentation of Ayn Rand's philosophy, Nathaniel conceived the idea of organizing Nathaniel Branden Lectures. He prepared a course of twenty lectures, "Basic Principles of Objectivism," which presented Ayn Rand's philosophy, including many aspects not yet covered in her written works, and, in addition, developed some of its most significant implications for the science of psychology. Intellectually, these lectures had Ayn Rand's complete approval; but as a business venture, they were Nathaniel's own independent undertaking. After graduate school, he had been engaged in the practice of psychotherapy and in writing a book on his psychological theories; now, he closed his practice to devote his time to his book (which, at present, is nearing completion) and to Nathaniel Branden Lectures.

When the course was given for the first time in the spring of that year, he had twenty-eight students. When the course was given again in the fall, there were forty-five students; when it was given the following February, the enrollment rose to sixty-five. Today, "Basic Principles of Objectivism" is given twice yearly in New York, with an average attendance of one hundred and eighty students. I give the same course in Philadelphia. Word of the lectures spread rapidly, and we began to receive mail from across the country—later, from all over the world—asking if this course could be made available. At present, "Basic Principles of Objectivism" is given via tape recordings to groups in major cities of the United States and Canada. In New York, with the co-operation of a number of associates, we give additional, more specialized courses in philosophy, psychology, economics and esthetics. In December of 1961, Nathaniel Branden Lectures was incorporated under the title of Nathaniel Branden Institute; besides its plans for an expanded schedule of lecture courses, it has begun to publish papers on Objectivism and its application to the various social sciences.

We are often asked what kind of people attend the lectures, in terms of age, educational background and profession. The average age of the students is the early thirties. In one series, the youngest student was a sixteen-year-old high school girl; the oldest was a sixty-year-old teacher of physics. This range is typical. The professional range is as varied: there are college students, secretaries, businessmen, housewives, writers, artists, teachers, lawyers, psychologists, psychiatrists.

During the past several years, there has been a growing stream of invitations for Ayn Rand to address student bodies on campuses across the country. One of the most interesting facts about her following, which we have observed among our students and on the many campuses where she has lectured, is that a considerable number of her readers and admirers are former "liberals." They are people who had been attracted to "liberalism" because it had promised a scientific approach to social problems; they were disillusioned when they saw the horrors which modern collectivist "liberalism" was achieving in practice; but they knew of no alternative. They were contemptuously indifferent to the advocates of capitalism who had no better arguments to offer than appeals to mystical faith and tradition. What they found in *Atlas Shrugged* was the fulfillment of the promise that collectivist "liberalism" had dismally failed to keep: a *rational* social philosophy. It was *Atlas Shrugged* that convinced them and turned them into advocates of capitalism, by teaching them to question—and to reject—the ethics of altruism.

Speaking of the success of *Atlas Shrugged*, Bennett Cerf remarked to Ayn Rand: "It's remarkable! In all my years of publishing, I've never seen anything like it. To break through against such enormous opposition!"

On a television interview, Mike Wallace once asked Ayn Rand what she thought of the attacks against her. She answered by quoting a line from Kipling's poem "If": ". . . if you can bear to hear the truth you've spoken twisted by knaves to make a trap for fools . . ." and by adding, "I can bear it. It's not fools that I seek to address."

In March of 1961, Random House published *For the New Intellectual: The Philosophy of Ayn Rand*—an anthology of the main philosophical passages from her four novels, plus an introductory essay, "For the New Intellectual," which is an analysis of the development of Western culture, the causes of its present crisis and the road to an intellectual renaissance.

"The world crisis of today," she wrote, "is a *moral* crisis—and nothing less than a moral revolution can resolve it: a moral revolution to sanction and complete the political achievement of the American Revolution. . . . The New Intellectuals must assume the task of building a new culture on a new moral foundation . . . They will have to be *radicals* in the literal and reputable sense of the word: 'radical' means 'fundamental.' The representatives of intellectual orthodoxy, conventionality and *status quo*, the Babbitts of today, are the collectivists. Let those who do care about the future, those willing to crusade for a perfect society, realize that the new *radicals* are the fighters for capitalism.

"It is not an easy task and it cannot be achieved overnight. But the New Intellectuals have an inestimable advantage: they have reality on their side."

Such, then, is the direction and goal of the Objectivist movement: to pave the way for a cultural renaissance.

Ayn Rand's present task is "The Objectivist Newsletter," which began publication on January 1, 1962, with Ayn Rand and Nathaniel Branden as its editors and publishers. It is a monthly newsletter in form and a journal of ideas in content; its purpose is to discuss the application of the Objectivist philosophy to the contemporary problems of our culture.

Ayn Rand's long-range assignment is a full, detailed treatise on Objectivism. The book will deal especially with epistemology, which she regards as the most important branch of philosophy; no social system and no code of ethics can be more secure than their epistemological foundation.

Shortly before the publication of *Atlas Shrugged*, when the youngest member of the "class of '43" expressed an inordinate optimism about the speed with which the ideas of *Atlas Shrugged* would spread through today's culture, Nathaniel told him: "Don't delude yourself. Things don't happen that fast—when you consider the enormity of what we're challenging and the scale of what we want to achieve. There's great deal of work—of writing—that we'll have to do, and one can predict when the results will begin to show. But if *Atlas Shrugged* sells fifty thousand copies, this culture is cooked." At present, the combined sale of the hard-cover and paper-back editions of *Atlas Shrugged* is approaching one million copies.

* * *

A child of thirteen faced a bandit's gun and thought: If it is the end, still, I have had something great in my life, I have had the image of Enjolras, I want to be worthy of him. . . . "My philosophical views are not part of the history of philosophy yet. But they will be." . . . "She had a tremendous capacity for enjoyment. Whether it was a piece of music she liked or a story or some present I brought her that cost a dollar—she was so expressively and radiantly delighted. . . . She was absolutely determined that she would get where she wanted to go. It didn't matter how difficult it was, or what hell she had to go through." . . . "I'm not brave enough to be a coward—I see the consequences too clearly." . . . "What if I went on strike? What if *all* the creative minds of the world went on strike?" . . . "My only love, the only value I care to live for, is that which has never been loved by the world, has never won recognition or friends or defenders: human ability. That is the love I am serving—and if I should lose my life, to what better purpose could I give it?" . . . "I know that I am challenging the cultural tradition of two and a half thousand years."

Has it been said that the kind of hero Ayn Rand writes about could not possibly exist . . . ?

And be sure to read

WORKERS' PARADISE LOST

by Eugene Lyons

"If you want to understand how Russia reached its present state of international power, if you want to make sense out of the distorted and conflicting claims of Soviet achievements and ambitions, and if you want to be able to answer the appeasers and the apologists for the Soviet Union, WORKERS' PARADISE LOST is most enthusiastically recommended. It is a work of eloquence and integrity: it deserves the widest possible audience."

—THE OBJECTIVIST

55-623, 95¢
